HACCP

HACCP

A practical approach

Sara Mortimore
Quality Assurance Manager
Grand Metropolitan Foods
UK

and

Carol Wallace
Product Safety Manager
J Sainsbury plc
UK

CHAPMAN & HALL

London · Glasgow · Weinheim · New York · Tokyo · Melbourne · Madras

**Published by Chapman & Hall, 2–6 Boundary Row,
London SE1 8HN, UK**

Chapman & Hall, 2–6 Boundary Row, London SE1 8HN, UK

Blackie Academic & Professional, Wester Cleddens Road, Bishopbriggs,
Glasgow G64 2NZ, UK

Chapman & Hall GmbH, Pappelallee 3, 69469 Weinheim, Germany

Chapman & Hall Inc., One Penn Plaza, 41st Floor, New York NY 10119,
USA

Chapman & Hall Japan, Thompson Publishing Japan, Hirakawacho
Nemoto Building, 6F, 1-7-11 Hirakawa-cho, Chiyoda-ku, Tokyo 102,
Japan

Chapman & Hall Australia, Thomas Nelson Australia, 102 Dodds Street,
South Melbourne, Victoria 3205, Australia

Chapman & Hall India, R. Seshadri, 32 Second Main Road, CIT East,
Madras 600 035, India

First edition 1994

© 1994 Sara Mortimore and Carol Wallace

Typeset in Palatino 10/12 pt by Cambrian Typesetters, Frimley, Surrey

Printed in Great Britain by St. Edmundsbury Press, Bury St. Edmunds,
Suffolk

ISBN 0 412 57020 3

A catalogue record for this book is available from the British Library

Library of Congress Catalog Card Number: 94-70262

♾ Printed on permanent acid-free text paper, manufactured in accordance
with ANSI/NISO Z39.48-1992 and ANSI/NISO Z39.48-1984 (Permanence
of Paper).

To Dave and Bill for all their help,
support and encouragement
throughout this project.

Contents

Series editor's foreword

As a long-standing protagonist of good manufacturing practice in the food and drink industry, I was more than pleased to be invited to edit a series of books on practical approaches to food control. The series does not set out to re-invent the wheel, but rather to draw together collective wisdom in respect of particular food control issues and to present them in a way which will allow relevant managers, management or practitioners to address them on a practical level. It also tries to give a practical perspective for those concerned with law enforcement, some of whom will be newly challenged in face of EEC food control legislation.

I am particularly delighted that the first in the series should be on the subject of hazard analysis and that the authors have real experience of HACCP applications within major and highly respected organizations. Sainsbury's and Grand Metropolitan are to be commended for the support that they have given to this initiative, as are others who have endorsed contributions from their employees.

I have also been impressed with the quality and scope of the input from the authors of this publication, Sara Mortimore and Carol Wallace, and hope that the example of practical application which runs as an ongoing theme throughout the book will help those applying HACCP for the first time to weave through the inevitable difficulties without undue shedding of blood, sweat and tears.

With both the publishers and contributors, I anticipate that the works in this series will be complementary, and that they will cover some of the grey areas between the straightforward application of food science and technology and its integration with other disciplines and the outside world. With this in mind, we are planning to address shortly the questions of crisis management and of laboratory accreditation, both of which can be perceived as having potential important interfaces with HACCP and vice versa.

This volume recounts and elaborates the principles of HACCP originally developed in support of the National Aeronautics and Space Administration (NASA) programme some thirty years ago by Bauman and his colleagues at Pillsbury to give the best possible assurance that astronauts would be safegarded against possible food poisoning risks during NASA space missions. Since that time the provenly successful philosophy has been widely and efficaciously applied, not only to safeguard against potential microbiological hazards, but also to evolve protective mechanisms against a wide spectrum of other problems ranging through foreign body incursion and other contaminants to aspects of general consumer protection, product liability and precautions against malicious tampering. It is more than appropriate that one of the authors is from the company that ultimately came to own the Pillsbury business.

We anticipate that most of the publications in this series will reflect the dynamic nature of food control and hazard management, and hence reader reaction will be welcomed by the publishers, the authors and the series editor, both in respect of current content and need for future inclusions. We all hope that you will enjoy reading this publication and that you will find it of value in contributing to your work.

Keith G. Anderson
February 1994

Foreword

It is nearly three decades since the Pillsbury Company pioneered the HACCP concept in the food industry. Awareness and adoption of the HACCP approach to food safety progressed steadily, albeit slowly, until about 1985. Since then the rate of progress has accelerated dramatically for two principal reasons.

Firstly, many previously unrecognized (or perhaps previously non-existent) microbial foodborne hazards have emerged since the 1960s. Microorganisms such as *Listeria monocytogenes*, *Campylobacter jejuni*, *Yersinia enterocolitica*, verotoxigenic *Escherichia coli*, and a new strain of *Salmonella enteritidis* have stressed food safety systems and the regulator's capacity to protect public health, leading to legislative demands in some countries for improved consumer protection. Not known to present food-borne hazards before 1963, these microorganisms now demand considerable attention. Moreover, the psychrotrophic nature of some has forced alterations in process controls and environmental sanitation programmes.

Secondly, the rapidly increasing global sourcing of raw materials and distribution of finished products make it imperative that governments cooperate at an international level to provide assurance of food safety.

HACCP is now widely embraced by the food industry and by government regulatory agencies because it has proven to be a cost effective means to prevent the occurrence of identifiable food-borne biological, chemical, and physical hazards.

Those who have significant industrial experience with the implementation of HACCP have learned the necessity of training and maintenance activities to properly apply and control a HACCP System. Most currently available publications or training programmes are quite inadequate in this regard. They are often rather dull expositions of HACCP principles, providing little or no guidance in matters of HACCP implementation, maintenance and training.

HACCP: A practical approach promises to improve this situation. It is a refreshingly concise, yet detailed treatment of hazard analysis and risk assessment; and HACCP Plan development, implementation and maintenance, written by two food safety professionals who have many years of practical experience in the United Kingdom's leading food companies. I expect that this book will be a very valuable resource to those who must understand and apply HACCP in their food manufacturing or regulatory activities

William H. Sperber, PhD
Director, Microbiology and Food Safety
The Pillsbury Company/Grand Metropolitan Food Sector
Minneapolis MN USA

Acknowledgements

Dr. W.H. Sperber (The Pillsbury Co.)
Mr. D.J. Phillips (Grand Metropolitan Foods Europe)
Dr. M.C. Easter (Reading Scientific Services Ltd)
Dr. G.D. Spriegel (J Sainsbury plc)
Mr. A.L. Kyriakides (J Sainsbury plc)
Mr. L.J. Cosslett (Britvic Soft Drinks)
Mr. P. Catchpole (Express Foods Ltd.)
Mr. P. Sockett (CDSC)
Mr. D.B. Rudge (Grand Metropolitan Foods Europe)
Mr. A.W. Roberts – Cartoonist

Case studies

Mr. T. Mayes (Unilever Research Laboratory)
Mrs. N.S. Hagger (Britvic Soft Drinks)
Mr. D.J. Phillips (Grand Metropolitan Foods Europe)
Ms. L. Karnes and HACCP Team (Memory Lane Cakes)
Mr. J. Hughes (J Sainsbury plc)

Corrections, helping with understanding and support.

W.W. and M. Mortimore
C.J. Wallace
D. MacMillan

Typing

M. Morris
B. Harris

Special thanks to Wyn for his wonderful cartoons and to Martin for providing technical support.

Disclaimer

The material in this book is presented after the exercise of care in its compilation, preparation and issue. However, it is provided without any liability whatsoever in its application and use.

About this book

The purpose of this book is to explain what HACCP really is and what it can do for any food business. It will lead you through the accepted international approach to HACCP and will show you how to do it, from start to finish of the initial study, through to continuous maintenance of your system. The information given within the book may also be used as a basis for developing a HACCP training programme.

You may have a number of reasons for wanting to know more about HACCP. If you are running a food business, you may already have decided that HACCP is the best control option available or you may have been asked to implement it by customers or regulatory authorities. You may be a regulatory authority and wish to enhance your understanding of the techniques. Alternatively you may be studying it as part of a broader course on food control or have noted the increasing recommendation for HACCP in legislation and guidelines.

Whatever your motivation for reading this book, there are a number of questions you will probably want to ask.

- What is HACCP?
- Where did it come from?
- Why should I use HACCP?
- Is HACCP applicable to everyone?
- How does HACCP help?
- What are the benefits?
- Are there any drawbacks?
- What are the principles of HACCP?
- Is it difficult?

The questions are answered in brief within Chapter 1 and are more fully explained in subsequent text, along with some of the support techniques which will be useful to you.

The book has been designed to lead you through to a successful HACCP programme. It is based upon the international HACCP approach advocated by the Codex Alimentarius Committee on Food Hygiene (1993) and the National Advisory Committee on Microbiological Criteria for Foods (NACMCF, 1992) in the United States of America. The former is a committee of the WHO/FAO Codex Alimentarius Commission.

It is recommended that you read the book from start to finish before going back over the 'doing' sections as you begin the process. As each of the HACCP techniques is explained, completed examples have been provided and there are additional case studies in Appendix A which can be used to look at different styles of application and documentation. Further useful reference information on hazards and their control can be found in Appendices B and C.

1

An introduction to HACCP

HACCP is an abbreviation for Hazard Analysis Critical Control Point and has become a buzz word in recent years. It is frequently heard and talked about at conferences and within companies, but is also often misunderstood and poorly applied in real situations. The HACCP concept has been around in the food industry for some time but only recently has undergone some major updates. These developments mean that the HACCP techniques have progressed considerably since their early beginnings, and have meant that some companies have found their systems to be out of date.

Those not familiar with HACCP often hold the misconceived belief that it is a difficult, complicated system which must be left to the experts. True, you do need a certain level of expertise to carry out HACCP, but this expertise is a thorough understanding of your products, raw materials and processes, along with factors which could cause a health risk to the consumer. HACCP itself is a straightforward and logical system of control based on the prevention of problems – a common sense approach to food safety management.

HACCP will be a key element of a complete product management or good manufacturing practice system. In brief, HACCP is applied through taking a number of easy steps:

- look at your process/product from start to finish;
- decide where hazards could occur;
- put in controls and monitor them;
- write it all down and keep records;
- ensure that it continues to work effectively;

Where did HACCP come from?
HACCP was originally developed as a microbiological safety system in the early days of the US manned space programme, as it

1

was vital to ensure the safety of food for the astronauts. At this time most food safety and quality systems were based on end product testing, but it was realized that this could only fully assure safe products through testing 100% of the product, a method which obviously could not have worked as all product would have been used up. Instead it became clear that a preventative system was required which would give a high level of food safety assurance, and the HACCP System was born.

The original system was drawn up by the Pillsbury Company working alongside NASA and the US army laboratories at Natick. It was based on the engineering system, Failure, Mode and Effect Analysis (FMEA) which looks at what could potentially go wrong at each stage in an operation along with possible causes and the likely effect, before deploying effective control mechanisms.

Like FMEA, HACCP looks for hazards, or what could go wrong, but in the product safety sense. Control and management systems are then implemented to ensure that the product is safe and cannot cause harm to the consumer.

Figure 1.1 'Origins of HACCP'.

Why should I use HACCP?
HACCP is a proven system which gives confidence that food safety is being effectively managed. It will enable you to maintain focus

on food product safety as the top priority, and allow for planning to prevent things going wrong rather than waiting for problems to control.

Because HACCP is a recognized, effective method, it will give your customers confidence in the safety of your operation and will indicate that you are a professional company which takes its responsibilities seriously. HACCP will support you in demonstrating this under food safety and food hygiene legislation, and in some countries is actually a legislative requirement. To implement a HACCP System, personnel from different disciplines across the company need to be involved, and this ensures that everyone has the same fundamental objective – that safety is more important than anything else. This is often otherwise difficult to achieve in the real world where there is constant pressure from a number of different areas, (e.g. customer/commercial pressures, brand development, profitability, new product development, health and safety, environmental/green issues, headcount restriction, etc.).

Is HACCP applicable to everyone?
Yes, you may be a multinational food corporation who will be starting from within a sophisticated quality management system with documented procedures and well defined practices, or a small manufacturer of goat's cheese in a shed on the farm, or a street vendor of ready-to-eat pizza slices. No matter, HACCP can be effectively applied to businesses at both ends of the spectrum.

How does HACCP help?
The primary area where HACCP will help is in the processing of safe food. It helps people to make informed judgements on safety matters and removes bias, ensuring that the right personnel with the right training are making decisions. As HACCP is a universal system, it can be passed on to your suppliers to assist in assuring raw material safety, and will also help to demonstrate effective food safety management through documented evidence which can be used in the event of litigation.

What are the benefits?
HACCP is **the** most effective method of maximizing product safety. It is a cost-effective system which targets resource to critical areas of processing, and in doing so reduces the risk of manufacturing and selling unsafe products.

Users of HACCP will almost certainly find that there are additional benefits in the area of product quality. This is primarily due to the increased awareness of hazards in general and the participation of people from all areas of the operation. Many of the mechanisms that are controlling safety are also controlling product quality.

Are there any drawbacks?

If HACCP is not properly applied then it may not result in an effective control system. This may be due to improperly trained or untrained personnel not following the principles correctly or it may be through lack of maintenance of the HACCP System, e.g. if a company implements a system and stops there, paying little or no heed to changes which occur in the operation. The effectiveness may also be lost if the company carries out the hazard analysis and then tries to make its findings fit in with existing control mechanisms and management systems. As we will see HACCP is compatible with existing quality management systems but you must ensure that product safety is always given priority.

Other problems may arise if HACCP is carried out by only one person, rather than a multidisciplinary team, or where it is done at the corporate level with little or no input from the processing facility.

Some critics may say that HACCP is too narrow in that it focuses only on food safety. How wrong they are! HACCP was designed for food safety and, as we have outlined, safety should always come first, but the HACCP techniques are flexible and can be applied to other areas such as product quality, work practices and to products outside the food industry. We will see later how HACCP can be applied beyond food safety but the key issue is to make sure you don't try to do too much and end up with a complicated system which is difficult to control (e.g. quality, legality and safety mixed together in the same system). Instead, the same techniques can be applied separately to establish distinct systems which are equally effective and easy to manage.

1.1 What are the Principles of HACCP?

The HACCP System consists of seven Principles which outline how to establish, implement and maintain a HACCP Plan for the operation under study. The HACCP Principles have international acceptance and details of this approach have been published by the Codex Alimentarius Commission (1993) and the National Advisory Committee on Microbiological Criteria for Foods (NACMCF, 1992).

We are now going to introduce a number of terms which may be unfamiliar to you. Don't worry. There is a glossary in Appendix D and an abbreviations list in Appendix E, and we will be discussing these again in full in Chapter 6 when we look at applying the principles.

1.1.1 *Principle 1*

Conduct a hazard analysis. Prepare a list of steps in the process where significant hazards occur and describe the preventative measures.

Principle 1 describes where the HACCP Team should start. A Process Flow Diagram is put together detailing all the steps in the process, from incoming raw materials to finished product. When complete, the HACCP Team identify all the hazards which could occur at each stage and describe preventative measures for their control. These may be existing or required preventative measures.

1.1.2 *Principle 2*

Identify the Critical Control Points (CCPs) in the process.

When all the hazards and preventative measures have been described, the HACCP Team establish the points where control is critical to managing the safety of the product. These are the Critical Control Points.

1.1.3 *Principle 3*

Establish Critical Limits for preventative measures associated with each identified CCP.

The critical limits describe the difference between safe and unsafe product at the CCPs. These must involve a measurable parameter and may also be known as the absolute tolerance for the CCP.

1.1.4 *Principle 4*

Establish CCP monitoring requirements. Establish procedures from the results of monitoring to adjust the process and maintain control.

The HACCP Team should specify monitoring requirements for management of the CCP within its critical limits. This will involve specifying monitoring actions along with frequency and responsibility.

1.1.5 *Principle 5*

Establish corrective actions to be taken when monitoring indicates a deviation from an established critical limit.

Corrective action procedures and responsibilities for their implementation need to be specified. This will include action to bring the process back under control and action to deal with product manufactured while the process was out of control.

1.1.6 *Principle 6*

Establish effective record-keeping procedures that document the HACCP System.

Records must be kept to demonstrate that the HACCP System is operating under control and that appropriate corrective action has been taken for any deviations from the critical limits. This will demonstrate safe product manufacture.

1.1.7 *Principle 7*

Establish procedures for verification that the HACCP System is working correctly.

Verification procedures must be developed to maintain the HACCP System and ensure that it continues to work effectively.

In the Codex document, Principles 6 and 7 are the other way round, while the above approach is consistent with the NACMCF. It really doesn't matter which way round these principles come in the list, as long as both elements are covered in your HACCP System.

2

Why use HACCP?

One of the first questions that will be asked within your organization is, 'Why use HACCP?' It is important to answer this so that all personnel have

- the same understanding of the motives behind the introduction of the system;
- commitment to developing an effective system.

In this chapter, we have endeavoured to cover some of the reasons for using the system – obviously for the management of food product safety, but perhaps less obviously because end product inspection and testing has limitations, and pressure from government, customers and the media for safe food is ever increasing.

2.1 Management of product safety

Within the food industry, the safety of our products must without question be considered top priority. That food is 'safe' is often an unwritten requirement of many customer specifications. It goes without saying, and unlike many of the other attributes of the product (appearance, taste, cost) it is **not** negotiable. Consumers expect safe food and we in the food industry have a responsibility to meet their expectations. Why should we use HACCP to assist us in meeting these requirements?

HACCP is a system of food control based on prevention. In identifying where the hazards are likely to occur in the process we have the opportunity to put in place the measures needed to prevent those hazards occurring. This will facilitate the move towards a preventative quality assurance approach within a company, reducing the traditional reliance on end product inspection and testing. HACCP is logical in its systematic assessment of all aspects of food safety from raw material sourcing, through processing and distribution to final use by the consumer. All types of food safety hazards are considered as part of the HACCP System – biological, chemical and physical. Use of a HACCP System should therefore give us as manufacturers, caterers and retailers, confidence that the food we sell is safe. Effective HACCP Systems involve everyone in the company and each employee has a role to play. The culture that evolves through this approach makes it much simpler to progress additional programmes such as quality improvement, productivity and cost reduction.

HACCP can, after the initial setting up of the system, be extremely cost effective. Firstly, because by building the controls into the process there will be less product rejected at the end of the production line. Secondly, by identifying the critical control points, a limited technical resource can be targeted at the management of these. Thirdly, the disciplines of applying HACCP are such that there is almost always going to be an improvement in product quality.

HACCP was developed as a simple method of helping manufacturers assure the provision of safe food to the consumer but many companies are only recently starting to fully realize the potential of the system. Let us consider where HACCP could have prevented the following food safety incidents from occurring.

2.2 Examples of food safety incidents

As we have seen the main reason for using HACCP is to manage food safety and prevent food poisoning incidents. Let's consider the possible consequences when food safety is not adequately managed.

When something goes wrong with a food product there may be localized or widespread illness and suffering, and the cost to the company concerned can be huge. Even when no illness has been caused, the discovery of safety hazards in a product intended for consumption can lead to prosecution for the company. Routine prosecutions often result from foreign material being discovered in food, but microbiological hazards have the potential to cause a much greater impact.

Table 2.1 contains a number of food safety incidents which have occurred in recent years, along with an estimate of the likely cost.

The true costs associated with such incidents are seldom documented, but where they have been established they can be shown to be substantial both to the industry and to society.

For example, in the case of the *Salmonella napoli* outbreak in chocolate, the quoted costs relate solely to the health care costs and

Table 2.1 Examples of food poisoning incidents*

Year	Country	Food	Number reported ill	Causative organism	Cost (£)
1965	USA	Cheddar cheese	42	Staphylococcus aureus	250 000
1977	Canada	Cheddar cheese	15	Staphylococcus aureus	300 000
1981	Holland	Salad in catering operation	700	Salmonella indiana	200 000
1982	UK (Italy)	Chocolate bar	245	Salmonella napoli	505 000
1983	USA	Pasteurized milk	49 (14 deaths)	Listeria monocytogenes	294 000
1984	Canada	Cheddar cheese	2700	Salmonella	5 880 000
1985	USA	Pasteurized milk	18 000 (2 deaths)	Salmonella	Dairy closed
1985	USA	Mexican-style cheese	142 (47 deaths)	Listeria monocytogenes	Reported lawsuit of 411 764 000
1985	UK	Infant dried milk	76 (48 infants) (1 death)	Salmonella ealing	22 058 000
1986	UK	Pasteurized milk	54	Salmonella	167 650
1987	Switzerland	Vacherin Mont D'Or cheese	30 deaths	Listeria monocytogenes	882 352
1988	UK (Germany)	Pepperami	81	Salmonella	> 1 000 000
1989	UK	Hazelnut yogurt	27 (1 death)	Clostridium botulinum Type B toxin in hazelnut purée	?
1992	France	Pork tongue	279 (63 deaths)	Listeria monocytogenes	?

*Information taken from Beckers et al. (1985); CDR Weekly (1992); Shapton (1989).

do not include the costs associated with withdrawing 2.5 million chocolate bars from the market.

A review by P.N. Socket (1991) of the Communicable Disease Surveillance Centre at Colindale in the UK reported that the costs associated with ten *Salmonella* incidents in catering establishments in the USA and Canada ranged from US$57 000 to US$700 000, and the direct costs only of five *Salmonella* incidents in manufactured foods ranged from US$36 000 to US$62 million.

It is also significant that the incidents in Table 2.1 involved both large and small companies and crossed international boundaries. Many of the companies involved received enormous publicity but for the wrong reasons and not all are still in business. Can you afford to be a statistic in someone else's table?

An effective HACCP System is one way of preventing incidents such as the above from happening. It is a system where all hazards to food safety are identified and effective control mechanisms are put in place. The continued monitoring of these control mechanisms, and maintenance of the system, ensure that any potentially unsafe situations which occur are highlighted, and this means that the company can take appropriate steps to prevent a food safety incident.

2.3 Limitations of inspection and testing

So, what is wrong with what we are doing already – inspecting and testing? There are several points which you might like to consider here – firstly, 100% inspection where every single product manufactured is inspected. This would seem to be the ultimate approach to product safety or would it? An easy way to find out for yourself is to make up an overhead or slide of the following piece of text:

'When Freddie fries his fish he finds that the fat used in frying is an important factor in producing a perfect finished fish dish'

Ask people within your organization to count the number of letter 'i's in the text within a given time (try 10 seconds). Very rarely will anyone find the right number – there are 15. This exercise is essentially a 100% inspection and can be used to demonstrate that it is not reliable as a control technique. Yet how often we rely on it, particularly for finished products going down the production line, or ingredients during the weighing-up stage. Fruit is a good example of this where we look for physical contamination – stalks, stones, leaves, insects, etc.

Employees get distracted in the workplace by other activities going on around them, such as the noise of the production line,

Figure 2.1 The limitations of inspection and testing.

fellow workers talking about their holiday plans or what was on television the night before. The human attention span when carrying out tedious activities is short and 'hazards' could be easily missed during visual inspection. Because of this people are often moved from task to task, in order to give some variety. However, this in itself brings problems along with line changes or shift changes; different personnel may be more aware of one hazard than another.

Of course, the main difficulty with a 100% inspection when it is applied to biological and chemical hazards is that there would be no product left to sell because biological and chemical testing is nearly always destructive. This leads us on to the use of sampling plans.

Many businesses randomly take a sample(s) from the production line. This can be daily, by batch, or even annually in the case of a seasonal vegetable or fruit crop. Statistically the chances of finding a hazard will be variable. Sampling products to detect a hazard relies on two key factors:

1. The ability to detect the hazard reliably with an appropriate analytical technique.
2. The ability to trap the hazard in the sample chosen for analysis.

Analytical methods for the detection of hazards vary in their sensitivity, specificity, reliability and reproducibility. The ability to

11

trap a hazard in a sample is, in itself, dependent on a number of factors including:

1. The distribution of the hazard in the batch.
2. The frequency at which the hazard occurs in the batch.

Hazards distributed homogeneously within a batch at a high frequency are naturally more readily detectable than hetero-geneously distributed hazards occurring at low frequencies.

For example, in a batch of milk powder contaminated with *Salmonella* distributed evenly at a level of 5 cells/kg, a sampling plan involving testing ten randomly selected samples each of 25 g would have a probability of detection of 71%. For powder contaminated at 1 cell/kg, the probability of detection using the same sampling plan would be only 22%.

This naturally assumes that the detection method is capable of recovering the *Salmonella* serotype contaminating the batch. Few of the methods for *Salmonella* detection would claim an ability to detect in excess of 90% of the 2000 serotypes and most of the methods probably have a success rate of less than 75%. Therefore the low probability of 22% will be further reduced.

The probability of detecting a hazard distributed homo-geneously in a batch is improved quite simply by increasing the overall quantity of the sample taken and is relatively unaffected by the number of samples taken. Therefore, ten samples of 25 g would have the same probability of detection as one sample of 250 g.

In the majority of cases, hazards, particularly microbiological, are distributed heterogeneously, often present in small clusters in a relatively small proportion of a batch. The probability of detecting a hazard distributed in this way is extremely low if low numbers of samples would be lower than 2%. Interestingly, even if the hazard occurred at high levels within 1% of the batch (10 000 batch, the probability of detecting the hazard taking ten 25 g samples would be lower than 2%. Interestingly, even if the hazard occurred at high levels within 1% of the batch (10 000 *Salmonella* cells/kg), the probability of detection would still be lower than 15%.

Such a situation cannot be rectified without recourse to a higher number of samples. In fact the probability of detecting the hazard in this scenario is greatly improved by merely taking more frequent samples from a batch, using a continuous sampling device.

For example, if 100 g of the milk powder was removed from every tonne by a continuous sampler and a well mixed subsample was tested (5 g from each tonne), the probability of detecting *Salmonella* heterogeneously distributed at 5 cells/kg would increase from 2% to >90%. However, even with exhaustive statistical sampling techniques, detection can never be absolute unless the entire batch is analysed and in most cases few manufacturers understand or can afford to operate rigorous statistical sampling procedures.

2.4 External pressures

2.4.1 Government

Government recognition of HACCP as the most effective means of managing food safety is increasing on a world-wide basis. The difficulty in focusing on specific pieces of legislation is that legislation is ever changing. However, in Europe one of the most powerful driving forces legally is the European Community Directive 93/43 EC (1993) on the Hygiene of Foodstuffs.

The Directive, while not using the precise wording of Codex Alimentarius or NACMCF, in Article 3 states that food business operators shall identify any step in their activities critical to ensuring food safety and ensure that adequate safety procedures are identified, implemented, maintained, and reviewed. The Directive lists the first five principles required to develop the system of HACCP. These principles have virtually the same interpretation as Codex/NACMCF with the exception of any specific reference to record keeping. Article 8 of the Directive dictates that competent authorities shall carry out controls to ensure that Article 3 is being complied with by food businesses; obviously evidence of compliance will be required, i.e. records. Article 9 states that where failure to comply with Article 3 (use of HACCP) might result in risks to the safety or wholesomeness of foodstuffs, appropriate measures shall be taken which may extend to the withdrawal and/or destruction of the foodstuff or to the closure of the business for an appropriate period of time.

The adoption of the Directive will mean that all food businesses throughout Europe are strongly recommended to use the HACCP approach. It will also more specifically require that food businesses who are certified to the international quality standard ISO 9000 will be forced to include HACCP within the scope of their Quality Management Systems as under this standard all relevant legislation must be complied with in full.

In the UK, the statutory defence of Due Diligence contained within the Food Safety Act (1990) requires that the person prove that he took 'all reasonable precautions and exercised all due diligence to avoid the commission of the offence by himself or by a person under his control'. A defendant using this defence would certainly have a stronger case if it could be proved that HACCP was in place.

The UK Government has recognized HACCP in several specific reports and no doubt this will increase. In New Zealand, the Ministry of Agriculture is considering making HACCP mandatory for all food producers. In the USA the HACCP techniques were used to identify the controls specified in the Low Acid Canned Food Regulations. The US Department of Agriculture has recently announced that HACCP programmes will be required for all meat and poultry processing facilities. It is also being applied in the area of seafood inspection.

The trend seems to indicate that HACCP will eventually be mandatory not only for all US food processing facilities but also all food processors who are exporting into the United States from anywhere else in the world.

In summary, it is clear that international legislation is moving more and more towards making HACCP a mandatory requirement for the food industry. Key indicators include the legal requirement for use of HACCP in specific sectors of the food industry and the strong recommendation from many governments through directives, and food safety reports and surveys.

2.4.2 Customers

While the end consumer may not know what HACCP means, those of you who are supplying to customers are most likely being asked to implement a HACCP System. Indeed it may be one of the main driving forces behind the purchase of this book. For the retailer and caterer the customer is the end of the supply chain – the consumer of the food. For the grower and food manufacturer quite likely the customer is a caterer, a retailer or another manufacturer. Whatever the situation, customers want to be confident that the food being purchased is safe. They want to have confidence in you as their supplier.

HACCP is an excellent way of assuring the safety of the food because not only must it be carried out and verified by experts, it must also be maintained. Gone are the days when a large customer inspection meant a walk around the factory to check hygiene and housekeeping followed by a pleasant lunch. A crucial factor in any supplier inspection these days is an assessment of the competence of the management. An effective HACCP System can go a long way in demonstrating to the customer that the supplier is managing the risks. One of the main reasons for the change in supplier/customer relationships in the UK has been the Food Safety Act (1990) where a company must prove that it 'took all reasonable precautions and acted with all due diligence' – the supplier inspection is very much about this – establishing faith in your suppliers. You in turn may want to consider asking your own suppliers, particularly of high risk materials, whether through safety or commercial reasons, to implement a HACCP System. Perhaps you could give a preferred supplier status to those who have done so. Your suppliers may then be encouraged to pass the disciplines back through the supply chain to their suppliers, and so on.

No one wants to be buying in a problem. If a food safety incident was attributed to your product but was eventually traced to an ingredient, would you or your supplier be held responsible? It may turn out to be the supplier; however, what damage will have been done to your business in the interim period if the media have taken an interest and your brand is involved?

2.4.3 Enforcement authorities

The role of the enforcement authority is to ensure that legislation is being correctly complied with. In the UK this falls to the Local Authority Environmental Health Departments, but there are equivalent or similar bodies elsewhere.

Environmental Health Officers (EHOs) are provided with Codes of Practice by the Department of Health. These offer guidance on the interpretation and enforcement of specifically The Food Safety Act (1990). 'Code of Practice No. 9: Food Hygiene Inspections' (1991) makes reference to the use of Hazard Analysis systems in relation to inspection of food businesses. Either the EHO would review a HACCP System already in place, i.e. evaluate the understanding, or instead use the Hazard Analysis techniques to determine which hazards will need to be controlled in order to ensure safe food production. The latter approach may be used in smaller businesses where fully documented HACCP Systems are not being implemented by the company itself.

2.4.4 Media

Most companies are aware of the power of the media but perhaps feel complacent when it comes to their own businesses, 'it will never happen to us', 'we are in control', etc. HACCP provides a means of ensuring that incidents, which could have been pre-vented, are prevented. Food safety scares have become big business; the media are always looking for a good story and consumers feel encouraged to go to the press, lured by both the publicity and the cash rewards.

Sometimes the issues may be very real, but not always. If a consumer goes to the press you will need to have evidence in order to answer the claims made against you. This is particularly important if the consumer has falsified claims and the Police are drawn into the case. Fully documented evidence, through HACCP records which have been efficiently maintained are essential. Someone within the company who is trained in media handling and an effective incident management system could be vital in ensuring that the company remains in business and the risk to the public minimized in the event of an incident occurring.

2.4.5 *International standardization*

Since the early days in Pillsbury, HACCP principles have become accepted internationally. Two important documents published within the last two years have assisted with this common understanding; these are the Codex and NACMCF approaches. Both contain the seven HACCP principles which were outlined in Chapter 1. From these principles many manufacturing companies, committees, consultancy groups, governments and Food Research Associations – large and small – have taken a lead.

This has steered the way towards harmonization world-wide in HACCP terms. It means that the HACCP System implemented by one company is based on the same principles as the one installed by its competitor. What remains then is the interpretation of the principles. This book has the objective of contributing to a common understanding of HACCP and is based both on the Codex and NACMCF approaches.

2.5 Prioritization for improvement

HACCP is a system of managing food safety but once you have learnt the technique it can be applied to other aspects of the business. One of the main benefits in the early stages of implementation is its help in setting priorities. Mistakenly, many people feel that HACCP can only be used by mature businesses who have Good Manufacturing Practices and Quality Management Systems such as ISO 9000 series already in place. It should fiercely be argued that HACCP is especially important for those businesses who do not fall into this category. HACCP can be used to prioritize areas for improvement. This can seem a daunting task when a customer inspection results in a ten-page audit report listing areas for change!

By systematically analysing the hazards at each stage in any food production chain and determining at which points control is critical to food safety you can see whether you already have these controls in place or not. The same discipline can be used to determine where control is crucial to end product quality, (appearance, taste), shelf life (what factors are important to control spoilage?) and legality (e.g. weight control). A HACCP Study can also be used to assess where priorities lie in terms of Supplier Quality Assurance. For all materials an agreed specification will be needed but how do you know which suppliers to visit, whether a certificate of analysis will be necessary, and when to sample and test at your own factory? Again, by determining which of your raw materials are themselves Critical Control Points, i.e. control is critical to the safety of the end product, you can start to prioritize activity and make effective use of the resource available.

What about training? Where do you start and what type of training will be needed? In undertaking the HACCP Study, you will be able to see where for example basic food hygiene training is essential in a manual operation, which controls need to be monitored and therefore where monitor training will be needed. Awareness in HACCP itself will be required throughout the company, but consider also the availability of specialist skills in for example microbiology, food technology, engineering, statistical process control (SPC), toxicology, auditing and interpersonal skills such as the training of trainers, communication, project planning and leadership skills. Don't worry if you don't have all of these disciplines available within your organization. You should identify your weak areas and plan to address them by making appropriate external contacts.

Key objectives may include:

- **Producing safe product every time.**
- **Providing evidence of safe production and handling of food products.** This is particularly useful during regulatory inspection or prosecution.
- **Having confidence in your product** and thereby ensuring that customers have confidence in your ability.
- **Satisfying a customer request for HACCP** to an international standard.
- **Compliance with the regulatory guidelines.**

Additional objectives may include:

- **Involving personnel from all disciplines** and at all levels in HACCP implementation – the management of food safety becoming everyone's responsibility.

- **Moving the company towards a Quality Management System** which may be certified to ISO 9001 – HACCP being seen as one of the key steps.
- **Cost effective use of resources** – where the limited technical resource is focused and targeted, and also where capital expenditure should be directed.

3

Preparing for HACCP

Before you get too far down the road, you need to consider the level of expertise you have in your organization. In this chapter we will look at how to plan the implementation of the HACCP Principles. This includes an indication of how to plan the project, the types and numbers of people needed, along with what they should be capable of achieving.

3.1 Who should be involved?

3.1.1 Senior management

Early involvement of senior management is fundamental to the effective implementation of HACCP. Real commitment can only be achieved if there is complete understanding of what HACCP actually is, what benefits it can offer to the company, what is really involved and what resources will be required. This understanding will be achieved not only by reading books such as this one but also by attending a HACCP briefing session, as a senior management group. This may be undertaken by a reliable consultant if there is no one able to do it internally. Open discussion should then follow with the end result that the decision to go ahead is given fill support by the board, and at this stage the Project Sponsor could be appointed.

Senior management from all disciplines must be encouraged to actively show their support and be unanimous in their approach. It would be a pity if the credibility was lost through the Sales Director continuing to make rash promises to the customer 'Yes, we can develop and produce this completely untried and tested high risk product for you within 3 days – no problem', or through the

Engineering Manager purchasing equipment that is unable to achieve the process criteria needed to make a safe product or be cleaned properly.

3.1.2 What types of people?

HACCP is carried out by people. If the people are not properly trained and experienced then the HACCP System is likely to be ineffective and unsound. It is important that HACCP is not carried out by one person alone but is the result of a multi-disciplinary team effort – **The HACCP Team**. It is recommended that as a minimum the core HACCP Team consists of the experts (expert meaning knowledge **and** experience) from the following areas:

1. Quality Assurance/Technical – providing the expertise in microbiological, chemical and physical hazards, an understanding of the risks of the hazards occurring, and knowledge of measures that can be taken to prevent the hazards occurring.
2. Operations or Production – the person who has responsibility for and detailed knowledge of the day-to-day operational activities required in order to produce the product.
3. Engineering – able to provide a working knowledge of process equipment and environment with respect to hygienic design and process capability.
4. Additional expertise – may be provided both from within the company and from external consultancies.

(a) Internal expertise

- Supplier Quality Assurance – essential in providing details of supplier activities and in assessment of hazard and risk associated with raw materials. Also the person responsible for auditing suppliers will have a broad knowledge of best practices gained through observing a wide range of manufacturing operations.
- Research and Development – if the company is one where new products and processes development is a continuous activity then input from this area will be essential. Early involvement at the product/process concept stage could prove invaluable.
- Distribution – for expert knowledge of storage and handling throughout the distribution chain. This is particularly important if strict temperature control is essential to product safety.
- Purchasing – perhaps an unlikely choice for a HACCP Team but could be useful in a company involved in purchasing factored

goods for onward sale or in a food service operation. The participation of purchasing personnel will mean that they are made fully aware of the risks associated with particular products or raw materials and can assist with early communication of a proposed change in supplier.

(b) External expertise

(Possibly you will have some of these disciplines internally)

- Microbiologist – if the company has its own microbiologist then certainly their expert knowledge will be needed on the HACCP Team. Many smaller companies do not have this option and should identify a source of expert help from either a Food Research Association or from a reputable local analytical laboratory.
- Toxicologist – likely to be located in a Food Research Association or University, a toxicologist may be needed particularly for knowledge of chemical hazards and methods for monitoring and control.
- Statistical Process Control (SPC) – there are many courses now available which will be sufficient to give members of the HACCP Team enough knowledge to carry out basic SPC studies on their process operations. This will be important in assessing whether a process is capable of consistently achieving the control parameters necessary to control safety. In some instances, however, it may be advisable to have an external expert in on the HACCP Team as a temporary co-opted member. Useful in setting up sampling plans or for more detailed assessment of process control data.
- 'HACCP' experts – deliberately left to last but by no means least, it may be appropriate to initially co-opt an external 'expert' in HACCP on to the HACCP Team. This may be useful in helping the company team to become familiar with the HACCP System, and could also be extremely important in helping the company to determine whether they have got the right people on the team and as an early assessment of whether the initial HACCP studies are correct.

It may be difficult initially for individuals not used to working as part of a team to adjust to this approach. It should be explained that as a team effort the HACCP Study will have input from a much greater diversity of knowledge, skill and experience, far beyond that of any one individual. The team is made up of people with a real working knowledge of what happens in each area and therefore processes which cross departments can be more accurately tackled. You should consider too that HACCP studies may well result in recommendations for changes to processes and products and even on occasions capital expenditure. These recommendations are far more likely to be accepted by senior management if they are supported by knowledgeable people across all disciplines within the company.

We have considered the disciplines within the team and in summary it should be emphasized that expert judgement is essential in assessment of hazards and risks. What else is important with respect to the type of people involved in the team? Personal attributes will include:

1. Being able to evaluate data in a logical manner – using expertise within the team and perhaps using published data for comparison.
2. Being able to analyse problems effectively and solving them permanently, treating the cause not the symptom of the problem.
3. Being creative – looking outside the team and the company for ideas.
4. Being able to get things done – make recommendations happen.
5. Communication skills. The HACCP Team will need to be able to effectively communicate both within the team and without, across all levels of the company.
6. Leadership abilities.

Leadership skills of some degree will be useful in all members of the team. After all they are leading the company in its HACCP approach to food safety management. It is recommended that one member of the team is appointed to HACCP **Team Leader**. This is often the QA Manager but consider carefully what the leadership of a team entails. Your Personnel or Human Resources department may be helpful in identifying suitable courses for development of these skills if they are not already sufficient.

The Team Leader role will be a key one in the success of the HACCP System and he or she is likely to become the company HACCP expert and be regarded as such. In the leadership role the Team Leader will be responsible for ensuring that the team members have sufficient breadth of knowledge and expertise, that their personal attributes are taken into account, that individual training and development needs are recognized. The Team Leader must be able to organize the team, making time available for them to review their progress on an ongoing basis. The behaviour within the team must be supportive, encouraging all members to participate. With all team members fully committed to producing and maintaining an effective HACCP System – there should be no time for arguments or internal politics.

The Team Leader will also be responsible for assessing whether all skills, resources, knowledge and information needed for the HACCP System are available from within the company and if not, together with the Project Manager (if this is someone different) identifying useful external contacts.

So far we have considered involvement from senior management within the company including the HACCP Team. Also involved will be personnel further down the management chain, line supervisors, operators, incoming goods inspectors, cooks and point of sale personnel. It is important that these people too are fully briefed on their role within the system, particularly if they are monitors of the controls critical to food safety.

3.1.3 How many people?

Within the HACCP Team itself, consider the range of disciplines required. In smaller companies the same person may be responsible for both QA and Operations. In terms of team size however between four and six people is a good number. This is small enough for communication not to be a problem but large enough to be able to designate specific tasks.

In very large organizations there may be more than one HACCP Team. It was stressed earlier that the members of the team must have a good working knowledge of what actually happens in practice. In large companies the 'experts' and senior people in the three main disciplines of QA, Production and Engineering may not be close enough to the operation. It may then be more effective to have a series of smaller departmental factory teams, still made up of the three main disciplines but at a less senior level. The departmental teams then carry out the HACCP Study for their own areas and when satisfied with the resulting HACCP Plan, pass it up to a senior 'core' HACCP Team for review and approval. This is ensuring that both the true working knowledge of activities is captured and reviewed by the appropriate experts in each area. An example of this could be represented diagramatically, as in Figure 3.1.

Numbers of people needed in addition to the HACCP Team will be dependent upon the type of operation and number of controls which need to be monitored. There should always be a sufficient number of people to ensure that the critical points are effectively monitored and that records are reviewed.

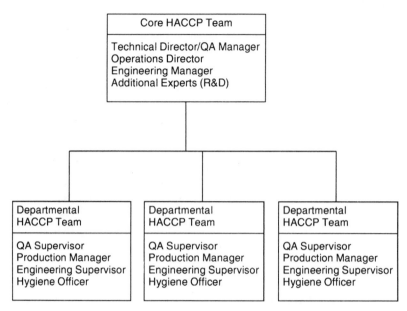

Figure 3.1 Example of HACCP Team structure in a large organization.

3.2 What training?

HACCP is only going to be effective as a means of managing food safety if the people responsible for it are competent. As a result training becomes the single most important element in setting up a HACCP System. Training not only provides the technical skills required in implementing HACCP, it also helps in changing attitudes of people. In our experience there are a number of key attributes and skills which are required of HACCP teams. A balance of these attributes throughout the team is necessary.

3.2.1 HACCP Team training

The level of technical expertise required by the HACCP Team is obviously far beyond that needed by the rest of the company. The training of these people is an investment and should be taken seriously. A suggestion as to how these skills may be provided if not already available within the team has been made in Table 3.1

You should, having looked at the table, realize that the HACCP Team members need to be provided with many additional support skills as well as the technical expertise, such as hazard and risk assessment, drawing process flow diagrams and collating data onto control charts, etc. in order for your system to work really well.

Table 3.1 Suggested sources of Key HACCP Team skills

	Skill	Means of providing it
1	Principles and techniques of HACCP	Training courses available through Food Research Associations, Universities, training organizations and consultants. Check for practical hands-on content as well as theory. Minimum duration should be 2 days for HACCP Team members, longer for Team Leaders. Reference books and scientific papers: Pierson and Corlett (1992); Campden Food and Drink Research Association (1992); ICMSF (1988)
2	Be able to draw Process Flow Diagrams	Practice within the factory and use of a HACCP 'expert' to confirm comprehension in early stages. Problem solving skills will be helpful.
3	Understanding of the types of hazards which could occur and methods of prevention. For example, in relation to food-borne pathogens this should include the frequency and extent of their occurrence in different foods. The severity and risk of transmitting food-borne pathogens and toxins through different foods. The means of and influence on contamination of all types and elimination or reduction by processing and procedures, i.e. the preventative measures.	With a good mix of disciplines on the team this area should be covered, provided the team members between them have both academic background, i.e. qualified to degree or equivalent in microbiology or a food science-related subject, and many years food industry experience. Useful courses in understanding hazards are provided by many food RAs if a refresher is needed. Additionally, an advanced qualification in food hygiene is highly recommended. In the UK this is provided by several reputable bodies such as the Royal Institute of Public Health and Hygiene, Institute of Environmental Health Officers and the Royal Society of Health. Use of hazard databases available through food RAs, universities. Use of reference books: ICMSF (1980); ICMSF (1986); Sprenger (1991)

Table 3.1 *continued*

	Skill	Means of providing it
4	Detailed knowledge of Good Manufacturing Practices	Essential food industry experience as above. Reference books: Shapton and Shapton (1991)
5	Be able to identify where the critical control points are in the process and method of monitoring. Establish sampling plans and corrective action in the event of a deviation.	As previous – 3.
6	Team working skills, including communication skills (especially important if this is a new way of working for most team members).	Personnel department may be able to assist with some in-house building training for the HACCP Team. External team building training courses are available, often about a 5-day length.
7	Project planning and management skills (the HACCP implementation project may have a separate Project Manager but if the team itself is responsible, this skill will be invaluable).	External courses run by management consultancies or training organizations. Use of an on-site consultant in the early stages. Reference books: Brown (1992); Bird (1992); Oates (1993)
8	Auditor training – essential for the verification of the flow diagram and HACCP Plan.	A Quality Management Systems auditor course is recommended (Internal Auditors level is sufficient which is usually 2 days). These can be run on your own site if numbers justify. Available from Food RAs, ISO 9000 assessment bodies such as Lloyds Register Quality Assurance or Training Consultants.

9	Statistical Process Control (a working knowledge in order to make valid process capability assessment and in data handling)	External Management consultancy groups who often provide training packages. Lasermedia. This is a system of training developed by the Ford Motor Company and can be purchased or hired on weekly basis from Lasermedia[a]. Reference books: Rowntree (1981); Price (1984)
10	Problem-solving techniques – in order to tackle recurring problems in a structured way and ensure permanent solutions are found. Can be very useful in learning how to draw Process Flow diagrams and in handling data.	Training packages can be purchased from management and training consultancy groups Courses available also through the above. Recommend an on-site session tailored to the need (HACCP) in order for it to be really understood and applied after the event.
11	Trainer training skills – essential if HACCP training is to be carried out in-house.	Food industry courses are now being run by many of the Food RAs. Management and training consultancies may also be able to provide this type of training. Effective Presentation courses may be a good foundation. Liaison with Personnel department recommended. Reference books: Jay (1993)

[a]Lasermedia Statistical Process Control Interactive Video Training Package, Arundel, West Sussex

Figure 3.2 'How do you draw a Process Flow Diagram?'.

3.2.2 CCP monitor training

These people will need training in two ways:

1. Awareness of what HACCP is and why it is being used. In relation to this, how crucial their role as Monitors of the Critical Control Points is to the safety of the finished product.
2. Specific training in the job required whether it be checking a pH, controlling a cooking temperature and time, or testing a sensitive raw material for *Salmonella*.

They will also need to be trained in entering data on log sheets, how to maintain records, and in the event of a CCP failure, what corrective action to take and what procedures to follow.

3.2.3 *Company HACCP awareness training*

Senior management will be one of the first groups of company personnel to be trained but it is important that all company employees are made aware of and understand the following:

1. What HACCP is.
2. Why HACCP is required – benefits of using it and examples of failure.
3. Who will be involved and level of training needed.
4. What changes will be needed compared with the current way of working.
5. That Critical Control Points are those which must **not** be negotiated. They are minimized to those that in the event of a failure will very likely result in a food safety incident.
6. That commitment to the management of food safety is essential through the company.
7. An understanding that GMP and SQA will be prerequisites to an effective system.

For the company awareness training it is often a good idea if this is carried out by the HACCP Team members – it raises the profile of both HACCP and the Team itself. An in-house presentation is perfectly adequate – the information needed can easily be sourced from this book; alternatively a member of the Team could be sent on an externally run HACCP training course. Remember – properly trained trainers will be much more effective in running such sessions.

3.3 Getting started – the Project Plan

It is important in preparing to implement a HACCP System that you consider carefully the scale of the task before charging ahead. Just as HACCP is systematic you also need to be systematic in your approach and plan in a structured manner exactly how to proceed.

Firstly, the implementation of HACCP can be managed as a project. It will have a definite life cycle that is a start date and a finish date when HACCP can be said to be fully operational. The project may be managed by a temporary project team and the timetable and costs estimated where possible. This will involve the appointment of a few key people and the documentation of the actions and time scale required. The roles needed in managing the project are two key personnel plus supporting team.

3.3.1 *The Project Sponsor*

As the champion of the project, the Project Sponsor is likely to be your company Managing Director, Operations Director or Technical Director. Whoever takes on the role is likely to sit on the senior management team and have budgetary control. The main responsibilities are to:

- Provide funds.
- Approve and drive the company HACCP or food safety policy.
- Approve the business issues and ensure that the project continues to move forward and remains valid.
- Appoint a Project Manager and team.
- Ensure adequate resources are made available to the Project Team.
- Establish a progress reporting procedure.
- Ensure that the Project Plan is realistic and achievable.
- Approve any changes to the original project.

3.3.2 *The Project Manager*

This role is likely to be taken by the Production or Technical Manager who may also become the HACCP Team Leader. The responsibility centres on ensuring that the Project Plan is drawn up and objectives achieved within the agreed time scale. This requires effective project management skills. Specifically to:

- lead and direct the Project Team;
- produce an achievable Project Plan;
- provide a regular progress report to the Project Sponsor;
- liaise with other Project Managers to ensure areas of common interest are identified and resource used effectively in these areas.

There may well be other business improvement projects going on within the business at the same time. It is useful to establish what these are early on, for example as in Figure 3.3.

Other projects may include the setting up of a formal supplier Quality Assurance programme, the introduction of Statistical Process Control on certain lines, production rationalization, product development activities, cost of quality projects, and so on. The list is not exhaustive.

The main issue here is to define the HACCP implementation project – what are the objectives, the constraints and how will it be achieved within the constraints? The project team will need a complete understanding of the starting point. This will include a review of documented procedures already in place, environmental

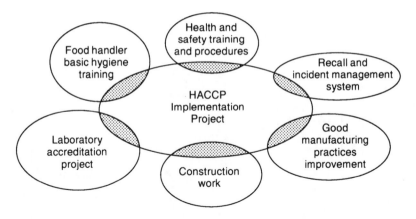

Figure 3.3 HACCP interaction with business improvement projects.

issues, GMP status, resource availability and current culture. In other words, how big is the task, what are our current capabilities and what additional resources will be required?

This will enable an implementation plan to be drawn up. A simple example of a single process operation is given below where each phase of the project has been defined as follows:

Phase 1: establish the HACCP Team
Phase 2: determine the scope of the HACCP System
Phase 3: establish Supplier Quality Assurance
Phase 4: prepare the HACCP Plan
Phase 5: Project sign off – implementation completed

Once this has been done each phase can be broken down into specific activities – a work breakdown structure. The start, finish and activity time is determined together with any dependencies (what needs to happen before this particular activity can take place?), and the resource allocated (who will make it happen?). This can be plotted on paper to provide an implementation timetable known as a Gantt chart. An example is given in Figure 3.4.

In looking at the Gantt chart, notice that while the duration of each task has been estimated, not all tasks can begin on Day 1. This is because some of them cannot start until another task has been completed – this is known as establishing the **dependency**.

Key terms are introduced on the chart:

- **Critical**: this means that the task is critical in terms of timing. If these tasks do not run to time then the project completion date will be affected – there is no slack.

HACCP Implementation – Gantt Chart

This is an imaginary outline plan for the implementation of HACCP into a model factory with one simple process line. The dependencies of the tasks are shown on the accompanying PERT chart.

ID	Name	Duration
1	**Phase 1 (Establish the HACCP Team)**	**32d**
2	Identify project sponsor and manager	0d
3	Awareness training of key personnel	2d
4	Decide on HACCP team structure and appoint team members	0d
5	Train team members in HACCP and support skills	10d
6	Set up external specialist support links	4w
7	**Phase 2 (Determine the scope of the System)**	**1d**
8	Write HACCP or food safety policy	1d
9	Publish scope and timescale for implementation	0d
10	**Phase 3 (Supplier Quality Assurance (SQA))**	**70d**
11	Write and agree raw material specificaions with suppliers	10w
12	Identify and train SQA personnel	2w
13	Set up SQA audit schedule and carry out agreed assessments	10d
14	**Phase 4 (prepare HACCP plan)**	**100d**
15	Draw and verify process flow diagram	2w
16	Conduct hazard analysis	1w
17	Establish critical control points	1w
18	Establish control procedures (HACCP control chart)	2d
19	Write procedures for CCP monitors	2w
20	Train CCP monitors	1w
21	Implement the HACCP plan	0d
22	Verification of the HACCP plan	3d
23	**Phase 5 (Project sign off)**	**0d**
24	Agree HACCP is fully implemented	0d

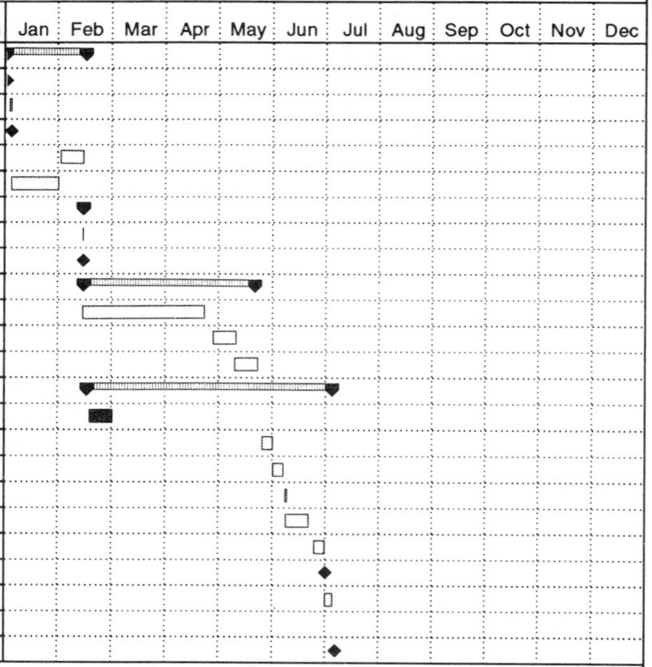

Critical / Noncritical / Milestone ◆ / HACCP Implementation / Summary

Figure 3.4 HACCP implementation – Gantt chart.

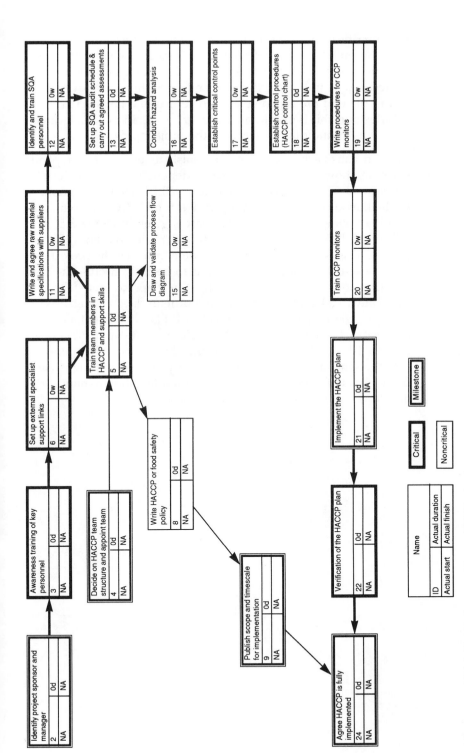

Figure 3.5 HACCP implementation – PERT chart.

- **Non-critical**: this doesn't mean that the tasks are any less important than those referred to as Critical. It just means that there is some slack in the timing. If they don't finish at the precise date indicated, then depending on how long over they run, the end project completion date may **not** be affected.
- **Milestone**: this is usually an event, or key decision date. It can be used as an indicator in terms of the project progress.

By then considering the start and finish times and the dependencies as shown on the Gantt chart, a dependency network can be established. This is also known as a PERT chart (**P**rogramme **E**valuation and **R**eview **T**echnique). For the HACCP Implementation Plan, an example of a PERT chart is given in Figure 3.5.

The PERT chart indicates the Critical Path (in bold lines) for the project. This is the shortest possible time in which the project can be achieved. It should be noted that to be truly useful, the task duration must be calculated using the elapsed time taken to complete a task and not the number of man days needed. As an example, the preparation of the HACCP Plan documentation has been set at 3 weeks + 2 days. This could be made up, for example, of 16 × 1-hour HACCP Team meetings held during that period.

Both Gantt and PERT charts can be produced through using computer software packages. The examples shown here were developed using Microsoft *Projects*.

4

An introduction to hazards – their significance and control

This chapter is designed to give you a clearer understanding of different types of hazards and their significance in foods. We will explore the mechanisms which can be used for their control and introduce the concept of critical control points. This information is intended for reading before you get going and will give a valuable grounding to the HACCP Team members. You may not initially have people who will understand the implications of all the information given here, but it will help you to get started and will highlight areas where you may need to bring in specialist help to your HACCP Team.

4.1 Hazards and how they can be controlled

A hazard is any factor which may be present in the product that can cause harm to the consumer either through injury or illness. Hazards may be biological, chemical or physical and are the basis of every HACCP System.

HAZARD:
a biological, chemical or physical property which may cause a food to be unsafe for human consumption.

Chemical hazards are often looked on as the most important by the consumer but in reality they often pose a relatively low health risk at levels likely to be found in food, and in general cause long-term effects. Biological hazards on the other hand usually present the greatest immediate danger to the consumer, through the potential to cause food poisoning.

4.1.1 Biological hazards

Most food processing operations will be at risk from one or more biological hazards, either from the raw materials or during the process, and the HACCP Plan will be designed to control these. Biological hazards can be either macrobiological or microbiological.

Macrobiological hazards, such as the presence of flies or insects, while unpleasant if found, rarely pose a risk themselves to product safety in its true sense. There are a few exceptions to this, such as poisonous insects, but on the whole the appearance of macrobiological hazards simply causes revulsion. However, they may be an indirect risk through harbouring pathogenic microorganisms and introducing these to the product.

For example, an insect harbouring *Salmonella* would pose a major risk to the consumer if it gained access to a fresh, ready-to-eat product. However, the same insect gaining access to a canned product before retorting would not be a true food safety issue as it would be sterile in the finished product.

Obviously it is important to ensure that your products are free from macrobiological hazards and you may want to consider them as part of your HACCP Study, but it is important to understand where the real safety risk arises.

Pathogenic or food-poisoning microorganisms exert their effect either directly or indirectly on humans. Direct effects result from an infection or invasion of body tissues and are caused by the organism itself, e.g. bacteria, viruses and protozoa. Indirect effects are caused by the formation of toxins (or poisons) that are usually preformed in the food, e.g. bacteria and moulds (or fungi).

Bacteria are broadly divided into two types depending on a simple colour reaction produced by the Gram stain. Bacteria are therefore classified as either Gram-positive or Gram-negative. As a general rule, Gram-negative bacteria tend to exert their efforts through invasion of the host whereas the effects of Gram-positive bacteria is usually mediated via a preformed toxin. Consequently the infections caused by Gram-negative bacteria generally have an onset period of 24 hours, they are long lasting and debilitating. They are rarely fatal in healthy individuals but can cause death in the young, old, ill or immunocompromized, e.g. *Salmonella*. Illness caused by preformed toxins of Gram-positive bacteria have a rapid onset period of 1–6 hours, they are short lived (lasting 24–48 hours) and are not usually fatal, e.g. *Staphylococcus aureus*. This is an over-simplification and as with most biological systems, there are always exceptions. For example Gram-positive *Clostridium botulinum* produces a lethal toxin, *Listeria monocytogenes* causes abortions and meningitis, and the effects of some Gram-negative bacteria, e.g. *E.coli* are mediated via toxins. Accordingly the reader is strongly advised to seek expert professional advice.

(a) Pathogenic Gram-negative bacteria

The Gram-negative pathogenic bacteria typically associated with foods include *Salmonella, Shigella, Escherichia coli, Campylobacter jejuni* and *Vibrio parahaemolyticus*.

These are usually present in the intestine and faeces of man, animals and birds. Consequently they can also be found in soil, water, raw agricultural products such as raw milk and raw meat (particularly poultry) and shellfish.

These bacteria are not heat resistant and cause problems as a result of poor sanitation, inadequate personal hygiene and the cross-contamination from raw materials to work surfaces, utensils, processing equipment/machinery, finished products and packaging. The hazards they represent must be either eliminated or controlled by heat processing (e.g. pasteurization), segregation of raw and cooked foodstuffs, good hygienic working practices and/ or formulating and storing the product such that the pathogen is inactivated or prevented from growing (e.g. fermented raw sausage).

Salmonella spp., *Shigella* spp. and *E.coli* are closely related and have similar properties; however there are also notable differences. There are over 2000 strains of salmonellae many of which affect man, but some are specific to birds and certain animals, and some are primarily spread by water as a result of poor sanitation, e.g. *S.typhi* which causes typhoid. *Shigella dysenteriae* causes bacillary dysentery and its infection is mediated by toxin. Four types of food poisoning have been described for *E.coli* i.e. enteropathogenic, enterotoxigenic, enteroinvasive and enterohaemorrhagic. Certain types of enterohaemorrhagic *E.coli* (such as 0157 H7) produce very unpleasant and debilitating symptoms (sometimes called bloody diarrhoea) and can cause renal failure resulting in death.

Camplyobacter jejuni is the most common cause of bacterial gastroenteritis in the UK. It is found principally in raw poultry and, unlike the other enteric pathogens, it does not grow well in foods as it requires exacting conditions for growth. The food itself is merely a vehicle (or vector) for cross-contamination, so segregation and inactivation via thermal processing are the most effective control measures.

Vibrio parahaemolyticus is more salt tolerant than the other Gram-negative pathogens and is found in marine environments and animals. This bacterium is typically associated with raw or under processed sea food, and accounts for 50–70% of food poisoning in

Japan. Other species can also cause gastroenteritis such as *V. cholerae*, which is asociated with water-borne gastroenteritis.

(b) Pathogenic Gram-positive bacteria

The Gram-positive bacteria are a diverse and unrelated group of organisms such as *Clostridium botulinum, Clostridium perfringens, Bacillus cereus, Staphylococcus aureus,* and *Listeria monocytogenes.*

Species of the genus *Clostridium* are anaerobic, i.e. they grow in the absence of oxygen, and produce heat-resistant spores. They are generally widely distributed in nature but are usually found in soil, vegetation and fresh water and marine sediments and animal faeces. Consequently their elimination and control is achieved by processing with high temperatures (such as involved in canning) and product formulation, e.g. adding acids (pickling) or reducing the available water (preserving with sugar or salt).

Clostridium botulinum is important because it produces a lethal toxin which paralyses the nervous system. Historically, food poisoning has been associated with inadequate heat processing and/or formulation, or ineffective seals on cans which are subsequently cross-contaminated during cooling. There are several types of *Cl. botulinum* which produce seven different toxins (distinguished alphabetically A–G). The majority grow at room temperature and will also spoil proteinaceous foods such as meat and fish. However some species are non-proteinaceous and can grow and produce toxin at much lower temperatures (albeit slowly). These organisms will be important as new food manufacturing processes are developed, e.g. sous vide.

In comparison, the mode of action of *Cl. perfringens* is quite different. Food poisoning due to this organism is usually associated with undercooked and/or inadequately reheated meats and sauces, particularly in catering operations. The organism grows to large numbers in the food and produces its toxin during spore formation in the intestine after consumption. The toxin causes diarrhoea and nausea but is not normally fatal. The controls required are effective thermal processing, segregation of raw and cooked materials, chilled storage of cooked meat before consumption, and adequate reheating and hot storage before consumption.

In contrast to the clostridia, species of the genus *Bacillus* are normally aerobic spore forming, i.e. they need oxygen to grow. *Bacillus cereus* also produces two types of toxins; a very fast acting emetic toxin, causing vomiting and a diarrhoeal toxin. It is widely distributed and commonly found in soil, vegetation and raw milk. Food poisoning is frequently associated with cooked rice and other starchy products, where the spores have not been inactivated by the initial heat process and have subsequently been allowed to germinate and grow due to inadequate handling and poor temperature control.

Bacillus subtilis and *B. licheniformis* are spore-forming bacteria that are historically associated with the spoilage of bread. More recent incidents of food poisoning have been associated with bread, pies and pasties where high numbers of these bacteria were present. The symptoms were similar to those shown by *B. cereus* . These bacteria are found in soil and vegetation, and their spores are heat resistant and will survive baking. Strict control of the temperature and humidity during subsequent cooling and storage is essential to prevent their germination and growth.

Unlike the other Gram-positive pathogenic bacteria, the sources of *Staphylococcus aureus* are human in origin, i.e. from the skin, nose, throat, cuts and sores. Consequently it is easily transmitted to any foods by handling and poor hygienic practices. If the bacterium is allowed to grow in foods, it will produce a toxin which is stable to further heat processing and therefore cannot be made safe again.

Staphylococcus aureus does not form heat-resistant spores and is more versatile than other pathogens because it is able to tolerate a greater range of growth conditions. Accordingly strict personal hygiene is of paramount importance for the control of this organism, as well as thermal processing and segregation.
and segregation.

The importance of *Listeria monocytogenes* as an agent of food-borne disease has only recently become fully recognized. It is important because it has a high mortality rate, it is ubiquitous and can grow at lower temperatures than many other pathogens.

Listeria does not produce spores or toxins and causes meningitis, septicaemia and abortion. It can be isolated from a wide variety of raw foodstuffs but is inactivated by normal pasteurization procedures. The ubiquitous nature of the organisms means that it represents a major post-process cross-contamination hazard, particularly for chilled processed foods.

(c) Emerging pathogens

The term 'emerging pathogens' is used to describe those organisms that have not historically been recognized as agents of human disease. Evidence is now available which demonstrates that the following bacteria may cause gastroenteritis: *Yersinia enterocolitica*, *Aeromonas hydrophila*, *Plesiomonas shigelloides* and *Vibrio vulnificus*.

Yersinia enterocolitica is a Gram-negative bacterium which belongs to the same family as *E.coli* and *Salmonella*. It is a ubiquitous organism which has been associated with a wide variety of foodstuffs and like *Listeria*, has the ability to grow at low temperatures. It can also produce an enterotoxin. The major sources of pathogenic types of *Yersinia* are from raw pork, raw milk and water. Outbreaks have been associated with these sources and from pasteurized milk. Thermal processing and the prevention of post-process cross-contamination are the principal methods of control.

Aeromonas hydrophila and *Plesiomonas shigelloides* are Gram-negative bacteria that are closely related. They are both aquatic bacteria that can also be recovered from a variety of terrestrial and aquatic animals. Both are associated with diarrhoea in man, but whether either is a primary pathogen is not entirely clear.

Vibrio vulnificus, like the other species of *Vibrio*, is associated with seafood and the marine environment. The organism is highly invasive and causes primary septicaemia. Its virulence appears to be enhanced in individuals suffering from hepatitis or chronic cirrhosis where it can be fatal.

Yersinia, *Aeromonas*, *Plesiomonas* and *Vibrio* are all inactivated by pasteurization and the controls required are thermal processing and the prevention of cross-contamination. However these procedures may not be appropriate for raw seafood and shellfish, where the hazards must be recognized and accepted or other decontamination procedures established.

(d) Viruses

Viral gastroenteritis is believed to be second only to the common cold in frequency and greatly exceeds the incidence of food-borne bacterial gastroenteritis. There are a number of types of viruses but the greatest number of outbreaks are due to Hepatitis A and Small Round Structured Viruses (SRSV) such as the Norwalk virus. Shellfish (particularly molluscan shellfish) are the most common food source because they concentrate the virus from contaminated water. Despite this, much less is known about the incidence of viruses in food than about bacteria and fungi. This is because viruses are obligate parasites, they do not grow on culture media or in foods (food is a vector only), they are very small and therefore very difficult to detect.

Viruses are present in man, animals, faeces, polluted waters and shellfish. They are transmitted from animals to people and from person to person by contaminated body fluids. Hence high standards of personal hygiene are essential. The Norwalk virus is characterized by a very rapid, sudden onset, explosive vomiting and is also spread by aerosols and cross-contamination of work surfaces, utensils and food. Viruses can be destroyed by the heat efficiency of the thermal process. This is dependent on both the type of virus present and the foodstuff itself.

(e) Parasites and protozoa

The larva of parasites such as pathogenic flatworms, tapeworms and flukes may infect man via the consumption of the flesh of infected pork, beef, fish and wild game. Examples include *Taenia saginata* (beef tapeworm), *Trichinella spiralis* (nematode), and *Clonorchis sinensis* (trematode or fluke from Asian fish).

Prevention of parasite infestation is achieved by good animal husbandry and veterinary inspection, along with heating, freezing, drying and/or salting. The most effective methods being heating (>76 °C) and freezing (-18 °C).

Protozoa such as *Toxoplasma gondii*, *Giardia intestinalis (lamblia)* and *Cryptosporidium parvum* produce encysted larvae which subsequently infect man on ingestion. Infected meat and raw milk serves as the sources for *Toxoplasma*, whereas raw milk and drinking water are the sources of *Giardia* and *Cryptosporidium*. Human infection can also be contracted by direct contact with infected pets and animals. The oocysts of *Cryptosporidium* and *Giardia* are resistant to chemical disinfection, but can be inactivated by heating and drying.

(f) Mycotoxins

Mycotoxins are produced as secondary metabolites of certain fungi, and they can cause long-term carcinogenic or short-term acute toxic effects in mammals at high levels of exposure. Although a large number of mycotoxins have been isolated, only a very small minority have been shown to be toxic to mammals. Mycotoxins are being considered here under biological hazards because they are products of microbial growth.

The mycotoxins of concern in food production are aflatoxins, patulin, ergot and tricothecenes, and may be consumed by humans via two routes. Firstly, direct consumption, e.g. contaminated grain or, secondly, indirect consumption via animal products, e.g. milk and turkey meat.

Aflatoxins are the most important group of food-borne mycotoxins, and are normally controlled through legislation in various foodstuffs. These mycotoxins are produced by *Aspergillus flavus* and other moulds growing on foodstuffs. There are six aflatoxins of concern, four of which (B1, B2, G1 and G2), occur in various foods and two of which (M1 and M2) are metabolites found in the milk of lactating animals which have eaten aflatoxin contaminated feed. Aflatoxin B1 is most commonly found and occurs in groundnuts and in grain crops, particularly maize.

Aflatoxins normally contaminate crops during the growing or storage periods. During the growth period the aflatoxin contamination risk is increased by environmental conditions which stress the plants and allow contamination with the mould, for example insect damage or drought conditions. Poor storage conditions such as dampness and humidity will increase the chance of unacceptable contamination. In order to control aflatoxins in your products you must understand the risks associated with each raw material source and with storage at your facility. Appropriate control can then be built in as part of your HACCP System.

Patulin is a mycotoxin associated with fruit and fruit juice products. It is considered to be a carcinogen and high concentrations may cause acute effects such as haemorrhages and oedema. The presence of patulin in food products is normally associated with the use of mouldy raw materials, and this can be prevented by building effective control measures into your HACCP System.

Ergot is perhaps the best known mycotoxin as its presence and effects have been reported through history, as for back as the 9th and 10th centuries AD. It occurs in cereals, particularly in rye, and has two main effects on man. The first form is gangrenous ergotism, and has been historically recorded, while the second affects the nervous system. Although ergotism is now rare in humans, the potential for contamination of the raw materials should be considered.

Tricothecenes are mycotoxins which are mainly found in grain crops, particularly wheat. This group includes zearalenone, T–2 toxin and deoxynivalenol (also known as vomitoxin). Deoxynivalenol is of particular importance and has been found in crops world-wide. It is produced by the mould *Fusarium graminearum* and its presence is promoted by wet weather conditions. This mycotoxin is known to cause toxic effects in animals and human illness has been reported. It is controlled through legislation in some countries where there have been particular problems, and should be considered as a raw material issue in the HACCP Study.

Many other mycotoxins are produced by fungi, but none of these are currently considered to be of risk in the food supply. However you must ensure that your HACCP Team have access to sufficient expert knowledge so that any newly discovered mycotoxin issues can be considered for your products.

4.1.2 *Chemical hazards*

Chemical contamination of foodstuffs can happen at any stage of their production, from growing of the raw materials through to consumption of the finished product. The effect of chemical contamination on the consumer can be long term (chronic) such as for carcinogenic or accumulative chemicals (e.g. mercury) which can build up in the body for many years, or it can be short term (acute) such as the effect of allergenic foods. The current main chemical hazard issues in food products are as follows:

(a) Cleaning chemicals

In any food preparation or production operation, cleaning chemicals are one of the most significant chemical hazards. Cleaning residues may remain on utensils or within pipework and equipment and be transferred directly onto foods, or they may be splashed onto food during the cleaning of adjacent items.

It is therefore vitally important that the HACCP Team members consider the implications of the cleaning procedures in their operation. Problems can be prevented by the use of non-toxic cleaning chemicals where possible, and through the design and management of appropriate cleaning procedures. This will include adequate training of staff and may involve post-cleaning equipment inspections.

(b) Pesticides

Pesticides are any chemicals which are applied to control or kill pests and include the following:

- Insecticides
- Herbicides
- Fungicides
- Wood preservatives
- Masonry biocides
- Bird and animal repellents
- Food storage protectors
- Rodenticides
- Marine anti-fouling paints
- Industrial/domestic hygiene products

Pesticides are used in a wide range of applications all over the world, in agriculture, industry, shipping and the home. The use most relevant to food safety is in agriculture but contamination from other sources must also be considered.

In agriculture pesticides are used during production to protect crops and improve yields, and after harvest they are again used to protect the crops in storage. However, not all pesticides are safe for use in food production (for example, some of those used for the treatment of timber) and even those which are safe for food use may leave residues which could be harmful in high concentrations. To overcome these problems most countries have very strict control on the pesticides which can be used and on the residue limits which are acceptable. These are set through expert toxicological studies and are normally set down in legislation.

From the food safety point of view you need to know which pesticides have been applied to all your raw materials at any stage in their preparation. You must also understand which pesticides are permitted for use and what the maximum safe residue limits are in each case. Control can be built in to your HACCP System to ensure that the safe levels are never exceeded in your products.

In addition to raw materials which have direct pesticide contact, you must also consider the possibility of cross-contamination with pesticides at any stage in food production. This could be cross-contamination of your raw materials or it could happen on your site, e.g. from rodenticides. These issues should again be considered as part of your HACCP Study.

(c) Allergens

Some food components can cause an allergic or food intolerance response in sensitive individuals. These reactions can range from mild to extremely serious, depending on the dose and the consumer's sensitivity to the specific component.

The control options open to the food processor manufacturing products with allergenic components are effective pack labelling, control of rework and effective cleaning of equipment. The label must accurately describe the product contents, highlighting any potentially allergenic components. Special care must be taken when declaring a generic category of ingredient such as 'fish' or 'nuts', where certain individuals may be allergic to specific species of fish or type of nut. A manufacturer or caterer who produces several different products must also consider the chance of cross-contamination of allergenic components into the wrong product where they will not be labelled. This is particularly important in the case of recycling loops and rework of product, and these issues should be considered as part of the HACCP Study.

(d) Toxic metals

Metals can enter food from a number of sources and can be of concern in high levels. The most significant sources of toxic metals to the food chain are:

- environmental pollution
- the soil in which food stuffs are grown

- equipment, utensils and containers for cooking, processing and storage
- food processing water
- chemicals applied to agricultural land

Particular metals of concern are tin (from tin containers), mercury in fish, cadmium and lead, both from environmental pollution. Also significant are arsenic, aluminium, copper, zinc, antimony and fluoride, and these have been the subject of research studies.

As for the other chemical hazards, you need to understand the particular risk of toxic metals to your products, and this is likely to be associated with the raw materials, metal equipment and finished product packaging. Control can be built in as part of your HACCP System.

(e) Nitrites, nitrates and *N*-nitroso compounds

Nitrate occurs naturally in the environment and is present in plant foodstuffs. It is also a constituent of many fertilizers which has increased its presence in soil and water.

Nitrites and nitrates have historically been added to a number of food products as constituents of their preservation systems. This deliberate addition of nitrite and nitrate to food is closely governed by legislation as high levels of nitrites, nitrates and *N*-nitroso compounds in food can produce a variety of toxic effects. Specific examples include infantile methaemoglobinaemia and carcinogenic effects.

N-nitroso compounds can be formed in foods from reactions between nitrites or nitrates with other compounds. They can also be formed *in vivo* under certain conditions when large amounts of nitrites or nitrates are present in the diet. Nitrate can cause additional problems in canned products where it can cause lacquer breakdown, allowing tin to leach into the product.

The HACCP Team must ensure that nitrite and nitrate being added to products do not exceed the legal, safe levels and must give appropriate consideration to the risk of contamination from other sources and other ingredients, giving an increased overall level.

(f) Polychlorinated biphenyls (PCBs)

PCBs are members of a group of organic compounds which have been used in a number of industrial applications. Because these compounds are toxic and environmentally stable, their use has been limited to closed systems, and their production has been banned in a number of countries. The most significant source of PCBs in foodstuffs is through absorption from the environment by fish. PCBs then accumulate through the food chain and can be found in high levels in tissues with high lipid content. This issue should be considered by HACCP Teams dealing with raw materials of marine origin.

(g) Plasticizers and packaging migration

Certain plasticizers and other plastics additives are of concern if they are able to migrate into food. Migration depends on the constituents present, and also on the type of food, for example fatty foods promote migration more than some other foodstuffs.

The constituents of food contact plastics and packaging are normally strictly governed by legislation, along with the maximum permitted migration limits in a number of food models. The HACCP Team should be aware of current issues for both food packaging and plastic utensils, and should build control into the HACCP System. This might mean the requirement for checks on migration at the packaging concept stage.

(h) Veterinary residues

Hormones, growth regulators and antibiotics used in animal treatment can pass into food. Hormones and growth regulators have been banned from food production in many countries, and the use of antibiotics and other medicines are tightly controlled. Carry-over of antibiotics can cause major problems due to the potential for serious allergic responses in susceptible individuals. Similarly hormones and growth regulators can cause toxic responses when consumed. The HACCP Team should consider the risks of contamination in their product so that appropriate control and monitoring can be instigated. This will include control at the primary producer and may also involve monitoring at the incoming raw material stage.

(i) Chemical additives

Additives are used not only to make products safe and hygienic, but also to assist processing and to enhance or beautify what would otherwise be bland but nutritious products. They may also be beneficial as in the case of vitamins.

The use of chemical additives is governed by regulation in almost all countries in the world. In Europe it is the Directive 89/107/EEC (1989) which not only classifies additives according to their purpose (such as preservative, acidulant or emulsifier) but also lays down guidelines and limitations for their use across various categories of foodstuffs. This is, in effect, a positive listing of permitted additives. Therefore, if an additive appears in this or other countries' positive legislation, it may be assumed to have undergone appropriate toxicological testing and be deemed, by advisory committees of experts, to be safe. This testing procedure led to the European 'E' number system of classification for approved and tested materials and also to the ADI (Acceptable Daily Intake) levels set by such organisations as JECFA (Joint Expert Committee on Food Additives) and WHO (World Health Organisation).

Nevertheless, it is still possible to imagine situations where careless or unnecessary use of additives poses a potential hazard in a foodstuff. For instance, in the choice of preservative one might avoid the excessive use of sodium metabisulphite in acidic products as the resultant sulphur dioxide gas may be injurious to asthmatics both in the workplace and as consumers. Similarly, nitrates and nitrites could be avoided if there are suitable alternatives, without compromizing food safety and quality. There are some synthetic colours, such as tartrazine, for which a causative relationship has been suggested, but not proven, for hyperactivity in children. It would obviously be sensible to use more natural alternatives in cases where the product is targeted at young consumers. Even then it is wise to remember that 'natural' does not always mean 'safer'. Many natural plant extracts, for instance, are acutely toxic. Generally, materials can be used only if they are derived from normally consumed foodstuffs. Care must also be taken so that the 'natural additive' is not offered in amounts greatly in excess of those encountered in the native foodstuff.

Additives may be beneficial, benign or, if misused, harmful. Great care and understanding must be exercised in their selection and use.

4.1.3 Physical hazards

Physical hazards, like biological and chemical hazards, can enter a food product at any stage in its production. There is a huge variety of physical items which can enter food as foreign material, some of which may also be described as macrobiological, but only a few of these are hazards to food safety. Here we must ask ourselves very carefully whether or not any potential foreign material items are likely to cause a health risk to the consumer. Only if they are should they be considered in the main food safety HACCP Study. If, however, you choose to use the HACCP techniques separately in other areas such as quality (see Chapter 9) you may wish to extend your terms of reference to include all potential foreign material as hazards. It should be noted that you could be prosecuted for the presence of foreign material in a product regardless of whether or not it is a true safety hazard, but simply because the product is not of the true nature and substance demanded by the consumer.

It is important to remember that any foreign material item could be a safety hazard if it has the potential to make the consumer choke. This is particularly important in foods which may be consumed by children, where even pieces of paper sacks or boxes could pose a safety risk. As with macrobiological hazards, it should also be noted that any foreign material item could transport microbiological hazards into the product and this is particularly significant if they gain access after all processing steps which would control these hazards.

Your procedures for Good Manufacturing Practice should ensure that these issues are considered as part of the building environment and should prevent any physical hazards from being brought into the production area by employees. The main physical food safety hazards are as follows:

(a) Glass

Glass fragments can cause cuts to the customer's mouth and could have very serious consequences if swallowed. Smooth pieces of glass, e.g. watch glasses, could also cause injury by choking or could be broken into sharp pieces when the consumer bites into the product.

Glass may be present in the raw materials, e.g. as foreign material from the growing site, or may be the raw material container. Containers made from glass should be avoided wherever possible and should be kept out of the processing area. In addition personnel should be prevented from bringing any glass items into production and equipment must not have sight glasses or glass gauges. Glass light fittings should always be sheathed with plastic to prevent product contamination if the light shatters.

It may be that your finished product is filled into glass containers. In this case it is obviously not possible to keep glass out of the production area, but it must be properly managed and you should always have stringent breakage control procedures in place.

Another control mechanism for glass in food products is the use of X-ray detection devices, although these are currently not widely used due to expense and application.

(b) Metal

Like glass, metal can enter the product from the raw materials or during production and can cause injury, as sharp pieces, or choking. It is particularly important with this hazard issue that you ensure that your equipment is properly maintained so that parts do not drop into the product. All engineering work must be properly managed and parts, e.g. nuts and bolts, must not be left lying around. Where raw materials are delivered in metal containers, these should be carefully opened to minimize swarf contamination. This should be done outside the main production area if possible.

All products should be metal detected at least once, and this should be at or as close to the end of production and filling as possible. Where the finished product is held in metal containers these should be adequately managed and product metal detection should take place immediately before product filling. Metal detectors should be carefully chosen and calibrated to pick up the smallest pieces of each potential metal type.

(c) Stones

Stones are most likely to originate in raw materials of plant origin, where they may be present within the plant, e.g. between leaves, or be picked up during harvesting. They can cause the consumer dental damage or choking, and sharp stones may cause similar problems to broken glass and metal.

Stones can most easily be prevented by careful choice of raw material supply, and can be removed by inspection or through the use of flotation tanks and centrifugal separators.

(d) Wood

Sharp splinters of wood could be a hazard to the consumer causing, for example, cuts to the mouth and throat. Pieces of wood could also get stuck in the consumer's throat and cause choking.

Wood can enter the production area and the product in a number of ways. It may be present in raw materials, e.g. in plant material brought in from the fields, or it may be part of the raw material packaging. Wooden crates and pallets should be avoided where possible, and must not be allowed into production areas. Where wooden packaging or pallets have to be used for your own products, these must be carefully managed, and must not be allowed access to production areas where product is exposed.

Ideally all wood should be contained in separate raw material handling and outer packaging areas. Production personnel must be prevented from bringing any wooden items into production areas. This should be part of every company's good manufacturing practices, and should be included in induction training for all staff.

Some products actually contain wood as one of their raw materials. These include ice lollies and traditional fish products such as herring rollmops. Obviously here it is not possible to keep wood out of the production area, but it should be obtained from an approved source and handled in a controlled manner to prevent any splintering.

If you are operating from an old manufacturing site it is possible that there is some wood built in to the processing area environment. Here you need to assess the risk of splinters breaking off into the product but from a general hygiene point of view you should put together a plan for its removal and replacement. The HACCP Team will be able to use the HACCP techniques they are learning to help prioritize the essential areas for improvement.

(e) Plastic

Plastic is often used to replace other physical hazards, such as glass and wood, although it should be noted that hard plastic shards can also be hazardous. Soft plastic is also used as packaging or for protective clothing such as aprons and gloves. While more shatterproof than glass, you should implement similar breakage control procedures for hard plastic as for glass. For soft plastic, visual inspection is important and soft plastic used during processing is often brightly coloured (usually blue) to assist with its identification.

(f) Pests

We have already considered pests as causes of biological hazards through the introduction of pathogenic microorganisms into foods. Pests may also be thought of as physical hazards as their presence in foodstuffs may cause injury or choking. Most important here are large insects and parts of rodents or birds. An effective pest control programme must be in place to control these hazards at every food production, storage or preparation premises.

Many of these physical hazard issues can be effectively controlled as part of Good Manufacturing Practice procedures at your facility. If you already have these procedures in place properly, then the HACCP Team will be able to concentrate on the critical product contamination areas. Further information on control of hazards can be found in Appendix B.

4.2 Understanding Control Points

It is likely that you will have many controlling steps in your process, some of which are controlling the hazards we have just mentioned, and others which are not directly associated with control of safety, i.e. are not CCPs. These will probably be points which are controlling the quality and legal attributes of your products and are normally called manufacturing or process control points. Control is effected at these points in the same way as at Critical Control Points (CCPs), but the important difference is that safety is not involved so the points are not truly critical.

Critical Control Points (CCPs) are the stages in a processing operation where the food safety hazards are controlled. These are the points which ensure that the hazard is not able, in the finished product, to cause harm to the consumer. In HACCP terms, a CCP is defined as follows:

CCP:
a point, step or procedure where control can be applied and a hazard can be prevented, eliminated or reduced to acceptable levels.

CCPs are essential for product safety, as they are the points where control is effected. However the CCP itself does not implement control. Instead it is the action which is taken at the CCP which controls the hazard. Controlling factors at CCPs are normally described as preventative measures, although you may also see them written as control options. These are normally defined as those factors which are required to eliminate or reduce the occurrence of hazards to an acceptable level.

PREVENTATIVE MEASURES:
physical, chemical or other factors which can be used to control an identified health hazard.

It is important that CCPs are kept to the points which are truly critical to product safety, and this means that their number is usually kept to a minimum in order to focus attention accurately on the essential controlling factors.

The HACCP Study is all about what is critical to product safety, and so the HACCP System is built up around CCPs. Although the same HACCP techniques can be used to help establish process control points (as we will see in Chapter 9), these process control points should be managed separately from the HACCP System, as their inclusion will make the system unwieldy and difficult to control.

If you are having difficulties in telling the difference between

Figure 4.1 'If I lose control, is it likely that a health hazard will occur?'.

CCPs and process control points, you should ask yourselves this simple question:

If I lose control is it likely that a health hazard will occur?

If the answer is yes, then the point must be managed as a CCP, while if the answer is no then a process control point is sufficient.

The effective operation of CCPs is crucial to the safety of the product. They must be established by the HACCP Team to control all identified hazards effectively.

5

Designing safety into products and processes

Effective HACCP Systems will manage and control food safety issues on an ongoing basis but what they cannot do is make a fundamentally unsafe product safe. It is essential that food safety is designed into a product at the development stage and this should be the responsibility of Product Development and the HACCP Team working together. Possibly your HACCP Team will include a member of the product development department who can introduce new product/process ideas at an early stage. There is no point in new product ideas being shown to marketing departments or to customers if there are inherent safety risks which cannot be controlled. These will just be highlighted when the HACCP Study is carried out and the product launch will have to be stopped, which is not helpful in gaining customer confidence.

There are a number of factors to be considered when designing food safety into a product, and the HACCP Team and other relevant specialists must be involved at the outset. In this chapter we will consider the product formulation and the importance of ensuring the safety of raw materials through Supplier Quality Assurance (SQA). We will also look at safe design of food processes and manufacturing areas. Finally, we will discuss the establishment of a safe and achievable shelf life.

5.1 Intrinsic factors

Intrinsic factors are the compositional elements of a food product and these can often have a controlling effect on the growth of microorganisms. The major intrinsic factors found in foodstuffs and considered here are pH and acidity, organic acids, preservatives, water activity and the ingredients themselves. The information given is an introduction only and, where necessary, HACCP Teams should refer to specific and more detailed reference books.

5.1.1 pH and acidity

Acidity is often one of the principal preserving factors in food products, preventing the growth of many food-poisoning or food-spoilage organisms at certain levels. In fact, fermenting and acidifying foodstuffs to low pH are food preservation techniques which have been used for thousands of years. Examples of foods which can be preserved safely by pH and acidity are yogurt, which is fermented to low pH by the action of starter cultures, and pickled vegetables, which are acidified with acetic acid (vinegar) and normally also pasteurized to prevent spoilage.

Although acidity measurement is still often used in manufacturing, the more useful parameter of measurement from the food safety viewpoint is that of pH. This is because information on the growth and survival characteristics of microorganisms at different levels of acidity is normally based around the pH scale.

There is a characteristic pH range across which microorganisms can grow and the limiting pH for growth varies widely between different species. Most microorganisms grow best at around neutral pH 7, but may also grow at values ranging from pH 4 to 8. A small number of bacteria can grow at pH <4 or >8 but those able to grow at pH <4 are not normally associated with food poisoning. However, the growth of these acid-tolerant organisms could have food safety implications if their growth in the foodstuff is involved in raising the pH to a level where other microorganisms, including pathogens, can grow. This is also true for yeasts and moulds which can grow at pH values considerably lower than pH 4.

It should also be remembered that microorganisms may survive at pH values outside their range for growth. This has significance for food safety when other factors cause the pH to change. For example, spores of *Bacillus cereus* might be present in a low pH raw material where it is unable to grow. If this is then added with other raw materials to make a higher pH product the spores may be able to germinate and grow to dangerous levels.

The pH limits for growth of a number of potential food pathogens can be found in Appendix C. The data shown in the Appendix are absolute limits for growth, many of which have been established in pure culture experimental studies. In real food situations the organisms may not be able to grow to these extremes for a number of reasons. These include water activity, oxygen concentration, heat or cold damage, and competing microflora. The effect of pH on growth is particularly affected by temperature and an organism which can grow at pH 4.5 at 30 °C may not be able to do so at 5 °C, and vice versa. The tolerance of microorganisms to pH can also be greatly affected by the type of acid used.

5.1.2 Organic acids

Certain organic acids are widely used as preservative factors in food manufacture, although some of these are only permitted to be used in defined concentrations. The antimicrobial activity of organic acids is due to the undissociated molecules, although the exact mechanism of their action is unknown. The effectiveness of these acids is related to the pH of the sample, as the dissociation of the molecules is pH dependent. For example, the level of sorbic acid (usually added to a product as potassium sorbate) which will be effective in product at pH 7 will be only 0.48% compared with 97.4% in a product at pH 3. Tables 5.1 and 5.2 (adapted from

Table 5.1 Percentage of organic acid undissociated at various pH values

| Acid | pH value | | | | |
	3	4	5	6	7
Acetic	98.5	84.5	34.9	5.1	0.54
Citric	53.0	18.9	0.41	0.006	< 0.001
Lactic	86.6	39.2	6.05	0.64	0.064
Benzoic	93.5	59.3	12.8	1.44	0.144
Sorbic	97.4	82.0	30.0	4.1	0.48
Propionic	98.5	87.6	41.7	6.67	0.71

Table 5.2 Percentage of undissociated acid which inhibits growth of most strains

Acid	Entero-bacteriaceae	Bacillaceae	Micro-coccaceae	Yeasts	Moulds
Acetic	0.05	0.1	0.05	0.5	0.1
Citric	> 0.005[a]	> 0.005	0.001[b]	> 0.005	> 0.005
Lactic	> 0.01	> 0.03	> 0.01	> 0.01	> 0.02
Benzoic	0.01	0.02	0.01	0.05	0.1
Sorbic	0.01	0.02[c]	0.02	0.02	0.04
Propionic	0.05	0.1	0.1	0.2	0.05

[a]Actual inhibitory concentrations likely to be far in excess of these values.
[b]This value is for *Staphylococcus aureus*; micrococci are more resistant.
[c]Clostridia are more resistant.

ICMSF, 1980) illustrate the antimicrobial activity of organic acids and pH dependence.

Organic acids are most effective against microorganisms in combination with other preserving factors although there are several drawbacks to their use.

1. Resistance of individual strains of microorganisms to organic acids varies considerably.
2. Organic acids are less effective if high levels of microorganisms are present initially.
3. Microorganisms may become resistant to their use.
4. They can be utilized as carbon sources by many micro-organisms.

Organic acids commonly used as preserving factors in foods include acetic, citric, lactic, benzoic, sorbic and propionic acids. Acetic, citric and lactic acids are often added as part of the formulation from the flavour point of view, while benzoic, sorbic and propionic tend to be only used for their preservative action. The specific organic acid chosen depends on the target microflora for inhibition, along with the formulation and other intrinsic factors present in the foodstuff.

5.1.3 Preservatives

Chemical preservatives can be added to certain foodstuffs to inhibit the growth of food poisoning and spoilage organisms. There are usually carefully controlled legal limits for addition and different preservatives are effective against different groups of micro-organisms. Examples of preservatives commonly used in foods are sodium nitrite which is often used in cured meat products, and potassium sorbate, which is used in many areas including bread, cake and jam manufacture. Other food preservatives include nisin, sodium nitrate, sulphur dioxide, sodium benzoate, sodium and calcium propionate, and sodium metabisulphite.

Sodium nitrate and nitrite have long been used in meat curing to reduce spoilage and stabilize colour. Their safety effect is to prevent the germination of spores thus controlling pathogens such as *Clostridium botulinum*. Their effectiveness depends on a number of factors including the types and numbers of microorganisms present, the curing temperature and the meat pH.

As we saw in the previous section, potassium sorbate or sorbic acid is effective in acid foods, particularly against yeasts and moulds. It will also limit the growth of micrococci, enterobacteria and bacilli, although not clostridia. Similarly, sodium benzoate or benzoic acid is also effective mainly in high-acid foods. It will inhibit the growth of yeasts and moulds and is commonly used in pickles, salad dressings and fruit juices.

Nisin is an antibiotic which prevents the growth of many bacteria, and which has been used in cheese manufacture and canned foods. This preservative tends to be relatively expensive and this has limited its application.

Sulphur dioxide is an antioxidant which inhibits the growth of bacteria and moulds, and which can be used in gaseous or liquid form. It is commonly added to beers and wines, and to comminuted meat products.

The propionates, sodium and calcium, are used to control moulds in low acid foodstuffs such as cakes and bread.

The smoking of food also has a preservative effect due to chemical compounds present in the smoke. Although the exact mechanism of preservative action is poorly understood, smoking is a traditional method of food preservation which has remained popular, e.g. for smoked salmon. In recent years it has become fairly common to add smoke flavour to food rather than using the smoking technique. This has little or no preservative effect.

5.1.4 Water activity

Water activity (a_w) is a measure of the availability of water in a sample. As microorganisms can only grow in the presence of an available form of water, they can be controlled by controlling the a_w. The a_w is the ratio of the water vapour pressure of the sample to that of pure water at the same temperature.

$$a_w = \frac{\text{water vapour pressure of sample}}{\text{pure water vapour pressure}}$$

Pure water has an a_w of 1.0, and as solutes are added making a more concentrated solution, the vapour pressure decreases and along with it the a_w. The a_w is directly related to the equilibrium relative humidity ($a_w = $ ERH/100), as well as to the boiling point, freezing point and osmotic pressure of the sample.

Traditionally, a_w has been used as a preservative factor against microorganisms in foods through the addition of salt and/or sugar and the reduction of moisture content through drying. Sugar has traditionally been added to fruit products, such as jams and soft drinks, while salt has wide application in products such as pickled, salted fish and dry cured meats. The minimum a_w values permitting growth for a number of food pathogens is given in Appendix C.

5.1.5 Ingredients

The individual ingredients and their interactions with each other should also be considered as intrinsic factors. Particular attention needs to be paid to hazards entering the product in this way.

- Do the ingredients contain hazards? For example, *Salmonella* in raw milk.
- Would the wrong quantity of an ingredient be hazardous? For example, too little of a preservative or acid added.
- Are any ingredients allergenic? For example, nuts.
- Could ingredient interactions cause a hazard? For example, by neutralizing the preserving acid.

Recent tends have been to design products which have fewer inherent preservation factors, for example, less sugar, less salt, less fat, and no preservatives. As this affects the stability and safety of the product, the HACCP Team should be aware that the significance of safe raw materials and control during processing has increased.

5.2 Establishing a safe raw material supply

In order to make safe products you must understand the hazards and risks associated with your raw materials. The raw materials should either contain no hazards, or any hazards present must be controllable by the process. This can be achieved through a planned and managed programme of Supplier Quality Assurance (SQA).

In establishing the level of control required for each of your raw materials it is important to think about how they will be handled and processed. The same raw material may require different levels of control for two different products, e.g. herbs going into a cooked product may require less emphasis on microbiological control at the raw material stage than the same herbs being used as a garnish on a ready-to-eat product. In order to assist in identifying the level of control needed a question decision tree has been developed (Figure 5.1).

Following the questions in the decision tree will give you an understanding of the level of control required for each of your raw materials. Work through the decision tree as follows:

Q1 Is there a hazard associated with this raw material?
This first question may be obvious but it focuses the mind on identification of all food safety hazards associated with the raw material. If no hazards are identified then you should move on to

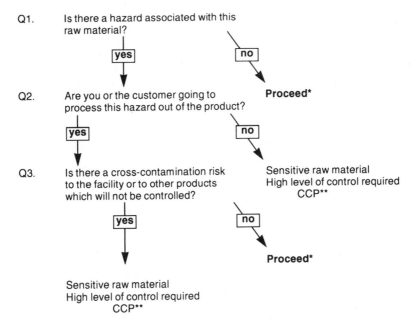

Q1. Is there a hazard associated with this
raw material?

yes   no

Proceed*

Q2. Are you or the customer going to
process this hazard out of the product?

yes   no

Sensitive raw material
High level of control required
CCP**

Q3. Is there a cross-contamination risk
to the facility or to other products
which will not be controlled?

yes   no

Proceed*

Sensitive raw material
High level of control required
CCP**

* Proceed to your next raw material

** Following the hazard analysis, you are likely to find that this raw material must be
managed as a CCP

Figure 5.1 Raw material Control Decision Tree.

the next raw material, but if hazards are identified you should
consider Question 2 for each one.

Q2 Are you or the consumer going to process this hazard out of the product?

If the answer to this question is no, then you could potentially have
the hazard in your finished product, if you do not implement
effective control at the raw material stage. This is therefore a very
sensitive raw material and must be subjected to a high level of
control, probably as a CCP in your process. If, however, the
answer to this question is yes, then you should go on to consider
Question 3.

Q3 Is there a cross contamination risk to the facility or to other products which will not be controlled?

This question investigates whether the hazard could be carried
through to your products by direct cross-contamination or via
contamination of the facility. This is particularly important in a
facility where several different products are being made, as there
may be a lethal step built in to control the hazard in its intended

product but not in other products it might cross-contaminate. If the answer to this question is no, and there is no cross-contamination risk or any risk will be controlled effectively by existing mechanisms (e.g. plant layout), then you should move on to the next hazard or raw material. If the answer is yes, then control of the sensitive raw material must be effected here, and it is likely that this will be a CCP in the HACCP System.

Using the Raw Material Decison Tree will allow you to target SQA resource at the raw materials which are most critical to your operation and products. These raw materials should then be managed through your SQA system. Let's look at examples of its use.

Throughout the next two chapters we will be using an example of chocolate chip ice cream to illustrate the design and implementation of a HACCP System. This example assumes that the manufacturer is a small/medium sized, one-product, one-process operation, operating to acceptable industry Good Manufacturing Practice standards. The product is packed in family-sized plastic tubs for retail sale.

Iced Delights Ice Cream Manufacturers
Development Specification:
Chocolate Chip Ice Cream
Recipe

Skimmed Milk Powder (SMP)
Cream (40% fat)
Liquid sugar (80° Brix)
Milk chocolate chips (5-mm discs)
Water
Natural vanilla extract (liquid)
Stabilizer (lecithin)

Packaging

2 kg plastic tubs

Target Consumers

A luxury ice cream for family use

contd

Provisional Manufacturing Outline

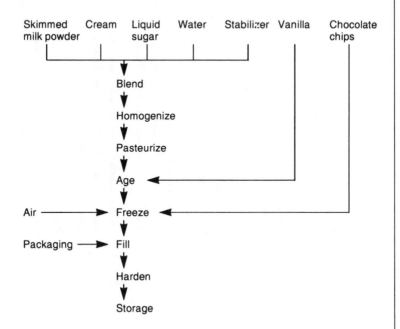

Provisional Microbiological Guidelines

	n	c	m	M
TVC	3	1	5×10^4	5×10^5
Coliforms	3	1	10	1×10^3
E. coli	3	0	Absent/g	Present/g
Salmonella	3	0	Absent/ 25 g	Present/ 25 g
Listeria monocytogenes	3	0	Absent/ 25 g	Present/ 25 g
Staphylococcus aureus	3	1	1×10^2	1×10^3

For definitions of n, c, m and M refer to Appendix E

Let's now look at the ingredients for this product using the Raw Material Decision Tree. We will consider the hazards associated with each raw material in Table 5.3.

Table 5.3 Chocolate chip ice cream – raw material decision matrix

Raw Material	Q1	Q2	Q3	CCP?	HACCP Team notes
Skimmed Milk Powder (SMP)					
– Salmonella	Y	Y	N	N	When we consider SMP, the answer to Q1 is yes. Because of associated risks of salmonella, however, the answer to Q2 is also yes as this ingredient will undergo a heat process which is lethal to vegetative pathogens. There is no cross-contamination risk at this facility as there is already full segregation of the raw materials before pasteurization from the post-process area, and from other sensitive raw materials such as chocolate chips. This raw material therefore does not require to be managed as a CCP at the SQA stage for this hazard.
– Foreign material	N	–	–	N	Foreign material is not normally associated with SMP because the milk is filtered before drying and powder is sieved immediately before bagging.
– Antibiotic residues	Y	N	–	Y	Antibiotic residues may carry through to the final product and will not be removed by the heat process. So, as part of SQA, the raw milk supply into the dairy must be monitored.

Cream					
– Vegetative pathogens (e.g. Salmonella, Listeria, E. coli)	Y	Y	N	N	This hazard is most likely to occur through post-process contamination, e.g. through poor tanker hygiene. However, the answer to Q2 is Yes and Q3 No, for the same reasons as SMP.
– Foreign material	N	—	—	N	The answer to Q1 is No as there is an in-line filter in place at the supplying dairy.
– Antibiotic residues	Y	N	—	Y	As per SMP.
Liquid sugar	N	—	—	N	No hazards were identified.
Milk choc chips					
– Salmonella	Y	N		Y	For chocolate chips there is a hazard of Salmonella being present. The chocolate chips will be added to the ice cream after the heat process, and the consumer will eat the product without any further preparation. This leads us to the decision that a high level of control is required with this raw material, i.e. it will be a product CCP, and we should focus SQA resource here accordingly.
– Chemical – pesticide residues	Y	N	—	Y	These hazards could occur at the growing and raw material storage stages. The answer to Q2 is No, so it is important to ensure that these issues are controlled by the supplier.

Table 5.3 continued

Raw material	Q1	Q2	Q3	CCP?	HACCP Team notes
Water – Microbiological	Y?	Y	Y	Y	As an ingredient in this product there would be minimal risk from microbiological hazard due to the heat process. However, the use as wash water for post-heat process equipment would need to be managed as a CCP through control of the water supply.
– Chemical, e.g. Toxic metals pesticides, nitrites	Y	N	—	Y	As an ingredient, control of the supply is critical as these hazards may not be processed out.
– Foreign material	N	—	—	N	Automatic filtration in place.
Natural vanilla extract – Microbiological – Physical	N N	— —	— —	N N	The processing by the supplier will eliminate any risk of either microbiological or physical hazards.
Stabilizer (lecithin)	N	—	—	N	No hazard identified.
Plastic tubs and lids – Chemical (plasticizers and additives)	Y	N	—	Y	There may be chemical leeching into product. The SQA process must ensure that all chemical constituents are legal and are within chemical migration limits for a high-fat ice cream product.

5.2.1 Elements of a Supplier Quality Assurance (SQA) System

There are a number of different elements to an effective Supplier Quality Assurance programme, including having agreed specifications, auditing suppliers and Certificates of Analysis. Supplier approval will depend on having confidence in the supplier's operation, that they are competent at managing the hazards present. It is therefore vital to develop good customer/supplier relationships – partners in the management of safe raw materials and products.

(a) Specifications

It is vital that all raw materials are purchased from approved suppliers to an accurate and up to date agreed specification. The specification is the cornerstone of your SQA system, detailing all the accepted criteria against which raw material quality and safety are measured. It should clearly define all the factors which you consider important to the raw material, and should include limits or tolerance of acceptability/unacceptability. The document can be as lengthy or as concise as you wish but should always include your minimum acceptance criteria.

A typical raw material specification would include the following. If you are buying in a finished product these issues will also need to be addressed:

- Details of supplier and manufacturing/supply site;
- A description of the raw material and its functionality;
- An ingredients breakdown;
- Details of all intrinsic factors with tolerance limits, e.g. pH, a_w, salt, alcohol etc;
- Microbiological acceptance criteria, e.g. absence of identified hazard organisms;
- Analytical and microbiological sampling plans;
- Labelling requirements;
- Storage and distribution conditions;
- Safe handling and use instructions;
- Description of pack type, size and quantity.

A description of how the raw material is processed, or Process Flow Diagram, and a site plan is helpful to the HACCP Team in ensuring that they have fully identified all hazards of concern in the raw material. These can form part of the specification or can be separate documents, and are essential for all high-risk raw materials. These documents can also be used to draw up a checklist of questions before the supplier audit. If your supplier is unwilling to provide processing information, perhaps for reasons of confidentiality, then you must be able to assure yourself that the raw material is safe by some other means. This may be through an understanding of the raw material's critical intrinsic factors along with the structured audit of the suppliers operation.

---

1. Company name, address, contacts and ownership details, including organizational structure and number of personnel.

2. Production site for this product.

3. How long has the factory been in operation?

4. Was the building purpose built?

5. Are any other types of product manufactured at this facility?

6. Does the company operate a food safety management system based on HACCP?

7. Does the manufacturing site operate to a formal quality system such as ISO 9000, and is it certificated?

8. Is microbiological testing carried out on site, and if so does this include pathogen testing?

9. Are any external contract laboratories used?

10. Have on-site and contract laboratories been accredited to an independent laboratory quality standard?

11. Is the manufacturing site covered by a pest control contract and, if not, what pest control procedures are in place?

12. Where is protective clothing laundered? If a contract laundry is used, has it been audited?

13. Who is responsible for plant hygiene? If contract cleaners are used, how often do they visit?

14. Are any raw materials, intermediate or finished products stored off-site, and if so who is responsible for the condition of these facilities?

15. Are specifications held for all raw materials and finished products?

16. Are written work procedures available on site?

17. Are there written personal hygiene standards?

18. What training do food handlers receive?

19. What vehicles are used for distribution (own/contract), and who monitors their condition?

20. What legislation is considered applicable to the company's operations?

Figure 5.2 Supplier Quality Assurance pre-audit survey.

(b) Auditing

Auditing is one of the key functions in any SQA system, as it is through audit that confidence can be gained in the supplier's operation. Before auditing a supplier there are a number of questions you will want to ask (Figure 5.2). This information will also be important for low-risk raw materials where you do not intend to audit the supplier.

You will need to put together a programme of auditing covering all your raw material types. The raw material control decision tree can be used to help prioritize areas for attention and to help determine audit frequencies.

When you have constructed a programme of auditing requirements, it is important to think about how audits will be carried out. Do you, for example, have personnel who can carry out audits and are they trained appropriately? The SQA audit is important to the safety and quality of your products so it is vital that it is carried out effectively, and that you maintain good relationships with your suppliers. This can only be secured through choosing the correct type of personnel and training them properly.

We will discuss auditing in much more detail in Chapter 6, where we will be looking at auditing the HACCP System. The elements are the same for successful supplier auditing, except here we are looking more broadly at the supplier's entire operation.

Figure 5.3 'Establishing a safe raw material supply'.

(c) Certificates of analysis

Certificates of analysis can be obtained for batches of raw materials to confirm that these have been sampled for certain criteria and that they comply with specifications for these criteria. These certificates can form a useful part of the SQA system, but the limitations of end product inspection and testing (see Chapter 1) should be remembered, and they should not be the only way of verifying that the finished product is free from the hazard(s).

You should ensure that certificates of analysis are prepared only by laboratories who are competent to carry out the tests and provide accurate results. This is best attained through independent laboratory accreditation which we will discuss further in Chapter 8.

(d) Third party inspectors

If you do not have any or sufficient numbers of trained and experienced staff to carry out your planned programme of audits, then you may wish to use third party inspectors. You may be able to use experts from a Food Research Association, or you may need to look at commercial inspection organizations.

In choosing third party inspectors, you will need to consider the expertise and experience of the auditors at the third party inspection body. It is vital that the inspectors have sufficient experience both in the technology concerned and in auditing practices. You must be confident that they will highlight any potential food safety problems and help you to maintain good relationships with your suppliers. This can be achieved by going out and accompanying your suppliers' auditors to confirm that you are happy with their performance.

(e) Buying from agents and brokers

When you buy raw materials through agents or brokers, you lose out on direct contact with the supplier. This can have drawbacks where the agent has little or no technical knowledge of the raw material, but it can work if you manage the situation effectively.

You must know how your raw materials have been processed and handled at every stage, in order to establish whether the likely hazards are present at expected or increased levels, and also whether any new unexpected hazards have crept in. It is important that you can obtain the appropriate assurances from the agent, and possibly from the supplier via the agent, and you must ensure that appropriate control is built into your own operation to cope with the worst-case scenario.

Even with the best planned SQA system it is difficult to be absolutely sure that your raw materials always meet the required standards for safety and quality. In order to do this more effectively it is advisable to pass on to your suppliers the requirement to operate an effective HACCP System for food safety hazards. This requirement can be passed right up the supply chain so that at each stage, growers, processors, distributors and final manufacturers have the same level of confidence in the material at their stage in the chain, in the same way as the consumer can have in a finished product manufactured through an effective HACCP System.

5.3 Can it be made safely?

When designing a new food product it is important to ask if it is possible to manufacture it safely. In addition to the product's intrinsic factors and proposed shelf life this will involve choosing the correct process technology and understanding the factory layout where manufacture is proposed.

5.3.1 Process technologies

There is a wide variety of different process technologies available and it is necessary that the type of process being used is fully understood.

It is essential that any planned **thermal process**, in terms of heating, cooling and holding temperatures and times are known, along with their effect on potential hazards. Where the consumer is expected to cook or heat a product, the exact instructions to achieve the desired heat process should be determined. Often product development is carried out on samples manufactured in a laboratory or pilot kitchen. Where this is true the process requirements to achieve the correct heat profile when scaled up to the manufacturing environment must be understood. This will vary depending on the type of heat processor chosen, e.g. band oven, plate heat exchanger, rack oven, bulk vessel, microwave, etc.

Where a product is being made by **fermentation**, it is important to understand the chosen culture system and how it is controlled. Would you know if the fermentation failed, and would this allow microbiological hazards to grow?

In the production of a **dried product**, how is the final moisture controlled? The potential for the presence of microbiological hazards which have survived through the process or have entered through contamination must be established, as these could cause a problem when the product is reconstituted. This is particularly important for products which are reconstituted without further heating, e.g. dessert mixes.

In a **freezing process**, the length of time to freeze and any holding stages before freezing could be significant. The potential cross-contamination risk is important here also, particularly for foods to be consumed immediately after defrosting. If you are using frozen ingredients in a product you will need to consider whether or not these need to be defrosted before addition. Adding frozen ingredients may help with temperature control, but they may change the product's intrinsic factors as they defrost, e.g. diluting the dressing of a low pH salad and raising the pH.

Irradiation may be used to vastly improve the microbiological quality of certain foodstuffs. However, if the product has been mishandled before the irradiation process it is possible that microbial toxins could be present which would not be affected by the process. This could cause a major food poisoning risk in the finished product.

Will it be a **continuous process** or will there be a number of holding or delay stages? The maximum holding time or delay at all stages should be understood, along with the associated temperature at this stage. This information will need to be assessed during the hazard analysis to establish the potential for growth of microbiological hazards.

The chosen **packaging system** may have an impact on product safety so the influence that packaging has on the growth of microorganisms during the product shelf life should be established. The use of controlled and modified atmosphere packaging systems has increased in recent years along with that of vacuum packaging. The absence of oxygen means that only anaerobic or facultative organisms can grow, and so these systems have been promoted for the extension of product shelf life by reducing/preventing the growth of the normal microflora. However, they allow the growth of a different microflora which could include food pathogens. It is vital that these organisms cannot grow to hazardous levels during the proposed shelf life.

If any new or less well established process technologies are employed then the hazards associated with these must be determined for full consideration during the hazard analysis. An example here is ohmic heating, which allows the sterilization of liquid-based foods without overcooking the liquid phase. Here a voltage is applied between electrodes inserted in a tube though which a continuous stream of food passes. The food is sterilized by the heat generated in it due to its electrical resistance. Initial considerations of this technique suggested that toxicological hazards might be formed by metal ions from the electrodes leaching into the food, or by the formation of free radicals in the food through the heating process. Detailed examination of the technique by expert toxicologists found that free radicals were not likely to be formed, and that any traces of metal in the food from the electrodes would not represent a hazard to health. The technique was therefore cleared for these hazards.

5.3.2 Factory issues

When designing a new product or process to fit an existing factory layout, or when planning a completely new factory layout, there are a number of factors which should be considered. A key issue for product safety is the risk of cross-contamination occurring during the process from the internal factory environment. Cross-contamination could arise from a wide range of sources and the inherent risks in a particular processing area must be understood. Some of the main sources of potential cross contamination are as follows:

(a) Layout

The facility layout should be carefully considered to minimize the cross-contamination risks. This should include adequate segregation of raw materials and finished products. Depending on the type of operation full segregation between raw and cooked product may be required, and in most facilities the outer packaging stages, both for raw materials and finished products, should be kept separate from the main processing area.

When designing factory layouts the availability of the required services and facilities for manufacture of the product must be considered. This will include the availability of potable water, and adequate cleaning facilities for plant, equipment and environment, along with the connection of all required services in the correct area – steam heating, cooling facilities, etc.

The number of holding stages and associated times must also be considered at this stage as it is important that there is adequate space for holding the required amount of product at each stage without causing a cross-contamination risk, and that the appropriate temperature controlled facilities are available.

The traffic patterns for staff and equipment should also be considered here, with the provision of adequate hygiene facilities such as changing and rest rooms and handwash stations, along with canteen and recreational facilities.

(b) Buildings

The fabric of the building itself could pose a risk to the product, through harbourage of pests and other contamination, or through physical contamination due to poor design and maintenance. Surfaces should be non-porous and easy to keep clean, with all cracks filled and sealed, and overhead services should be kept to a minimum. All buildings should be well maintained to prevent physical hazards falling into the product, and drains should be designed and serviced so that the flow is always away from production areas, with no chance of back flow or seepage. Adequate pest proofing and cleaning schedules must be drawn up for all facility buildings.

All food manufacturing areas must be constructed such that these issues are managed.

(c) Equipment

Equipment should be designed to minimize any cross-contamination risk. This could arise through parts of the equipment breaking off and gaining entry to the product as physical hazards. Alternatively if equipment has any dead areas, is difficult to clean or is poorly cleaned, microbiological build-up could contaminate the product. Chemical contamination could arise through lubricants or cleaning residues remaining on the equipment food contact surfaces. Remember also to ensure that you can clean around and under equipment. If it is too close to the floor to clean underneath, the equipment should be sealed around the base.

You will also need to consider what the equipment is made of. For example, is it stainless steel or is it mild steel which may corrode leaving a surface prone to microbiological contamination? Is it painted and could your product be at risk from paint flakes? Does it have any wooden parts or brush attachments which cannot be effectively cleaned?

(d) People

Food handlers and other personnel with access to the food processing area could cross-contaminate the product with microbiological, chemical or physical hazards. The process layout and movement patterns should be considered in order to minimize this risk, along with the appropriate training programmes.

Here also you will need to look at the types of protective clothing required, along with frequencies of changing and laundering procedures. You should already have considered changing facilities, amenities and handwash stations as part of the building layout, but cross-check whether you have made sufficient provision.

(e) Cleaning

There must be sufficient facilities for cleaning and these should be situated to enable their convenient use. Cleaning areas should not cause a cross-contamination risk to the process. Cleaning schedules should be prepared for all areas and staff must be adequately trained to carry them out effectively.

(f) Chemicals

Storage facilities must be provided for any chemicals which are required for use in the manufacturing area. These must prevent the risk of product contamination. All chemicals must be properly labelled and must not be decanted into food containers.

(g) Raw materials

Raw materials can act as cross-contaminants if they gain access to different products, or if they are added in excess quantities. This can have serious consequences in the case of allergenic raw materials entering a product where they are not labelled. Raw material handling areas must be carefully planned, and areas used for more than one type of ingredient should be cleaned between use.

Make sure that you know how all your raw materials need to be handled and put appropriate measures in place. You may be buying in something in a safe condition but it is easy to make it unsafe through improper handling, e.g. leaving perishable goods sitting on a loading bay for several hours.

(h) Storage

Storage areas must be properly planned to minimize damage and cross-contamination issues. Consider whether you have adequate segregation, temperature and humidity control, and ensure that all storage areas are properly pest proofed. All materials should be stored off the floor and in sealed bags or containers. Part-used containers must be resealed after each use, and strict stock rotation should be employed.

(i) Products

Residues of other products can also cause a serious hazard if allergenic material is present or if they affect the intrinsic nature of the product which is contaminated. Production lines should be spatially separated to prevent cross-contamination, and handling and cleaning procedures should be planned appropriately. Consider any extra control required if personnel are switched between lines or departments – will there be an additional risk from their protective clothing?

(j) Packaging

Packaging areas and handling practices should be managed and controlled to prevent any cross-contamination risk. The packaging itself could be a major hazard, e.g. glass fragments, or could introduce microorganisms to the product. Make sure that your packaging is suitable for the job and won't be damaged during product storage and distribution, and consider whether you have the correct coding and use instructions printed legibly.

5.4 Establishing a safe and achievable shelf life

When you are designing your products, you will need to consider the shelf life which you and your customers would like for each product, and then go on to establish whether or not this proposed shelf life is safe and achievable. There is a wide variety of criteria which can influence your product's shelf life and these include:

- raw materials
- process technology used
- product intrinsic factors
- type of packaging
- conditions during storage, distribution and retail
- customer storage and handling.

The shelf life will be limited by factors which cause the product to become unsafe or deteriorate, and these will be influenced by the criteria listed above. As we are concentrating on safety in this text, we will consider only factors which cause the product to become unsafe here. However the HACCP techniques can be used to predict product deterioration or spoilage as we will see in Chapter 9. Further information on determining shelf life can be found in some excellent guidelines published by the UK Institute of Food Science and Technology (1993).

If you are a small manufacturer of high-risk products, you may wish to consider use of external experts to help with shelf life determination.

5.4.1 *What factors could cause the product to become unsafe?*

The main factors which can cause products to become unsafe during their shelf life are pathogenic microorganisms. Rancidity of fats can cause revulsion and sickness when consumed, but these are normally associated with spoilage rather than safety.

We have already discussed microbiological pathogens as hazards in Chapter 4, and have looked at intrinsic factors earlier in this chapter. The pathogen profiles in Appendix 3 may be helpful in deciding whether the product is likely to provide an environment favourable to pathogen growth. Pathogenic microorganisms may be present in your product from the raw materials, or from contamination during processing. These may be able to grow, depending on the intrinsic factors and packaging, along with the storage, distribution and handling conditions to which the product is subjected.

If you consider that a pathogen is likely to be present in your product, and that it will not be prevented from growth by the product's intrinsic factors, then you will need to investigate the degree of growth which is possible in the product. This, along with knowledge of the infectious dose for the organism in question, can be used to evaluate when the product will become potentially unsafe for consumption, and thus to limit the shelf life to a safe level. It is important to note that if pathogens with a low infectious dose are likely to be present at the start of shelf life, and the product is not due to be cooked thoroughly by the consumer, then the product is potentially unsafe and should be redesigned.

5.4.2 *How do you know when pathogens reach unsafe levels?*

Information on growth potential in foods, and with varying proportions of inhibitory intrinsic factors, can be found in the scientific literature. This can give you a good idea of the likely position in your product but should not be relied on absolutely for a safe shelf life. Mathematical modelling of pathogen growth in various concentrations and combinations of intrinsic factors can also be carried out. A number of computer models have been developed which can be used or accessed by the HACCP Team and expert consultants, the major one in the UK being the MAFF *Food Micromodel*, which can be accessed in the UK through Food Research Associations.

The theoretical safe shelf life obtained from literature values or mathematical modelling should be confirmed in practice for the product in question. This can be done through examination of the product for each microorganism of concern throughout and beyond the proposed shelf life. Product samples should be held under the expected storage and handling conditions, and it is prudent to build in an element of abuse, e.g. elevated temperature storage, to reflect possible product mishandling.

Where the microorganism(s) of concern may not be present all the time, or may be present at very low levels, it is more appropriate to carry out product challenge testing to evaluate potential for growth. Here each individual pathogen is inoculated into the product, which is then held at the expected storage and handling conditions. As for standard shelf life examination the product is tested at various intervals throughout and beyond the proposed shelf life and an element of abuse should be built in.

It is important to note that shelf life should always be confirmed on product samples which have undergone the same treatment as all product which goes on sale. This means that any shelf life proposed through theoretical studies, or through examination and challenge of development samples, must be verified on product which has been manufactured on the main production line, under the normal manufacturing conditions. For new products this will be done following the HACCP Study, but for existing products, where you are carrying out HACCP retrospectively, this verification can be going on while the HACCP Study takes place.

When you have established the safety of your product design, and decided on the likely shelf life, you can move on to look at how safety will be controlled from day-to-day during manufacture. This is through the establishment, implementation and maintenance of a HACCP Plan for the process, which we will now begin to consider.

6

How to do a HACCP Study

Now that we have discussed safe product design, we are ready to look at how to carry out the HACCP Study, and to find out how to apply HACCP to our products. In this chapter we will be identifying the potential hazards associated with our products and exploring the options for their prevention. In doing this we will be looking at a number of useful techniques such as brainstorming, grouping, and the use of hazard analysis charts, which will help the HACCP Team to structure their approach. We will then move on to the identification of CCPs and start to build up the information required in the HACCP Plan – critical limits, monitoring procedures, corrective action, and responsibility. This covers the requirements of HACCP Principles 1–5. We will continue to use the example product, chocolate chip ice cream. While going through this chapter you may wish to consider how to use HACCP in carrying out inspections of other businesses.

6.1 What is the HACCP Plan?

The HACCP Plan is a formal document which pulls together the key information from the HACCP Study, and holds details of all that is critical to food safety management. The HACCP Plan is drawn up by the HACCP Team and consists of two essential components – the Process Flow Diagram and the HACCP Control Chart – along with any other necessary support documentation. It is important that the HACCP Plan is focused on food safety management and therefore additional documentation should be kept to a minimum. However, it is often useful to include a product description, and details of record keeping and verification procedures may also be included, although these could be held as part of the documentation for a Quality Management System. You may also find it helpful to retain all preparatory documentation used by the HACCP Team which illustrate the hazard analysis thought process, although this documentation should not be part of the formal HACCP Plan.

6.1.1 *The Process Flow Diagram*

The Process Flow Diagram is a stepwise sequence of events through the whole process, giving a clear and simple description of how the end product is made. It is an essential part of the HACCP Plan which enables the HACCP Team to understand the production process, and is the basis for the hazard analysis. It includes details of all ingredients handling procedures and follows the process through to the consumer. Consumer actions may also be included, depending on the terms of reference drawn up by the HACCP Team (see section 6.2).

At the end of the HACCP Study all CCPs identified are highlighted on the Process Flow Diagram, thus tying it together with the HACCP Control Chart. The Process Flow Diagram is also useful in demonstrating control of food safety to customers and regulatory inspectors.

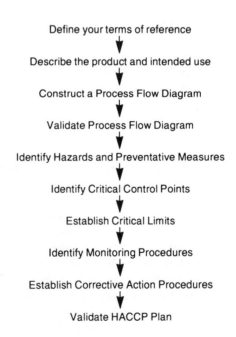

Figure 6.1 The HACCP Plan – step by step.

6.1.2 *The HACCP Control Chart*

The HACCP Control Chart contains details of all the steps or stages in the process where there are CCPs. It is normally documented as a matrix or table of control parameters, and contains details of the hazards and preventative measures associated with each CCP, along with the control criteria and responsibilities.

In order to put together a HACCP Plan we use the HACCP Principles and follow a number of steps as detailed in Figure 6.1.

6.2 Define your terms of reference

When your HACCP Team is ready to start their first HACCP Study, it is important to agree on the terms of reference or scope before they begin. It is essential that the correct focus is established to prevent the team being bogged down in unnecessary detail.

HACCP was originally designed as a food safety management tool and food safety should be your initial focus. However, as this is a very wide area in itself the HACCP Team must decide firstly where to start and also, just as important, where the study will end. There are a number of questions to help with these decisions:

1. Do you want to cover all types of hazards initially (i.e. microbiological, chemical and physical) or just one type, e.g. glass or microbiological?
An inexperienced HACCP Team may find it easiest to limit the number of hazard types in the initial study. It is much easier to revisit the process again afterwards to look at other hazard types than to try and do everything at once and find that you either miss some important hazards or get stuck because of the scope of the exercise. Experienced HACCP Teams who are used to the HACCP technique may find it straightforward to look at all types of hazards at once, and this is certainly better from the time management point of view.

2. Will the study cover a whole process or one specific part, and is this for one or a group of products?
You will want to consider the length and complexity of the process in answering this question. Does a long process subdivide logically into several distinct process areas which could be evaluated independently, for example? If the HACCP Team decides to look at individual sections of the process they may find the study easier to manage. However it is important that when the parts of the study are fitted together that no hazards have been missed, and it is

particularly important to investigate what happens to the product when it moves from one process area to the next.

If the process being studied is common for a number of products then these can be included in the scope, but it is essential that no hazards arising from slight differences in product formulation are overlooked.

3. Should the HACCP Study stop at the end of the production line or continue through distribution, retail and consumer handling?

To answer this question you will need to consider whether your product(s) is safe at the end of production, i.e. all hazards have been controlled, or whether the product(s) needs special handling. Is it a perishable product which could potentially be rendered unsafe by improper handling or are you actually relying on consumer action to control any hazards, e.g. in a raw meat product?

When you have answered the above questions you will be able to define your terms of reference for the HACCP Study.

Terms of Reference: Chocolate Chip Ice Cream

This HACCP Study considers biological, chemical and physical hazards throughout the entire process.

Biological hazards include vegetative pathogens such as *Salmonella* and *Listeria* and toxin formers such as *Staphylococcus aureus*. Chemical hazards could be associated with the raw materials, e.g. pesticides and antibiotics or with contamination during the process, e.g. cleaning chemicals. However for the purposes of this study, the HACCP Team decided that it would be easier to consider cleaning chemicals separately as a complete hazard analysis of the facility cleaning procedures. Therefore, the terms of reference exclude this hazard.

The HACCP Team considered that a wide range of physical hazards would affect the safety of this product, as it is likely to be consumed by small children who may be susceptible to choking on large items.

For this example, the HACCP Plan just covers one product, but additional products, undergoing similar processes, may be added to the plan at a later stage if the

---

company expands its product range. As the ice cream is to be sold as retail tubs and is unlikely to be affected by storage and distribution, the HACCP Study stops at the dispatch stage.

6.3 Describe the product and its intended use

At this stage it will be helpful to the HACCP Team to formally note what the product actually is and how/by whom it will be used. For the chocolate chip ice cream example, the HACCP Team noted the following:

Product Description: Chocolate Chip Ice Cream

This is a frozen, ready-to-eat product containing both pasteurized and unpasteurized components. The SMP, cream, sugar and water are pasteurized, while the flavouring and choc chips are added without further heat processing. Air is also whipped into the product at freezing.

The product will be consumed, without processing, by the general population including high-risk groups.

6.4 Constructing a Process Flow Diagram

6.4.1 Types of data

The Process Flow Diagram is used as the basis of the hazard analysis and must therefore contain sufficient technical detail for the study to progress. It should be carefully constructed by members of the HACCP Team as an accurate representation of the process, and should cover all stages from raw materials to end product, as defined in the HACCP Study terms of reference. The following types of data should be included:

- Details of all raw materials and product packaging, including format on receipt, necessary storage conditions and micro-biological, chemical and physical data.
- Details of all process activities including the potential for any delay stages.
- Temperature and time profile for all stages. This is particularly important when analysing microbiological hazards as it is vital to

83

assess the potential for any pathogens present to grow to hazardous levels.

- Types of equipment and design features. Are there any dead areas where product might build up and/or which are difficult to clean?
- Details of any product reworking or recycling loops.
- Floor plan with details of segregated areas and personnel routing. While it is possible to indicate process flow and floor plan on the same diagram, HACCP Teams often find it helpful to keep these as two distinct diagrams in the HACCP Plan.
- Storage conditions, including location, time and temperature
- Distribution/customer issues (if included in your terms of reference).

6.4.2 *Style*

The style of the Process Flow Diagram is the choice of each organization and there are no set rules for presentation. However, it is often felt that diagrams consisting solely of words and lines are the easiest to construct and use. Engineering drawings and technical symbols are used by some companies but, because of their complexity, these may cause confusion and so are not advised.

Whichever style of presentation is chosen, a key point is to ensure that every single stage is covered and in the correct order (p. 85). For large, complex processes it is often simplest to prepare a separate diagram for each operation. Where this is done, it is important to show exactly how each diagram fits together and the HACCP Team must ensure that no stages have been missed out.

6.4.3 *Verify during manufacture*

When the Process Flow Diagram is complete it must be verified by the HACCP Team. This involves team members watching the process in action to make sure that what happens is the same as what is written down, and may also involve going in on the night shift or weekend shift. It is essential to establish that you have got it right as the hazard analysis and all decisions about CCPs are based on this data.

6.5 Identifying hazards

When the Process Flow Diagram has been completed and verified, the HACCP Team can move on to the next stage of the HACCP

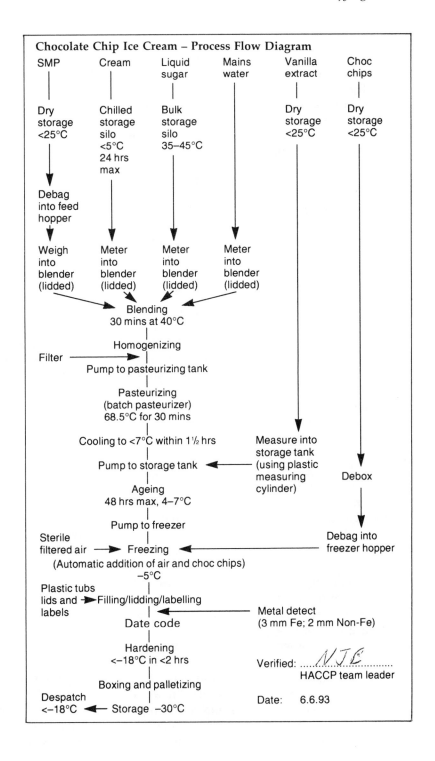

Chocolate Chip Ice Cream – Process Flow Diagram

SMP — Dry storage <25°C — Debag into feed hopper — Weigh into blender (lidded)

Cream — Chilled storage silo <5°C 24 hrs max — Meter into blender (lidded)

Liquid sugar — Bulk storage silo 35–45°C — Meter into blender (lidded)

Mains water — Meter into blender (lidded)

Vanilla extract — Dry storage <25°C — Measure into storage tank (using plastic measuring cylinder)

Choc chips — Dry storage <25°C — Debox — Debag into freezer hopper

Blending 30 mins at 40°C

Filter → Homogenizing
Pump to pasteurizing tank

Pasteurizing (batch pasteurizer) 68.5°C for 30 mins

Cooling to <7°C within 1½ hrs

Pump to storage tank

Ageing 48 hrs max, 4–7°C

Pump to freezer

Sterile filtered air → Freezing ← Debag into freezer hopper
(Automatic addition of air and choc chips) −5°C

Plastic tubs lids and labels → Filling/lidding/labelling

Date code ← Metal detect (3 mm Fe; 2 mm Non-Fe)

Hardening <−18°C in <2 hrs

Boxing and palletizing

Despatch <−18°C ← Storage −30°C

Verified: ....*N.J.C.*........
HACCP team leader

Date: 6.6.93

Study, the hazard analysis, as described by HACCP Principle 1. This is one of the key stages in any HACCP Study as the team must ensure that all potential hazards are identified and considered. There are a number of resources and techniques available to your HACCP Team to assist in this task, as described in the following sections. However, before starting out on the hazard analysis, all team members must be clear on the meaning of the word 'hazard'. Remember, a 'hazard' is normally considered to be a factor which may cause a food to be unsafe for consumption. Hazards can be of biological, chemical or physical nature.

HAZARD:
a biological, chemical or physical property which may cause a food to be unsafe for human consumption

6.5.1 *Reference materials – where to find them and how to use them*

A wealth of reference material is available to assist you in identifying and analysing the hazards in your process.

The members of your HACCP Team are the first important resource with their collective and multidisciplinary experience of the process and technology under study. Different team members will be able to contribute, for example, an indication of what hazards are likely to be found in the raw materials, where contamination could occur or build up in the process, what the process is capable of, etc. The team as a whole will be able to discuss the significance of these individual issues and ascertain the risk or likelihood of each hazard occurring.

In areas where the team expertise is limited it is important to know where information and advice can be obtained. It is essential that further expertise is secured when required as incorrect evaluation and predictions could have food safety implications.

Chapter 4 gives detail on a wide range of biological, chemical and physical hazards along with preventative measure options for their control. In addition, examples of practical hazard control can be found in Appendix B. Although this list of hazards and preventative measures in this appendix is not exhaustive, it can be a good starting point for the HACCP Team and can be used to spark off other ideas during a hazard brainstorming session (see later).

Examples of hazards in different product and raw material types can easily be found in the literature in the form of books, epidemiological reports and research papers. Here again information can be found on the likely behaviour of particular hazard types during the process along with possible controlling options. When using literature data to assist with hazard analysis it is vital that the HACCP Team are able to interpret this data and evaluate the significance to the process under study. Information may also be found in hazard databases and through the use of mathematical models. Legislation may also help where it highlights particular concerns with specific product types. Again it is important to be able to interpret the significance of any data found.

If you do not have sufficient expertise available there are a number of organizations and resources, where you may obtain support. These include industry bodies, research associations, higher educational establishments, regulatory enforcement authorities and external expert consultants.

6.5.2 *Questions to be considered*

There are a number of questions which can be asked by the HACCP Team, the answers to which will assist in decisions about potential hazards. The following is based on a list of questions put together by the NACMCF (1992); however, remember that it may not be exhaustive, and you may have some additional ideas.

(a) Raw materials

What hazards are likely to be present in each raw material and are these likely to be of concern to the process and/or product? Are any of the raw materials themselves hazardous if excess amounts are added?

(b) Design of plant and equipment

Where are there risks of cross-contamination occurring during the process and at any holding stages? Consider microbiological, chemical and physical safety issues. Are there any stages where contamination could build up or where microbiological hazards might grow to dangerous levels?

Can the equipment be effectively controlled within the required tolerances for safe food production? Can effective cleaning be carried out? Are there any extra hazards associated with particular equipment?

(c) Intrinsic factors

Do the product's integral factors (pH, a_w, etc.) effectively control all microbiological hazards likely to be present in the raw materials or which could enter the product as cross contaminants during the process? Remember there are different types of microorganisms which react in different ways – what will control one might not control another. Which intrinsic factors must be controlled to ensure product safety? Will microbiological hazards survive or grow in the product formulation?

(d) Process design

Will microbiological hazards survive any heating step in the process or is there a step which will destroy all pathogens? Does the use of reworked or recycled product during the process or in any of the raw materials cause a potential hazard? Consider carefully both microbiological hazards and their toxins. Is there a risk of recontamination between process stages?

(e) Facility design

Are there any hazards directly associated with the facility layout or internal environment? Is segregation adequate between raw and ready-to-eat product? Is positive-pressured filtered air necessary? Do movement patterns for personnel and equipment cause any hazards?

(f) Personnel

Could personnel practices affect the safety of the product? Are all food handlers adequately trained in food hygiene? Are occupational health procedures in place?

Do all employees understand the aims and significance of the HACCP System, along with where their role affects the process?

(g) Packaging

How does the packaging environment influence the growth and/or survival of microbiological hazards? For example, is it aerobic or anaerobic? Does the package have all required labelling and instructions for safe handling and use, and can these be easily understood? Is the package damage-resistant and are tamper-evident features in place where required?

(h) Storage and distribution – what could go wrong?

Could the product be stored at the wrong temperature and will this affect safety during the shelf life? Could the product be abused by the customer causing it to be unsafe?

6.5.3 *Handling hazard information through brainstorming*

Before you can progress in any HACCP Study you must be able to identify all the hazards. And this means not just hazards you already have experience of, but also what could conceivably occur.

At each stage in the Process Flow Diagram, the hazards and their causes should be brainstormed. This can be done either formally, through a structured brainstorming session, or informally, as part of a general discussion. Brainstorming is one of a number of standard problem-solving techniques which can be applied successfully to HACCP and is particularly useful at the hazard analysis step for a number of reasons:

1. Analytical thinking stifles creativity. Where team members are analytically or scientifically trained, lateral thinking and new ideas may be repressed.
2. The group is too close to the process and how it has always been done. This makes it difficult to challenge what is known or understood, and leads to assumptions being made and beliefs being accepted.
3. The belief that there is always one correct solution to every problem. This leads individuals into searching for the one correct answer, and in doing so overlooking alternative, less apparent solutions.

In order to overcome these barriers, brainstorming is a structured approach where each HACCP Team member offers an idea in turn. An individual is allocated the position of scribe to ensure that all ideas are recorded and a time limit is set to keep the pressure on. Brainstorming should be carried out as a quick-fire session and team members should say whichever hazards come into their heads, however outlandish they may initially seem. It is important to build on other people's ideas and to think laterally. Ideas are never praised, criticized or commented on and company status should be left outside the room.

As an example, at the freezing stage of the process flow diagram for chocolate chip ice cream, which includes the addition of the chocolate chips, the HACCP Team identified the hazards and their causes shown in Table 6.1 through brainstorming.

Table 6.1 Chocolate chip ice cream, freezing stage – hazard brainstorming

Hazard	*Cause*
Metal	*Blades of choc chip bag opening knives*
Jewellery	*Through debag operators not following personal hygiene policy*
Flaking paint	
Crawling insects	
Condensation	*Open top on choc chip hopper allows entry of*
Dust	*debris from overhead structure*
Rivets	
Rust	
Flying insects	*Insects flying into hopper*
Cardboard/polythene	*Poor operating practice at debagging*
Pathogenic microorganisms in air	*Filter malfunction*
— Salmonella	
Cross-contamination	*Poor freezer cleaning procedures*
— Microbiological	
— Chemical	

Following the brainstorming session, the HACCP Team should analyse all the hazard ideas but must be careful that no idea is rejected, unless all team members are confident that it does not exist as a hazard in the process under study.

6.5.4 The structured approach to hazard analysis

A structured approach to hazard analysis helps to ensure that all hazards have been identified. It really is crucial that you do not miss any hazards and this will be helped by having personnel from a wide range of disciplines in your HACCP Team, working from a verified Process Flow Diagram.

When your HACCP Team is new to hazard analysis, it is important to ensure that all potential hazards are identified before moving on to discuss possible preventative measures. More experienced teams may wish to discuss preventative measures, in place or required, at the same time as hazard identification, as it may be felt to save time. But – some words of caution – make sure that you do not miss any hazards out. It is often found that

Table 6.2 Chocolate chip ice cream – Hazard Analysis chart

Process step	Hazard	Preventative measure
Ingredient storage – SMP	Physical and microbiological contamination through pest infestation	
– Cream	Growth of pathogens due to temperature abuse	
– Liquid sugar	No hazard identified	
– Vanilla extract	No hazard identified	
– Chocolate chips	Physical and microbiological contamination through pest infestation	
Debag SMP into feed hopper	Paper/polythene from sacks Environmental contamination – foreign material. Metal from knives Jewellery from operators	
Weigh SMP into blender (lidded)	No hazard identified	

Table 6.2 continued

Process step	Hazard	Preventative measure
Meter liquid ingredients into blender (lidded)		
— Liquid sugar	No hazard identified	
— Cream	Introduction of high levels of pathogens/toxins through build up in uncleaned pipework/nozzle	
Blending	Introduction of high levels of pathogens/toxins through build up in uncleaned blender	
Homogenizing	Introduction of high levels of pathogens/toxins through build up in uncleaned equipment	
Pump to pasteurization tank	'Survival' of foreign matter through filter failure	
Pasteurizing	Survival of pathogens through not achieving correct heat process time/temperature	
Cooling	Outgrowth of spores due to slow cooling	
Pump to storage tank	Introduction of high levels of pathogens/toxins due to poor cleaning	
Measure vanilla extract into storage tank	No hazard identified	

Ageing	Growth of vegetative pathogens and spore outgrowth due to poor temperature control
Pump to freezer	Introduction of high levels of pathogens/toxins due to poor cleaning
Freezing	Foreign material in chocolate chips, from packaging, bag opening, knives, operators and equipment
	Environmental contamination through unlidded chocolate chip hopper – physical and microbiological
	Pathogens in air
	Introduction of high levels of pathogens/toxins through poor freezer cleaning
Filling, lidding, labelling	Introduction of high levels of pathogens/toxins from filling heads due to poor cleaning
	Metal contamination not identified due to equipment malfunction
Date coding	No hazard identified
Hardening	No hazard identified
Boxing and palletizing	No hazard identified
Storage/dispatch	No hazard identified as good distribution practice in place

personnel get into deep discussions about the merits of different preventative measures and that the hazard identification stage either loses momentum or loses its way completely. When this happens hazards may easily be missed, so it really is better to ensure you have identified them all first.

Some organizations have found it helpful to record all hazards as they are identified against the process steps where they occur in a structured manner. The documentation produced is then used as the basis for the hazard analysis and discussion of preventative measures. The use of such informal documentation helps to structure the thinking and discussions of the HACCP Team, and therefore helps to ensure that all potential hazards are covered. An example of a Hazard Analysis Chart for the chocolate chip ice cream product is shown in Table 6.2.

6.5.5 What is the risk?

During hazard analysis it is necessary to assess the significance of each identified hazard in order to build in appropriate control mechanisms. This procedure is known as risk assessment and must be understood by the HACCP Team.

What do we mean by risk? Risk is normally defined as the chance or probability that the hazard will be realized, i.e. the likelihood that the hazard will happen.

RISK:
the likelihood the hazard will happen.

Many people worry that risk assessment is difficult but it really is as simple as that. What is often more complicated is the decision as to whether or not a particular hazard is likely to happen. This can be particularly complex in the case of some chemical hazard issues, where the danger from different levels of exposure is unknown.

The HACCP Team need to consider the risk associated with each potential hazard. In other words you will be asking yourselves whether a particular issue is a significant or real hazard or not. For example, *Salmonella* spp. would only be a real hazard in a raw material if it was likely to be found from time to time, e.g. in raw milk. There is little point in setting up a HACCP System to control a potential hazard which will never occur. However, caution must be employed when ruling out potential hazards from a process. You must be absolutely sure that there is no risk and that they are never likely to occur. If in doubt, assume that the hazard may occur, and this will be addressed when the CCPs are determined.

Some previous approaches to HACCP (NACMCF, 1989, in Pierson and Corlett, 1992) have advocated the allocation of risk categories to the different potential hazards in a process but the question always came up – what should you do next? This type of approach is only of benefit if you then have a system for processing the different risk categories. In other words, if you categorize the risk of three different hazards occurring as serious, major and minor, should you not still have effective control mechanisms in place for the minor hazard as it may still occur and cause a food safety problem? The current international approach to HACCP (NACMCF, 1992; Codex, 1993) does not advocate categorisation and ruling out of hazards on the basis of risk categories, but instead **requires control of any hazard which can reasonably be expected to occur**. This is still a judgement of risk but in a more simple and straightforward manner.

The HACCP Team does not need to delve deeply into the theory of risk assessment for different hazard types, but they do need to know where to find the right expertise when unsure of the risk of a particular hazard occurring. The golden rule must always be that if in doubt, consider a potential hazard to be a real hazard and progress with your HACCP Study accordingly.

6.6 Identifying preventative measures

When all potential hazards have been identified and analysed, the HACCP Team should go on to list the associated preventative measures. These are the control mechanisms for each hazard and are normally defined as those factors which are required to eliminate or reduce the occurrence of hazards to an acceptable level. Examples of preventative measures can be found in Appendix B – Examples of practical hazard control.

PREVENTATIVE MEASURES:
factors which can be used to control an identified health hazard

When evaluating preventative measures it is necessary to consider what you **already have** in place and what **new** measures may need to be put in place. This can easily be done using your Process Flow Diagram and/or Hazard Analysis Charts as a guide.

Remember that more than one preventative measure may be required to control a hazard which occurs at different stages of the process; for example the potential for contamination with *Listeria monocytogenes* before and after cooking in a ready-to-eat product. For contamination before cooking the heat process might be the preventative measure while environmental control would be required to prevent contamination after cooking. Similarly, more than one hazard might be effectively controlled by one preventative measure, e.g. two microbiological pathogens by a heat process, or glass and metal by sifting.

The following completed Hazard Analysis Chart shows the hazards and preventative measures identified by the HACCP Team for our chocolate chip ice cream example.

Table 6.3 Chocolate chip ice cream – completed Hazard Analysis Chart

Process step	Hazard	Preventative measure
Ingredient storage – SMP	Physical and microbiological contamination through pest infestation	Effective pest control programme
– Cream	Growth of pathogens due to temperature abuse	Store at < 5°C for 24 hours max
– Liquid sugar	No hazard identified	—
– Vanilla extract	No hazard identified	—
– Chocolate chips	Physical and microbiological contamination through pest infestation	Effective pest control programme
Debag SMP into feed hopper	Paper/polythene from sacks Environmental contamination – foreign material Metal from knives Jewellery from operators	Fine mesh sieve on entrance to hopper Metal detection at later stage Operator hygiene training
Weigh SMP into blender (lidded)	No hazard identified	—

Table 6.3 continued

Process step	Hazard	Preventative measure
Meter liquid ingredients into blender (lidded)		
— Liquid sugar	No hazard identified	—
— Cream	Introduction of high levels of pathogens/toxins through build up in uncleaned pipework/nozzle	Effective cleaning (procedures and practices)
Blending	Introduction of high levels of pathogens/toxins through build up in uncleaned blender	Effective cleaning (procedures and practices)
Homogenizing	Introduction of high levels of pathogens/toxins through build up in uncleaned equipment	Effective cleaning (procedures and practices)
Pump to pasteurization tank	'Survival' of foreign matter through filter failure	Filter in place and intact
Pasteurizing	Survival of pathogens through not achieving correct heat process time/temperature	68.3°C/30 mins
Cooling	Outgrowth of spores due to slow cooling	Rapid cooling — chilled water jacket
Pump to storage tank	Introduction of high levels of pathogens/toxins due to poor cleaning	Effective cleaning (procedures and practices)
Measure vanilla extract into storage tank	No hazard identified	—

Process step	Hazard	Control measure
Ageing	Growth of vegetative pathogens and spore outgrowth due to poor temperature control	≤ 7°C for 48 hours max
Pump to freezer	Introduction of high levels of pathogens/toxins due to poor cleaning	Effective cleaning (procedures and practices)
Freezing	Foreign material in chocolate chips, from packaging, bag opening, knives, operators and equipment	Empty through magnetized grating; operator hygiene training; metal detection at later stage
	Environmental contamination through unlidded chocolate chip hopper — physical and microbiological	Install lid on hopper to remove hazard
	Pathogens in air	Effective filtration
	Introduction of high levels of pathogens/toxins through poor freezer cleaning	Effective cleaning (procedures and practices)
Filling, lidding, labelling	Introduction of high levels of pathogens/toxins from filling heads due to poor cleaning	Effective cleaning (procedures and practices)
	Metal contamination not identified due to equipment malfunction	Effective metal detection — calibrate and monitor detector
Date coding	No hazard identified*	—
Hardening	No hazard identified	—
Boxing and palletizing	No hazard identified	—
Storage/dispatch	No hazard identified as good distribution practice in place	—

*There is not strictly a food safety hazard here. However, in order to minimize the effect if a CCP fails somewhere in the process, it is vital to be able to trace and recall all products concerned. Therefore it may be appropriate to manage this as a CCP.

6.7 Where are the Critical Control Points?

6.7.1 *How to find them*

As we saw in Chapter 4, a Critical Control Point (CCP) is a point, step or procedure where a food safety hazard can be prevented, eliminated or reduced to acceptable levels.

CCP:
a point, step or procedure where control can be applied and a hazard can be prevented, eliminated or reduced to acceptable levels.

CCPs can be found by using your thorough knowledge of the process and all the possible hazards to decide on the best preventative measures for their control. The information established during the hazard analysis should allow the identification of CCPs through the expert judgement of the HACCP Team and specialist advisers.

However, the location of CCPs using judgement alone may lead to more points being managed as CCPs than are really necessary. There is always the tendency to err on the side of caution but designating too many points as CCPs, rather than correctly identifying the real CCPs, may mean that you lose commitment as you will always have some points where you are prepared to negotiate a deviation. For example, if a metal detector failed at a raw material stage you could switch it off and rely on the one at the end of the line, or if a pH check of a product component was wrong, you could test the final product and release if within specification.

On the other hand, too few CCPs would be even more disastrous and could cause the sale of unsafe food. It is important that control is focused where it is essential for food safety and so care should be employed to ensure that the CCPs are correctly identified.

To assist in finding where the correct CCPs should be, a tool is available known as the CCP Decision Tree (Figure 6.3). As we saw in Chapter 5, a decision tree is a logical series of questions which are asked for each hazard. In the case of the CCP Decision Tree this is for each hazard at each process step. The answer to each question leads the HACCP Team through a particular path in the tree and to a decision whether or not a CCP is required at the step.

Using a CCP Decision Tree promotes structured thinking and ensures a consistent approach at every process step and for each hazard identified. It also has the benefit of forcing and facilitating

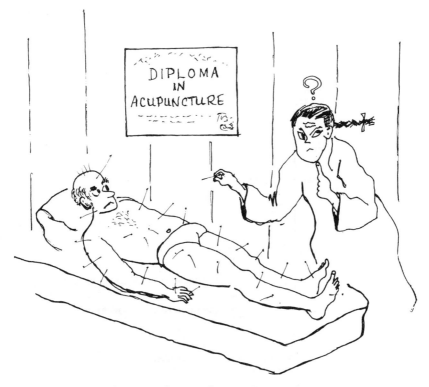

Figure 6.2 'Where are the Critical Control Points?'.

team discussion, further enhancing teamwork and the HACCP Study.

Several versions of the CCP Decision Tree have been published (NACMCF (1992), Codex (1993), CFDRA (1992)) with slightly different wording, although they display a common approach to CCP location. Figure 6.3 has been adapted from the above in order to simplify the approach.

6.7.2 Use of CCP Decision Trees

The questions in the tree should be asked for each hazard at each process step, including receipt and handling of raw materials.

If you have used the previous decision tree for raw materials at the sourcing or Supplier Quality Assurance stage (see section 4.2) you will already know where specific CCPs are required with incoming raw materials before they reach your site. If you were to put the same raw materials through the questions in the CCP Decision Tree you would find the same answers. However, you

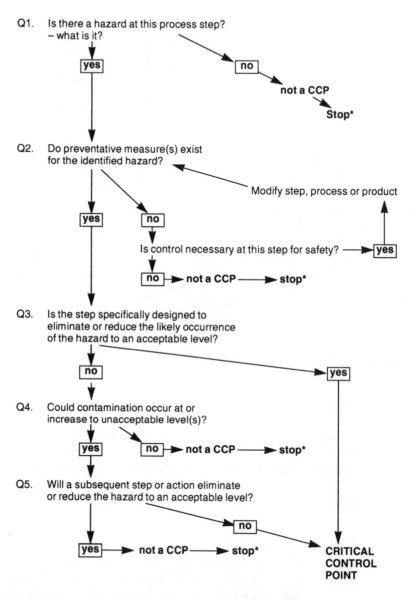

Q1. Is there a hazard at this process step?
– what is it?

yes   no

not a CCP

Stop*

Q2. Do preventative measure(s) exist
for the identified hazard?

Modify step, process or product

yes   no

Is control necessary at this step for safety? ⟶ yes

no ⟶ not a CCP ⟶ stop*

Q3. Is the step specifically designed to
eliminate or reduce the likely occurrence
of the hazard to an acceptable level?

no   yes

Q4. Could contamination occur at or
increase to unacceptable level(s)?

yes   no ⟶ not a CCP ⟶ stop*

Q5. Will a subsequent step or action eliminate
or reduce the hazard to an acceptable level?

no

yes ⟶ not a CCP ⟶ stop*   CRITICAL
CONTROL
POINT

* Stop and proceed with the next hazard at the current step or the next step in the
described process

Figure 6.3 The CCP Decision Tree.

will find that it helps to focus on raw materials first at the development stage, and should pick these up again with the CCP Decision Tree where they arrive as incoming goods at your facility.

Work through the CCP Decision Tree as follows:

Q1 Is there a hazard at this process step?
This first question will seem obvious but it helps to focus the HACCP Team's minds on the specific process step in question. It is particularly useful if there is a time delay between carrying out the hazard analysis and determining CCPs. Sometimes a 'hazard' identified during brainstorming turns out not to be a real hazard when challenged here. If there is a hazard then you should move on to Q2.

Q2 Do preventative measures exist for the identified hazard?
Here you need to consider the measures you already have in place along with what could be implemented, and this is most easily done using your Hazard Analysis Charts. If the answer to this question is yes then you should move straight on to question 3.

If, however, the answer is no and preventative measures are not and could not be put in place, then you must consider whether control is necessary at this point for food safety. If control is not necessary here then a CCP is not required and you should move on to the next hazard and start the decision tree again. However, make sure that if you are answering no here because there is control later on, that you actually pick up the later point as a CCP. An example of how this question loop works is for metal detection. Metal detection might not be required for safety at some of the early process steps although they may be associated with a metal hazard. It would, of course, be essential to have a metal detector at the finished product stage.

If members of the HACCP Team have identified a hazard(s) at a process step and there are no possible preventative measures at that or any following step, then you must modify either the process step, the process itself or the product such that food safety control is possible. For example if *Salmonella* is likely to be present and your heat process is not sufficient to destroy the organism, then you will need to look at increasing your heat process or building in some other control method. It should be noted that a process step can only operate as a CCP if preventative measures can be introduced. When the necessary modifications have been established you should ask Q2 again and progress through the tree.

It is important that any necessary changes highlighted at this stage by the HACCP Team, to the step, process or product, are agreed and implemented before the unsafe product goes into production. Here you may need to ensure that senior management fully accept the HACCP Team's findings, and provide the required back up for the change(s) to be implemented.

Q3 Is the step specifically designed to eliminate or reduce the likely occurrence of the hazard to an acceptable level?

The key thing to remember when asking this question is that it is the step and not the preventative measure which is being questioned. This question was originally developed to accommodate process steps which are specifically designed to control specific hazards. What the question is really asking is whether the step itself controls the hazard. For example, milk pasteurization at 71.7 °C for 15 seconds is specifically designed and will control vegetative pathogens, while ambient storage of raw materials is not specifically designed to control hazards such as pest infestation.

You should carefully consider your hazard analysis information along with the Process Flow Diagram to answer this question, and remember – it is just as important to consider mixing steps, where it is critical to get the product formulation right, as it is to consider the main processing steps. If the product is not properly mixed, then your intrinsic control mechanisms may not be effective, and an unmixed product may have detrimental effects on other processing steps, e.g. the heat process.

If the answer is yes then the process step in question is a CCP and you should start the decision tree again for the next process step or hazard. If the answer is no, move on to Q4.

Q4 Could contamination occur at or increase to unacceptable level(s)?

This question requires your hazard analysis information along with the HACCP Team's combined experience of the process, and processing environment. The answer should be largely obvious from the hazard analysis but make sure that you have covered the following issues.

- Is the immediate environment likely to include the hazard(s)?
- Is cross-contamination possible via personnel?
- Is cross-contamination possible from another product or raw material?
- Could composite time/temperature conditions increase the hazard?
- Could product build-up in dead space and increase the hazard?

- Are any other factors or conditions present which could cause contamination to increase to unacceptable level(s) at this step?

Where there is uncertainty about what constitutes unacceptable levels of a particular factor (i.e. where it becomes a hazard), it is important that the HACCP Team should seek expert advice before making a decision. However, if a completely new process is under study it may not be possible to obtain a definite answer. Here the HACCP Team should always assume that the answer is yes and proceed appropriately.

When considering how contamination could increase to unacceptable levels it is important to understand the possible additive effect during the process for each particular factor. This means that you may need to think not only about the current process step, but also whether any subsequent steps or holding stages between steps could cause the hazard to increase. For example, a number of steps being performed at ambient temperature might give the opportunity for a low initial contamination level of *Staphylococcus aureus* to grow to toxin-forming levels, and become a hazard.

If the answer to Q4 is yes, i.e. contamination could occur at or increase to unacceptable levels, move on to the next question. If the answer is no, go back to the beginning of the decision tree with the next hazard or process step.

Q5 Will a subsequent step or action eliminate or reduce the hazard to an acceptable level?

This question is designed to allow the presence of a hazard or hazards at a particular process stage if they will be controlled either later in the process or by consumer action. In this way it minimizes the number of process steps which are considered to be CCPs and focuses on those steps which are **crucial** for product safety.

If the answer to this question is yes, then the current process step is not a CCP for the hazard under discussion but the subsequent step/action will be. For example, correct consumer cooking will control some of the microbiological hazards present in a raw meat product. Similarly, metal detection of finished products at the packing stage will detect metal contamination which may be a hazard associated with the raw materials or an earlier process stage. If the answer is no, then the current process step must be a CCP for the hazard being considered.

Although this question allows the number of CCPs to be minimized, this may not be appropriate in all cases. In the above example of metal detection, the only CCP which is absolutely critical is metal detection at the finished product stage. However, from a commercial point of view, the early detection/control of metal or any other hazard where there is a high degree of risk will be advisable. When this is done it must be made clear that the purpose is to establish additional control in order to minimize product losses. The extra control points should not be called CCPs.

There may also be occasions where the cost of the preventative measure itself is prohibitive. An example of this may be the X-ray detection of bone in meat, where there may only be one X-ray detector available. Here it must be located at the CCP, as this takes priority over any additional manufacturing controls.

All CCPs identified by the HACCP Team must be implemented and cannot be replaced by other measures elsewhere in the process.

When working through the decision tree you may find it helpful to designate one member of the HACCP Team as question master and scribe. This will ensure that the discussions are structured and that the team do not become side-tracked. It is often also helpful to construct a question-and-answer matrix for each process step where a hazard has been identified. Do this on a flip chart so that all team members can see it. Alternatively, this could be an extension to the Hazard Analysis Chart.

Another useful way of carrying out and recording your decision process is to take a number of photocopies of the decision tree. Then use a separate copy for each hazard and follow through your decisions in coloured pen, noting the reasons in each case.

You should continue to work through the decision tree for each hazard present at each process step until all CCPs have been determined. When this has been achieved the HACCP Team should highlight the CCPs on the Process Flow Diagram and move on to building up the HACCP Control Chart.

Before moving on to look at how CCPs are controlled we will follow through the CCP Decision Tree for the chocolate chip ice cream example (Table 6.4).

Table 6.4 Chocolate chip ice cream – process step decision matrix

Process step and hazard	Q1	Q2	Q3	Q4	Q5	CCP?	HACCP Team notes
Ingredient storage SMP Physical and microbiological contamination through pest infestation	Y	Y	N	Y	Y	N	Physical contamination will be removed by the in-line filter before pasteurization and microbiological contamination by the pasteurization and microbiological contamination by the pasteurization step itself. 'Storage' in itself is not specifically designed to control the hazards identified
Choc chips physical and microbiological	Y	Y	N	Y	N	Y	There will be no later means of controlling hazards introduced at the storage stage
Debag SMP Paper/polythene frame sacks	Y	Y	N	Y	Y	N	Controlled through the in-line filter before pasteurization as previous
Environmental contamination (foreign material)	Y	Y	N	Y	Y	N	Controlled through the in-line filter before pasteurization as previous

Table 6.4 continued

Process step and hazard	Q1	Q2	Q3	Q4	Q5	CCP?	HACCP Team notes
Metal from bag opening knives	Y	Y	N	Y	Y	N	In line filter before pasteurization plus metal detection of finished product
Jewellery from operatives	Y	Y	N	Y	Y	N	In line filter before pasteurization plus metal detection of finished product
Meter liquid ingredients into blender							
Introduction of high levels of pathogens/ toxins through poor cleaning	Y	Y	N	Y	N	Y	The cleaning procedures will be a CCP for control of toxin producing pathogens — heat stable toxin will not be controlled by the pasteurization step
Blending Introduction of high levels of pathogens/ toxins through poor cleaning	Y	Y	N	Y	N	Y	As above
Homogenizing Hazard as above	Y	Y	N	Y	N	Y	As above
Pump to pasteurization tank Survival of foreign material through filter failure	Y	Y	N	Y	N	Y	Physical contamination must be removed at this stage as there are no more filtration steps

Process step and hazard					Justification
Pasteurizing Survival of pathogens through not achieving correct temperature and time	Y	Y		Y	Pasteurization is specifically designed to kill vegetative pathogens
Cooling Outgrowth of spores due to slow cooling	Y	Y		Y	Rapid cooling is essential in preventing spore germination and outgrowth. Tank cooled to $<7^{\circ}\text{C}$ within 1½ hours
Pump to storage tank Introduction of high levels of pathogens/toxins through poor cleaning	Y	N	N	Y	Vegetative pathogens are also considered now as we have passed the lethal heat treatment
Ageing Spore outgrowth due to poor temperature control	Y	N	N	Y	Temperature control will be critical in prohibiting spore germination and outgrowth
Pump to freezer	Y	N	N	Y	As pump to storage tank
Freezer Foreign material (choc chip bags, bag opening knives and operators)	Y	N	N	Y	While later metal detection will find any metal contamination the prevention of paper or other non-metal object ingress is critical at this stage

Table 6.4 continued

Process step and hazard	Q1	Q2	Q3	Q4	Q5	CCP?	HACCP Team notes
Pathogens in air	Y	Y	N	Y	N	Y	Effectively filtered air is essential
Introduction of high levels of pathogens and toxins through poor cleaning	Y	Y	N	Y	N	Y	As previous
Filling, lidding and labelling Introduction of high levels of pathogens and toxins through poor cleaning	Y	Y	N	Y	N	Y	As previous
Survival of metal contamination through metal detector malfunction	Y	Y	N	Y	N	Y	This is the final opportunity for metal detection before storage and dispatch to the consumer
Coding	No hazard was noted during the hazard analysis. However, the HACCP Team have decided that in order to minimize risk of illness or injury caused through inability to trace and recall, the step would be managed as a CCP.						

6.8 Building up the HACCP Control Chart

As we saw in section 6.1, the HACCP Control Chart is one of the key documents in the HACCP Plan, holding all the essential details about the steps or stages in the process where there are CCPs. This information could be documented separately elsewhere, but most companies find it easier to hold it all together in one matrix, as shown in Table 6.5.

Table 6.5 The HACCP Control Chart

Process Step	CCP No.	Hazard	Preventative measure	Critical limits	Monitoring Procedure	Monitoring Frequency	Corrective action	Responsibility

6.8.1 *What are the Critical Limits?*

When you have identified all the CCPs in your process, the next step is to decide how they will be controlled. You must establish the criteria which indicate the difference between safe and unsafe product being produced so that the process can be managed within safe levels. The absolute tolerance at a CCP, i.e. the division between safe and unsafe, is known as the **Critical Limit**. If the Critical Limits are exceeded, then the CCP is out of control and a potential hazard may exist.

CRITICAL LIMITS:
criteria which must be met for each preventative measure at a CCP. The absolute tolerance for safety.

Depending on the particular control criteria the CCP may have just one Critical Limit, or there may be an upper and a lower Critical Limit. The product will be safe as long as all the CCPs are managed within their specified Critical Limits.

(a) How do you set the Critical Limits?

Since the Critical Limits define the boundaries between safe and unsafe product, it is vital that they are set at the correct level for each criteria. The HACCP Team must therefore fully understand the criteria governing safety at each CCP in order to set the appropriate Critical Limits. In other words, you must have detailed knowledge of the potential hazards, along with a full under-standing of the factors which are involved in their prevention or control. Critical Limits will not necessarily be the same as your existing processing parameters.

Each CCP may have a number of different factors which need to be controlled to ensure product safety, and each of these factors will have an associated Critical Limit. For example, cooking has long been established as a CCP which destroys vegetative pathogens. Here the factors associated with control are temperature and time. The Critical Limits associated with industrial meat cooking are that the joint centre temperature achieves 70 °C for at least two months.

In order to set the Critical Limits all the factors associated with safety at the CCP must be identified. The level at which each factor becomes the boundary between safe and unsafe is then the Critical Limit. It is important to note that the Critical Limit must be associated with a measurable factor which can be routinely monitored. Some factors which are commonly used as Critical Limits include temperature, time, pH, moisture or a_w, salt concentration and titratable acidity.

As HACCP Team members you will have an in-depth knowledge of the hazards and control mechanisms of the process, and you may have an understanding of the safety boundaries. However, in a number of cases this may be beyond your in-house expertise and it is again important to know where you can obtain information and advice. Possible sources of information are as follows:

- **Published data** – information in scientific literature, in-house and supplier records, industry and regulatory guidelines (e.g. Codex, ICMSF, FDA, IDF, etc.).
- **Expert advice** – from consultants, research associations, plant and equipment manufacturers, cleaning chemical suppliers, microbiologists, toxicologists, process engineers.
- **Experimental data** – this is likely to support Critical Limits for microbiological hazards and may come from planned experiments, challenge studies where product is inoculated, or from specific microbiological examination of the product and its ingredients.
- **Mathematical modelling** – computer simulation of the survival and growth characteristics of microbiological hazards in food systems.

(b) Types of Critical Limit

The factors or criteria which make up the Critical Limit can be chemical, physical or microbiological, and will be related to the type of hazard that the CCP is designed to control.

- **Chemical limits** – these may be associated with the occurrence of chemical hazards in the product and its ingredients or with the control of microbiological hazards through the product formulation and intrinsic factors. Examples of factors involved in chemical limits are maximum acceptable levels for mycotoxins, pH, salt and a_w or the presence or absence of allergens.
- **Physical limits** – these are often associated with the tolerance for physical or foreign material hazards. However, they can also be involved in the control of microbiological hazards, where the survival or death of the microorganism is governed by physical parameters. Examples of factors associated with physical limits are absence of metal, intact sieve (sieve size and retention) and temperature and time. Physical limits can also be associated with other factors, e.g. the limit might be 'continued approved status' where the preventative measure is supplier assurance for particular hazards.

- **Microbiological limits** – these should be avoided as part of the HACCP System, apart from the control of non-perishable raw materials. This is because microbiological factors can usually only be monitored by growing the organism of concern in the laboratory, a process which may take several days. The monitoring of microbiological limits would therefore not allow you to take instant action when the process deviates. Instead you might have several days' production quarantined in storage, without knowing where the hazard is present. This is further complicated by the fact that microorganisms are rarely distributed homogeneously throughout a batch, and therefore may be completely missed (remember the limitations of inspection and testing as discussed in Chapter 2). It may be possible to use microbiological limits for positive release of raw materials, but only if the material is homogeneous and a representative sample can be taken.

Microbiological factors are best kept for verification purposes, i.e. where you perform additional tests to ensure that the HACCP System has been effective, as here the time scale involved does not create operational difficulties. One exception to this general rule is where rapid microbiological methods can be implemented, but even these need to be truly rapid, i.e. minutes rather than hours, to be effective. An example here is ATP bioluminescence which can be used to demonstrate the effectiveness of cleaning procedures or to estimate the total levels of microorganisms in a raw material.

When your HACCP Team have established appropriate Critical Limits for all CCPs, they should be added to the HACCP Control Chart as in the following example (Table 6.6).

Table 6.6 Chocolate chip ice cream – Critical Limits

Process Step:	CCP No.	Hazard	Preventative measure	Critical limits	Monitoring		Corrective action	Responsibility
					Procedure	Frequency		
Ingredients: Skimmed milk powder	1	Antibiotic residues	Effective supplier assurance: – Audit – Agreed specification (maximum acceptable levels)	Audit pass Legal limits				
Cream	2	Antibiotic residues	Effective supplier assurance: – Audit – Agreed specification (maximum acceptable levels)	Audit pass Legal limits				

HACCP plan Ref. HP001

Iced Delights
HACCP CONTROL CHART

Date 14.8.93 Supersedes: N/A
Approved by: ..N.J.B.......
HACCP Team Leader

Table 6.6 continued

HACCP plan Ref. HP001			Iced Delights HACCP CONTROL CHART						Date 14.8.93 Supersedes: N/A Approved by: ...N.J.K....... HACCP Team Leader	
					Monitoring				
Process Step:	CCP No.	Hazard	Preventative measure	Critical limits	Procedure	Frequency	Corrective action	Responsibility
Chocolate chips	3.1	Salmonella	Effective supplier assurance: — Audit — Agreed specification (maximum acceptable levels)	Audit pass Absent/50g				
	3.2	Pesticides	Effective supplier assurance: — Audit — Agreed specification (maximum legal levels)	Audit pass MRLS for each pesticide type used				
Water	4	Pathogens and chemical residues	Effective supplier assurance:					

	No.	Hazard	Control	Target
			– Positive reporting of problems by supplier named contacts	No problems reported
			– Confirm potability through analysis of on-site sample	Legal levels
Plastic, tubs and lids	5	Chemical plasticizers and additives – leach into product	Correct choice of container (agree in specification)	Suitable for food use: – High-fat product – Compliance with legal migration limits
			Effective supplier assurance: – Audit	Audit pass
Storage – Chocolate chips	6	Physical and microbiological contamination through pest infestation	Effective pest control procedures in place	Absence of pests in storage area

Table 6.6 continued

Iced Delights
HACCP CONTROL CHART

Date 14.8.93 Supersedes: N/A
Approved by: .N.J.D.......
HACCP Team Leader

Process Step	CCP No.	Hazard	Preventative measure	Critical limits	Monitoring		Corrective action	Responsibility
					Procedure	Frequency		
Pump to pasteurization tank	7	Survival of foreign matter through filter malfunction	Effective filtration	Intact filter in place				
Pasteurizing	8.1	Survival of vegetative pathogens	Correct heat process	65.6°C/ 30 minutes				
Cooling	8.2	Outgrowth of spores due to slow cooling	Rapid cooling – Chilled water jacket – Continuous mixing	<7°C within 1½ hours max				
Ageing	9	Spore outgrowth due to poor temperature control and batch stock rotation	Effective temperature control Effective stock rotation	7°C maximum 48 hours maximum				

Process step	No.	Hazard	Control measure	Critical limit			
Freezing	10.1	Ingress of foreign material at chocolate chip addition (non-metal)	Empty through grating (20 mm holes)	Intact grating in place			
	10.2	Pathogens in air	Effective filtration	Intact filter in place (BS Class E/F or equivalent)			
Filling, lidding and labelling	11	Metal in packed product	Effective metal detection	2.0 mm ferrous 3.0 mm non-ferrous			
Date coding	12	Inability to trace and recall product resulting in unfit product in market place	Effective date and batch coding	Correct code applied			
All process steps involving product in contact with production equipment (tanks, pipework, freezers, filler)	13	Introduction of high levels of pathogens/ toxins due to poor cleaning	Effective cleaning procedures	No product residues			

In addition to your Critical Limits you may find it beneficial to have another layer of control to help you manage the process. This can be done by setting up target or action levels within your Critical Limits. The target levels can be used as an additional measure to indicate drift in the process, and you can then adjust the process to maintain control before the CCP actually deviates from its Critical Limits. An example of target levels can be found at the pasteurization step during ice cream production. The Critical Limits for the destruction of vegetative pathogens through the heat process are 65.6 °C for 30 minutes. In order to make sure that deviation does not occur, the process parameters might be set at 68.5 °C for 30 minutes, the target levels.

TARGET LEVELS:
control criteria which are more stringent than Critical Limits, and which can be used to take action and reduce the risk of a deviation.

Operating your system to target levels should ensure that a deviation from the Critical Limits never occurs. They are set for day-to-day management of the process, and are not normally added to the HACCP Control Chart as too many control criteria here can cause confusion. However, if you choose to build target levels into your HACCP System you will need to ensure that they are documented and that they tie in with your monitoring procedures. The best way of doing this is to document the target levels on your monitoring log sheets, and you must ensure that all monitoring personnel understand how they work.

6.8.2 Finding the right monitoring procedure

Monitoring is the measurement or observation at a CCP that the process is operating within the Critical Limits. It is one of the most important parts of the HACCP System, ensuring that the product is manufactured safely from day to day.

The specific monitoring procedure for each individual CCP will depend on the Critical Limits, and also on the capabilities of the monitoring device or method. It is essential that the chosen monitoring procedure must be able to detect loss of control at the CCP (i.e. where the CCP has deviated from its Critical Limits), as it is on the basis of monitoring results that decisions are made and action is taken.

There are two basic types of monitoring procedure:

1. On-line systems, where the critical factors are measured during the process. These may be **continuous** systems where critical

data are continuously recorded, or **discontinuous** systems where observations are made at specified time intervals during the process.

2. Off-line systems, where samples are taken for measurement of the critical factors elsewhere. Off-line monitoring is normally discontinuous and has the disadvantage that the sample taken may not be fully representative of the whole batch.

By far the best type of monitoring procedure is an on-line continuous system which can be set up to detect drift in the process and cause change to prevent the CCP from going out of control. In other words, a system which is designed to detect and correct drift around target levels and thus prevents deviation beyond the Critical Limits.

Now you will probably have noticed that most monitoring systems (i.e. those which do not involve continuous on-line systems) are based on some form of inspection and testing. And this is after we pointed out the limitations of inspection and testing at the beginning of this book! Although end product inspection and testing procedures do have serious limitations as control criteria alone (preventative measures) these procedures must form part of the HACCP monitoring System. Here they are properly targeted on critical factors throughout the process, and set up through statistical means.

The frequency of monitoring will depend on the nature of the CCP and the type of monitoring procedure. It is imperative that the HACCP Team determines the appropriate frequency for each monitoring procedure. For example, in the case of a metal detector, the frequency of checks is likely to be every 30 minutes, while with a seasonal vegetable crop, the CCP for pesticides may be monitored by pesticide testing once per crop season.

It is vital that inspection and testing programmes being used to monitor CCPs are statistically valid, and these programmes will be of most benefit if established under a structured system of Statistical Process Control. This will be covered in the next chapter.

We can now fill in the monitoring procedures and frequencies in our HACCP Control Chart example, shown in Table 6.7.

6.8.3 *Corrective action requirements*

HACCP Principle 5 requires that corrective action be taken when the monitoring results show a deviation from the Critical Limit(s) at a CCP. However, since the main reason for implementing HACCP is to prevent problems from happening in the first place, you should also build in corrective actions which will prevent

Figure 6.4 'Establish corrective action to be taken when monitoring indicates a deviation from an established Critical Limit'.

deviation from happening at the CCP. Your HACCP Plan is therefore likely to have two levels of corrective action, i.e. actions to prevent deviation and actions to correct following deviation.

Corrective action procedures should be developed by the HACCP Team and should be specified on the HACCP Control Chart. This will minimize any confusion or disagreements which might otherwise have occurred when action needs to be taken. It is also important to note that it is critical to assign responsibility for corrective action both to prevent and correct deviations. This will be discussed in more detail in the next section.

As we have seen, there are two main types of corrective action:

1. Actions which adjust the process to maintain control and prevent a deviation at the CCP
This first type of corrective action normally involves the use of target levels within the Critical Limits. When the process drifts towards or exceeds the target levels it is adjusted, bringing it back within the normal operating bands.

This is typified by on-line continuous monitoring systems which automatically adjust the process, e.g. automatic divert valves in

Table 6.7 Chocolate chip ice cream – monitoring procedures

HACCP plan Ref. HP001			Iced Delights HACCP CONTROL CHART					Date 14.8.93 Supersedes: N/A Approved by: ..N.J.B.........	
Process Step	CCP No.	Hazard	Preventative measure	Critical limits	Monitoring		Corrective action	Responsibility (HACCP Team Leader)
					Procedure	Frequency		
Ingredients: Skimmed milk powder	1	Antibiotic residues	Effective supplier assurance: – Audit	Audit pass	Audit by trained SQA auditor	Annual		
			– Agreed specification (maximum acceptable levels)	Legal limits	Antibiotic testing by supplier – results provided	Quarterly		
Cream	2	Antibiotic residues	Effective supplier assurance – Audit	Audit pass	Audit by trained SQA auditor	Annual		
			– Agreed specification (maximum acceptable levels)	Legal limits	Antibiotic testing by supplier – results provided	Quarterly		

Table 6.7 continued

Process Step:	CCP No.	Hazard	Preventative measure	Critical limits	Monitoring		Corrective action	Responsibility
					Procedure	Frequency		
Chocolate chips	3.1	Salmonella	Effective supplier assurance: – Audit	Audit pass	Audit by trained SQA auditor	Annual		
			– Agreed specification (maximum acceptable levels)	Absent/50g	Check supplier certificate of analysis for compliance	Every batch		
					Salmonella test	Monthly		
	3.2	Pesticides	Effective supplier assurance: – Audit	Audit pass	Audit by trained SQA auditor	Annual		

HACCP plan Ref. HP001

Iced Delights
HACCP CONTROL CHART

Date 14.8.93   Supersedes: N/A
Approved by: .....N.J.B.........
HACCP Team Leader

Product	No.	Hazard	Control	Critical limit	Monitoring	Frequency
Water	4	Pathogens and chemical residues	— Agreed specification (maximum legal levels) Effective supplier assurance: — Positive reporting of problems by supplier named contacts — Confirm potability through analysis of onsite sample	MRLS for each pesticide type used No problems reported Legal levels	Pesticide testing — in-house and supplier Check emergency contact procedures and review previous quarter trends Review certificates of analysis	Annual Quarterly Quarterly
Plastic, tubs and lids	5	Chemical — plasticizers and additives — leach into product	Correct choice of container (agree in specification)	Suitable for food use: — High-fat product — Compliance with legal migration limits	Review component listing and supplier migration data against legislation	Every time pack type or packaging supplier changed

Table 6.7 continued

HACCP plan Ref. HP001			Iced Delights HACCP CONTROL CHART				Date 14.8.93 Supersedes: N/A Approved by: N.J.B......... HACCP Team Leader		
Process Step	CCP Nr.	Hazard	Preventative measure	Critical limits	Monitoring		Corrective action	Responsibility
					Procedure	Frequency		
	5 cont.		Effective supplier assurance: – Audit	Audit pass	Audit by trained SQA auditor	Annual		
Storage – Chocolate chips	6	Physical and microbiological contamination through pest infestation	Effective pest control procedures in place	Absence of pests in storage area	Inspection by trained pest control professional	Eight inspections per annum		
					Facility house-keeping inspection	Weekly		

No.	Step	Hazard	Control	Critical limit	Monitoring	Frequency
7	Pump to pasteurization tank	Survival of foreign matter through filter malfunction	Effective filtration	Intact filter in place	Visual inspection	Start-up and shut down daily
8.1	Pasteurizing	Survival of vegetative pathogens	Correct heat process	65.6°C/30 minutes	Chart recorder – visual inspection and sign off. Check temperature sensor against traceable calibrated thermometer	Each batch. Daily
8.2	Cooling	Outgrowth of spores due to slow cooling	Rapid cooling – Chilled water jacket – Continuous mixing	<7°C within 1½ hours max	As 8.1	As 8.1
9	Ageing	Spore outgrowth due to poor temperature control and batch stock rotation	Effective temperature control. Effective stock rotation	7°C maximum. 48 hours maximum	Chart recorder – visual inspection and sign off	Each shift

Table 6.7 continued

HACCP plan Ref. HP001				Iced Delights HACCP CONTROL CHART				Date 14.8.93 Supersedes: N/A Approved by: N.J.B......... HACCP Team Leader		
						Monitoring				
Process Step	CCP No.	Hazard	Preventative measure	Critical limits		Procedure	Frequency	Corrective action	Responsibility
	9 cont.					Check temperature sensor against traceable calibrated thermometer	Daily		
						Record date and time in and out of ageing tank	Every batch		
Freezing	10.1	Ingress of foreign material at chocolate chip addition (non- _____)	Empty through grating (20 mm holes)	Intact grating in place		Visual deception	Every batch		

Process step	No.	Hazard	Control measure	Critical limit	Monitoring	Frequency
Filling, lidding and labelling	10.2	Pathogens in air	Effective filtration	Intact filter in place (BS Class E/F or equivalent)	Microbiological analysis for indicator organisms in air sample	Monthly
	11	Metal in packed product	Effective metal detection	2.0 mm ferrous 3.0 mm non-ferrous	Check metal detector with test pieces	Start-up and half hourly
Date coding	12	Inability to trace and recall product resulting in unfit product in market place	Effective date and batch coding	Correct code applied	Visual inspection	Start-up and half hourly
All process steps involving product in contact with production equipment (tanks, pipework, freezers, filler)	13	Introduction of high levels of pathogens/toxins due to poor cleaning	Effective cleaning procedures	No product residues	Visual inspection Rapid hygiene check (ATP bioluminescence)	Every clean Before start-up – every batch

milk pasteurization which open when the temperature falls below the target level, sending milk back to the unpasteurized side. However, preventative corrective action can also be associated with manual monitoring systems where the CCP monitor takes action when the target levels are approached or exceeded, and thus prevents a CCP deviation.

The factors which are often adjusted to maintain control include temperature and/or time, pH/acidity, ingredient concentrations, flow rates and sanitizer concentrations. Some examples are as follows:

- Continue to cook for longer to achieve the correct centre temperature.
- Add more acid to achieve the correct pH.
- Chill rapidly to correct storage temperature.
- Add more salt to the recipe.

When adjusting the process to maintain control, you must ensure that you can do so without causing or increasing the hazard. For example, if the product temperature had risen above 5 °C and you implement rapid chilling to bring it back down, then you must know that the temperature has not risen high enough for long enough to allow the growth of any microbiological hazards which might be present.

2. Actions to be taken following a deviation at a CCP
Following a deviation it is important to act quickly. You will need to take two types of action and it is vital that detailed records are kept.

- Adjust the process to bring it back under control. Adjusting the process will take a similar form to that discussed above for the prevention of deviations. The only difference here is that the process will have to be adjusted further to return to its normal operating level. Possibly this will be through the provision of a short-term repair so that production can restart quickly with no more deviations, while the permanent corrective action takes a longer period of time, e.g. the provision of temporary off-line metal detection until the in-line metal detector is mended.
- Deal with the material which was produced during the deviation period.

In order to effectively handle non-complying materials you will need to implement a series of further corrective actions:

(i)   Place all suspect product on hold.
(ii)   Seek advice from the HACCP Team, facility management and other relevant experts. Here it is important to consider the risk of the hazard occurring in the product.
(iii) Conduct further tests, where appropriate, to assess safety.

When you have obtained sufficient information the decision about what should happen to the product can be taken. This would probably be to:

(i)   Destroy the non-complying product;
(ii)   Rework into new products;
(iii) Direct non-complying product into less sensitive products such as animal feed;
(iv)   Release product following sampling and testing;
(v)   Release product.

Destruction of the non-complying product is the most obvious action, and the main one to be taken when the risk of the hazard occurring, in products which cannot be reworked, is high. However, this has the disadvantage of being costly, and is therefore normally the action of last resort.

Reworking the product can be carried out where the hazard would be controlled through the reworking process. It is important to ensure that any reworking does not cause new hazards in the secondary product, e.g. when allergenic ingredients such as nuts are reworked into a product where they will not appear on the pack ingredients listing. The key here is to rework like with like.

If the product can be diverted into safe use then this is another option. This might involve packing as less sensitive animal feeds, or possibly diverting into another product where the hazard will be controlled, e.g. the use of cooked meats, contaminated with vegetative microorganisms, in pie fillings which will receive another cook. Here the presence of heat-stable toxins must be carefully considered. Again, the presence of allergenic materials must be controlled.

You may decide to sample and test the product to establish whether or not the hazard is present. As previously discussed, great care must be taken when implementing sampling regimes due to the statistical probability of detecting the hazard. Do you know what the probability of finding the hazard is using your chosen sampling plan, and if so, are you confident that the remaining product will be safe?

The final option is to simply release the product but this cannot ever be advised for safety. You have chosen to implement HACCP to prevent safety problems and are designing your HACCP Plan to control hazards. This is what your CCPs are set up for. Product safety is not negotiable and you must not simply release product manufactured during a deviation. Also consider what your legal position would be if hazardous products were knowingly sold by your company.

It is important that detailed records are kept of all stages. It is essential that you investigate the cause of the deviation, and take appropriate steps to ensure that it does not happen again. The defined corrective action procedures are added to the HACCP Control Chart and you should then consider responsibility, both for monitoring and corrective action.

6.8.4 Who should be responsible?

The most important issue with responsibility is that you ensure that it is properly defined. All personnel involved need to clearly understand what they are required to do, and also how to do it. These details should be decided by the HACCP Team in conjunction with other management and must be fully documented on the HACCP Control Chart.

(a) Responsibility for monitoring

As we have seen, monitoring is a key part of the HACCP System operation and it is therefore vital that the persons involved in monitoring understand and are fully accountable for their monitoring actions. Monitoring procedures are closely related to the production process so it is usually most appropriate that the responsibility for monitoring lies with the Production Department.

(b) Responsibility for corrective action

Responsibility for corrective action will again often lie with the Production Department who are implementing the HACCP Plan, but you should consider assigning particular responsibilities at different levels in the management structure.

On-line responsibilities of the CCP monitor or line operator will most likely involve the notification of a supervisor who will then coordinate further actions. However, you may wish to give responsibility at this level for stopping the line in order to prevent large quantities of product being made while the CCP is out of control.

Off line, more senior responsibility will be appropriate where the corrective actions involve shutting down the plant for periods of time or where disposition actions are required. These decisions need to be taken by personnel who have the knowledge to recommend the appropriate corrective action for product manu-factured during a deviation, as outlined in the previous section. This may involve the HACCP Team Leader in discussion with facility management. However if the HACCP Team Leader is an expert in HACCP techniques rather than in hazards and their associated risks, it is important that other experts should be involved in the decision making process, e.g. toxicologists, microbiologists, process specialists.

It is also important to ensure that the individuals who are responsible for documenting and signing off the corrective action procedures are defined. This information will be crucial in proving that the required action has been taken, particularly important for legal issues.

At this stage the HACCP Control Chart should be complete as in our example in Table 6.8.

The CCPs should then be added on the final Process Flow Diagram for retention in the HACCP Plan, as in Figure 6.6.

Table 6.8 Chocolate chip ice cream – completed HACCP Control Chart

HACCP plan Ref. HP001			Iced Delights HACCP CONTROL CHART					Date 14.8.93 Supersedes: N/A Approved by: ...N.J.B......... HACCP Team Leader	
Process Step	CCP No.	Hazard	Preventative measure	Critical limits	Monitoring		Corrective action	Responsibility
					Procedure	Frequency		
Ingredients: Skimmed milk powder	1	Antibiotic residues	Effective supplier assurance: – Audit	Audit pass	Audit by trained SQA auditor	Annual	Change supplier	Purchasing Manager
			– Agreed specification (maximum acceptable levels)	Legal limits	Antibiotic testing by supplier – results provided	Quarterly	Contact supplier Reject consignment	QA Manager
Cream	2	Antibiotic residues	Effective supplier assurance: – Audit	Audit pass	Audit by trained SQA auditor	Annual	Change supplier	Purchasing Manager
			– Agreed specification (maximum acceptable levels)	Legal limits	Antibiotic testing by supplier – results provided	Quarterly	Contact supplier Reject consignment	QA Manager

Product	No.	Hazard	Control	Target/critical limit	Monitoring	Frequency	Corrective action	Responsibility
Chocolate chips	3.1	Salmonella	Effective supplier assurance: — Audit	Audit pass	Audit by trained SQA auditor	Annual	Change supplier	Purchasing Manager
			— Agreed specification (maximum acceptable levels)	Absent/50g	Check supplier certificate of analysis for compliance	Every batch	Contact supplier Reject consignment	Goods Inwards Clerk
					Salmonella test	Monthly	Contact supplier Reject batch. Visit/change supplier	QA Manager
Water	3.2	Pesticides	Effective supplier assurance: — Audit	Audit pass	Audit by trained SQA auditor	Annual	Change supplier	Purchasing Manager
			— Agreed specification (maximum legal levels)	MRLS for each pesticide type used	Pesticide testing – in-house and supplier	Annual	Contact supplier Reject consignment	QA Manager

Process Step	CCP No.	Hazard	Preventative measure	Critical limits	Monitoring		Corrective action	Responsibility
					Procedure	Frequency		
Water	4	Pathogens and chemical residues	Effective supplier assurance: — Positive reporting of problems by supplier named contacts	No problems reported	Check emergency contact procedures and review previous quarter trends	Quarterly	Amend contact procedure	Facility Engineer
			— Confirm potability through analysis of onsite sample	Legal levels	Review certificate of analysis	Quarterly	Contact supplier for discussion	QA Manager
Plastic, tubs and lids	5	Chemical — plasticizers and additives — leach into product	Correct choice of container (agree in specification)	Suitable for food use: — High-fat product — Compliance with legal migration limits	Review component listing and supplier migration data against legislation	Every time pack type or packaging supplier changed	Change container/ supplier	QA and Purchasing Managers

5 cont. Storage – Chocolate chips	Effective supplier assurance: – Audit	Audit pass	Audit by trained SQA auditor	Annual	Change supplier	Purchasing Manager
6 Physical and microbiological contamination through pest infestation	Effective pest control procedures in place	Absence of pests in storage area	Inspection by trained pest control professional; Facility house-keeping inspection	Eight inspections per annum; Weekly	Call in pest control professional – Eradicate pests – Dispose of contaminated product; – Eradicate pests – Dispose of contaminated product	Site General Manager; QA Manager
7 Pump to pasteurization tank Survival of foreign matter through filter malfunction	Effective filtration	Intact filter in place	Visual inspection	Start-up and shut down daily	Replace filter. Quarantine product (rework or disposal)	Production Operator Operations Manager

HACCP plan Ref. HP001

Iced Delights
HACCP CONTROL CHART

Date 14.8.93 Supersedes: N/A
Approved by: ..N.J.B.........
HACCP Team Leader

Process Step:	CCP No.	Hazard	Preventative measure	Critical limits	Monitoring Procedure	Frequency	Corrective action	Responsibility
Pasteurizing	8.1	Survival of vegetative pathogens	Correct heat process	65.6°C/ 30 minutes	Chart recorder – visual inspection and sign off	Each batch	Contact QA and discuss: – continue heating /holding period	Production Operator
					Check temperative sensor against trace-able calibrated thermometer	Daily	Quarantine product (rework or disposal)	Operations Manager QA Technician
Cooling	8.2	Outgrowth of spores due to slow cooling	Rapid cooling – Chilled water jacket – Continuous mixing	<7°C within 1½ hours max	As 8.1	As 8.1	As 8.1	As 8.1
Ageing	9	Spore outgrowth due to poor temperature control and batch stock rotation	Effective temperature control	7°C maximum	Chart recorder – visual inspection and sign off	Each shift	Quarantine product. Contact QA and discuss	Production Operator

Step	Hazard	Control	Critical limit	Monitoring	Frequency	Corrective action	Responsibility
9 cont.		Effective stock rotation	48 hours maximum	Record date and time in and out of ageing tank	Daily	Quarantine product and discuss with QA	QA Technician
				Check temperature sensor against traceable calibrated thermometer	Every batch	Quarantine product and discuss with QA	Production Operator
Freezing 10.1	Ingress of foreign material at chocolate chip addition (non-metal)	Empty through grating (20 mm holes)	Intact grating in place	Visual deception	Every batch	Replace grating	Production Operator
10.2	Pathogens in air	Effective filtration	Intact filter in place (BS Class E/F or equivalent)	Microbiological analysis for indicator organisms in air sample	Monthly	Replace filter	QA Manager

HACCP plan Ref. HP001

Iced Delights
HACCP CONTROL CHART

Date 14.8.93 Supersedes: N/A
Approved by: ...J.B............
                    HACCP Team Leader

Process step	CCP No.	Hazard	Preventative measure	Critical limits	Monitoring Procedure	Monitoring Frequency	Corrective action	Responsibility
Filling, lidding and labelling	11	Metal in packed product	Effective metal detection	2.0 mm ferrous 3.0 mm non-ferrous	Check metal detector with test pieces	Start-up and half hourly	Repair recalibrate metal detector. Quarantine and recheck product back to previous good check	Production Operator/QA Supervisor
Date coding	12	Inability to trace and recall product resulting in unfit product in market place	Effective date and batch coding	Correct code applied	Visual inspection	Start-up and half hourly	Quarantine product and recode. Input correct code or repair as appropriate	Production Supervisor
All process steps involving product in contact with production equipment (tanks, pipework, freezers, filler)	13	Introduction of high levels of pathogens toxins due to poor cleaning	Effective cleaning procedures	No product residues	Visual inspection Rapid hygiene check (ATP bio-lumin-scence)	Every clean Before start-up – every batch	Reclean Reclean	Production Operator Production Operator

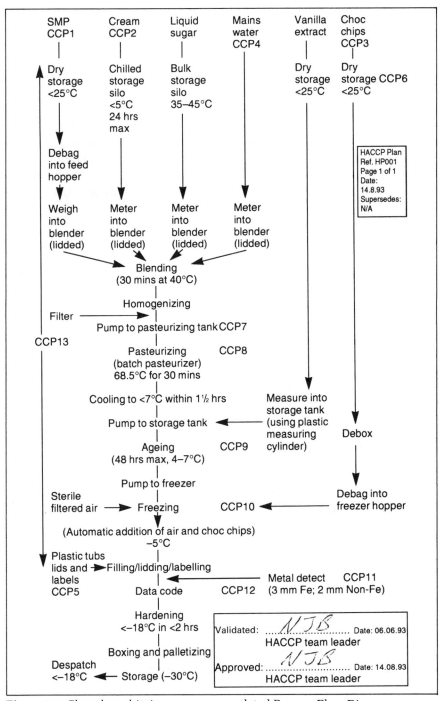

Figure 6.5 Chocolate chip ice cream – completed Process Flow Diagram.

6.9 The modular approach to HACCP

If your products are manufactured using a number of basic process operations in sequence, it may be possible to use the modular approach when putting together a HACCP Plan. This flexible approach allows hazard analysis to be carried out separately on each of the basic operations or modules. These are then added together to determine the CCPs for each product.

For example, in a facility producing a number of chilled ready meals, the following basic process operations may be in place, and each individual product will involve a combination (Table 6.9):

It is important to know where each module starts and ends so that no process step, and therefore no hazard, is missed when these are put together. When you have added up the correct sequence of process combinations (or modules), with their

Table 6.9 Process operation modules

PROCESS OPERATION MODULE

Storage
  chilled
  frozen
  ambient

Ingredient preparation
  can opening
  vegetable chopping/dipping/blanching
  weighing
  dry mixing
  pastry

Manufacturing
  mixing
  assembly
  baking
  meat cooking
  sauce cooking
  pasta/potato/rice cooking
  deep frying

Filling
  mechanical
  by hand

Packing
  mechanical
  by hand

Storage and despatch
  chilled
  frozen ambient

---

associated hazards and preventative measures, you can progress to determining CCPs in the normal way using the decision tree.

Note: It is vital that you do not try to determine CCPs for each individual module as CCPs for one product may not be automatically the same as for another.

6.10 Challenging your controls

You are now ready to implement your HACCP Plan and may wish to go straight on to validation, however, before going ahead it is worthwhile pausing to consider whether you really do have sufficient control for all possibilities. What happens, for example, when a CCP fails? Do you have the appropriate contingency plans in place?

It is important to challenge your controls and to understand what would happen in the event of a failure. This can be done using the structured approach through a number of different hazard cause and control identification systems. These include Hazard and Operability Study (HAZOP), Action Error Analysis (AEA), Management Oversight and Risk (MORT) and Failure Mode and Effect Analysis (FMEA), the system which HACCP was derived from (Suokas and Pyy, 1988).

HAZOP is a highly structured method which tries to identify all possible deviations from the way a system is designed to operate and to identify all hazards associated with these deviations. AEA, on the other hand looks at possible human failures, for example what happens when a step is forgotten or is implemented at the wrong time? The final system mentioned here, MORT, again looks at potential human failings, but this time as part of an investigation into the structure and functioning of the whole organization. It can be applied to potential deviations or deviations which have already occurred, and so can be useful in long term corrective action procedures, as well as to a general observation of potential safety failures in the organization.

All of these systems are fully described elsewhere in the scientific literature. Here we will concentrate on FMEA which is perhaps the most appropriate for challenging your HACCP Plan. FMEA, like HACCP, was designed to look at an operation and establish what could go wrong, so that appropriate control could be built in.

This system simply looks at the possible failure modes, the contributory cause(s) of the failure and considers what the effects would be. It then considers the current controls and recommends any additional controls required. What FMEA is actually doing is challenging the security of the CCPs, and increasing the effectiveness of the HACCP System.

Like HACCP, FMEA is a system which depends on teamwork and in particular the brainstorming approach to identify all the possible failure modes and their associated causes. It really does require the HACCP Team to think the unthinkable and challenge commonly held beliefs such that all potential outcomes are considered. When this has been done it is relatively straightforward to identify and implement an extra 'safety net' of controls so that deviations at CCPs are minimized, and equally important that deviations are not missed through failure in monitoring.

The most straightforward way to challenge controls through FMEA uses the structured FMEA chart shown below (Table 6.10).

Table 6.10 Failure Mode and Effect Analysis chart

Failure mode	Effect of failure	Cause of failure	Current control	Recommended controls
Failure to detect metal	Metal in product – injury	Metal detector breakdown	Metal detect and check metal detector hourly. Record result	Maintenance schedule
	– complaints of metal in product from customers	Metal detector not properly calibrated		Set up calibration schedule for correct sensitivity
	– lost credibility	Metal detector in wrong place in line		Move to just before packing
	– prosecution	Incorrect metal detector		Confirm sensitivity appropriate for all products
	– bad publicity	Rejects not controlled		Locked cage for rejects
	– lost customers	Damage in transit		Training for drivers. Standing instructions and audits

The HACCP Team should use brainstorming to fill in the first three columns, and then discuss whether the CCPs, Critical Limits and monitoring procedures (i.e. the 'current controls') identified during the HACCP Study are sufficient and effective. Following this exercise the final column can be completed as the HACCP Team consider any extra control criteria required for a more fail-safe system.

This example shows the considerations for metal hazards being found in the product.

When you are confident that all your proposed controls are sufficient for all possible outcomes you can move on to validation and implementation of your HACCP Plan.

6.11 Validation of the HACCP Plan

When you have completed your HACCP Control Chart and highlighted all CCPs on your Process Flow Diagram then the HACCP Plan is complete. However, before going on to implement the plan it is important to know that it is correct and valid – a final check that you have got it right. This should be carried out soon after the plan is completed so that implementation can follow without delay.

You should work through all the records in the Process Flow Diagram and HACCP Control Chart to make sure that all the details are actually relevant to the hazards, and that the control criteria, i.e. the Critical Limits, have been set at tight enough levels to ensure control of product safety. It is equally important that you ensure that no hazards have been missed during the study.

It is also important to inspect the processing area in order to make sure that all required preventative measures (particularly new measures) are in place. Critical process and monitoring equipment should also be examined to ensure that it is capable of achieving the desired control criteria and is appropriately calibrated.

Although members of the HACCP Team can carry out some or all of the HACCP Plan validation, it may be appropriate to use other experts to cross-check the study and ensure that no issues have been missed. It is really important to know that you have got it right, so if it is your first HACCP Plan then you should involve other relevant experts in the validation. This could be done by other experts within your company, e.g. at corporate level, or by external independent specialists and HACCP experts.

7

Putting the HACCP Plan into practice

Now that we have seen how to put together a HACCP Plan, the next step is to implement the HACCP Plan in your operation. You have made a commitment to implement the formal HACCP System in order to effectively control all safety issues. In order to do this properly you must ensure that sufficient resources are available, so that the identified CCPs are monitored, and that records are kept. In this chapter we will be considering each of these areas and, in addition, how to meet the requirements of HACCP Principles 6 and 7.

7.1 What resources are required?

The major resources required to implement the HACCP Plan are equipment, methods, facilities and people. We will discuss each one in turn.

7.1.1 Equipment

It is important to establish that you have the correct equipment for each situation. Can it, for example, carry out the process specified and achieve the desired control criteria ? Has it been properly calibrated and maintained, and will it be reliable when the HACCP System is implemented? Some important questions to consider at this stage are as follows:

- Do you have the right equipment in place or will you have to buy any new equipment?
- Is it appropriate to the task?
- Is it sensitive enough?
- Can it be calibrated?

- Does it require ancillary equipment, e.g. locked boxes for dud detectors on a can line?
- Is it easy to operate, e.g. a gas chromatograph?
- Can the operative interpret the results?
- Will it work on the line or does it require special facilities, i.e. will it withstand the rigours of the production environment?
- Is it cleanable?
- Are there any health and safety constraints?

7.1.2 Methods – use of statistical techniques

A method which may be useful to some organizations when setting up monitoring and verification systems is Statistical Process Control (SPC).

As part of the HACCP Plan the Critical Limits for each Critical Control Point within the process have been established. These limits may sometimes only be a minimum value, such as the time and temperature requirements for a heat treatment process, or the limits may be solely a maximum value such as cold storage temperature. Other CCPs may require a process to be contained between a minimum and a maximum limit, e.g. nitrite in bacon, where the minimum level controls microbiological safety but the maximum level is necessary to ensure chemical safety. Alternatively, it may also be necessary to have a minimum limit in terms of food safety, but also to have a maximum limit in terms of product quality (Figure 7.1).

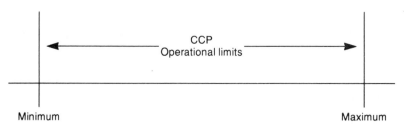

Figure 7.1 CCP operational limits.

For each CCP you will need to verify that, under normal operating conditions, the process can be realistically and consistently maintained within these defined limits. One way of assessing whether a process is capable is to use statistical analysis. Such statistical techniques have been developed and used for many years, predominantly for process monitoring and control in the engineering industry. The techniques are not really difficult to apply but for those with no prior knowledge, the use of a good reference book or, better still, an expert in the field will be invaluable.

(a) Process capability

The statistical verification of a process in order to establish the probability (confidence) of its ability stay within specified limits is known as establishing the **process capability** (Figure 7.2).

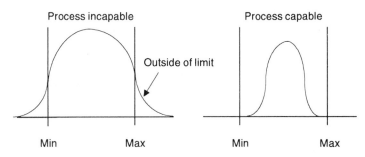

Figure 7.2 Process capability.

A stable process is one that is in a state of statistical control. In assessing the process capability we are doing two things:

1. Determining whether the process is capable of achieving the control criteria (the Critical Limits) that have been established.
2. Determining whether the process is capable of being controlled. All processes are subject to natural and inherent variability. This type of variation is known as 'common cause' variation and is usually the result of a combination of many small sources of variation within the process. If the common cause variation is known then we know over what range the process is capable of being controlled. Some processes are subject to 'special cause' variation, where the source can be attributed to an unexpected change. These special causes can usually be investigated and corrective action taken to prevent a recurrence.

In establishing the process capability we want to be sure that the process is only subject to common cause variation, i.e. in statistical process control, and that common causes are minimized (Figure 7.3).

There are a few basic requirements for the application of process capability.

1. A series of random samples/readings are taken from the process in consecutive groups of five to ten (with 50 to 100 samples taken in total). These measurements of the process must be

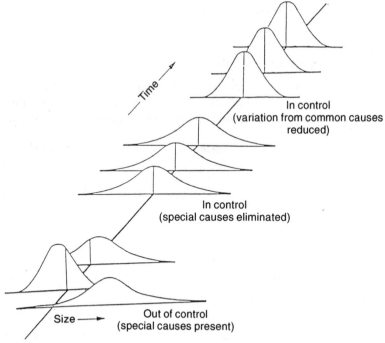

In control
(variation from common causes reduced)

In control
(special causes eliminated)

Out of control
(special causes present)

Figure 7.3 Stages of process improvement.

obtained at a time when all process controls were left untouched throughout the duration of the run.

2. These readings must be shown to be normally distributed. A normal distribution must meet mathematically defined requirements, and has a characteristic bell-shaped appearance (Figure 7.4). If this type of distribution can be verified as being contained with the defined limits throughout the process, then the process can be said to be running in 'statistical process control'.

3. The degree of natural variation (spread) of results within the normal distribution can be quantified numerically by statistical analysis. This measurement is known as the **Standard Deviation (SD)**. From the Standard Deviation it can be determined by calculation whether the process is capable, or not capable, of running within defined limits.

Standard Deviation × 2 = ± variation from the mean value within which 95.4% of the process readings/samples would be expected to be found.

Standard Deviation × 3 = ± variation from the mean value within which 99.7% of the process readings/samples would be expected to be found.

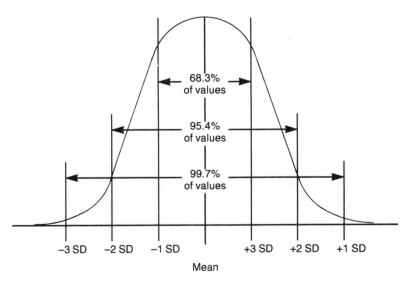

Figure 7.4 The normal distribution.

(b) Process Control Chart

Once a statistical analysis has been carried out for a particular process and has demonstrated that it is capable of achieving an acceptable level of performance, then the statistical profile which has been built up from the capability study can be used to produce a **Process Control Chart** for the control of a process and its parameters. Such a Chart takes the form of data capture with graphical plotting of the variations on a time or batch basis. By using the information of the process profile the process controller (with the aid of a control chart) will be able to tell whether variations in measurements taken of a process parameter are inherent and to be expected as a result of **natural random** fluctuations of the process (i.e. due to common causes), or whether the variations are of such a magnitude as to be statistically significant and indicate that this shift in the process must be due to some **assignable** reason (i.e. due to special causes). When a significant variation occurs it indicates that there has been a shift in the overall equilibrium of the process and that an adjustment must be made to restore the process, the shift may also indicate the failure of some plant component. The process control chart can be used very effectively as an on-line CCP log sheet which is filled in by the operative. The chart gives the operator a very rapid notification that the process is going out of control.

Process Control Charts can be used to analyse the process parameters in two respects: **Mean** and **Range** (or Standard

Deviation), measuring the **accuracy** and the **precision** of the process respectively. The control chart may have upper and lower **action limits** marked onto them (where appropriate) and can sometimes include intermediate upper and lower **warning bands**. By taking the mean of the process measurements (say four to five readings) the operator will get a 'consensus' reading of any overall shift in the process. American Process Control charts are only marked with upper and lower action limits, with no intermediate warning bands. The action and warning limits for the charts are derived from values generated from the Process Capability analysis and constants extracted from Statistical Process Control tables.

By looking at the range of the individual results used to produce the mean the operator gets an indication of the stability ('wobble') of the process. Excessive range variation may well indicate the start of plant failure (e.g. a sluggish control valve) – analogous to a spinning top just before falling over. Although the mean reading of all the wobbles may still indicate that it is stationary on its spot, the excessive wobbling (range) would indicate the inherent instability and that the spinning top is just about to fail (i.e. in this case fall over).

The information for a Process Control Chart could be captured on a table as set out in Table 7.1.

Table 7.1 Information gathering for Process Control Charts

Time/Batch No.		08:30	09:00	09:30
Measured values	1	6.5	7.6	8.3
	2	7.6	7.4	7.8
	3	7.5	8.2	7.5
	4	8.1	6.8	7.2
Sum		29.7	30	30.8
Average		7.4	7.5	7.7
Range		1.6	1.4	1.1

A Mean Range Chart would look as set out in Figure 7.5. The basic interpretation of the chart would be:

- Any result above the Upper Action Level (UAL) or below the Lower Action Level (LAL) should be considered highly significant and process adjustment should be considered.
- Any result between the Warning Levels (Upper and Lower) and the corresponding Upper and Lower Action Levels should be considered to be suspect; two results in a row in the same band

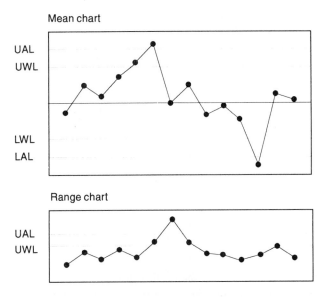

Figure 7.5 A Mean Range chart. UWL, upper warning level; LWL, lower warning level; UAL, upper action level; LAL, lower action level.

would be considered highly significant and process adjustment should again be considered.

- Any series of results that show a consistent upward or downward trend should also be considered to be significant.

The use of Process Control Charts is of most benefit when an immediate reading or measurement can be made for assessment in order to achieve instant process control and adjustment.

This section has been dealing predominantly with the interpretation of variable data, such as that obtained by measuring time, temperature, flow rate, etc. However, the application of Control Charts can be used equally effectively with **attribute** data, such as the YES/NO result obtained when checking that a metal detector is working.

(c) Microbiological applications

The requirement for rapid measurement at a CCP will usually preclude the use of microbiological analysis where results are usually obtained in terms of days rather than seconds. Also the application of mean to microbiological count results is not particularly appropriate as counts are not usually symmetrically (normal) distributed around the mean value, but vary more

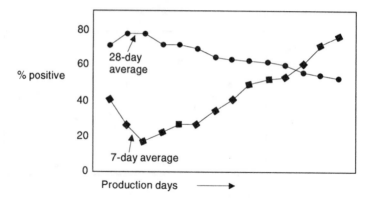

Figure 7.6 Moving Average Control chart.

typically on a log scale. For the monitoring of microbiological results and trends, on a more retrospective basis, the use of a rolling (moving) average of percentage samples that were either present/absent per unit weight, or the percentage of sample with counts that were either < or > a specification level per gram, can be particularly effective at picking up trends and eliminating fluctuations (Figure 7.6). (It is however important to respond to and investigate each individual incidence of unacceptably high microbiological results.) These rolling averages can be on a weekly, monthly or quarterly basis (as found to be most appropriate) and associated with each rolling average can be an assigned warning level. This may be particularly useful for monitoring the effectiveness of a cleaning schedule.

The basic concepts and the final application of Statistical Process Control in the form of Process Control Charts are relatively simple. However, care and understanding is required in the initial interpretation and the setting up of an effective system.

The use of the principles of Statistical Process Control can be a very powerful tool in the application of HACCP, for ensuring that the Critical Control Points are being effectively monitored and controlled.

7.1.3 Facilities

Different facilities are needed for the process itself and for the additional implementation requirements. You should consider the main facility (i.e. processing area) along with specific facilities required during the process. For example, do you have sufficient hand wash basins and are they correctly sited? Will the existing waste disposal system cope with additional waste from this process? Is there sufficient space for handling the packed product?

You will also need a briefing area so that you can brief staff and carry out any further specific training required. This may need to be capable of holding large numbers of employees during awareness briefing sessions, and smaller numbers, for example, during the training of CCP monitors.

7.1.4 *People*

People are a key resource in any HACCP System and you must ensure that they can be effective. Do you have enough personnel to adequately monitor the CCPs and are these the right people for that task? Do your chosen monitors have enough time to fit the monitoring procedures in with their other responsibilities? Have you considered the required level of supervision of CCP monitors, and is this in place?

The HACCP Team should consider all these issues in conjunction with other company management in order to identify all the resources required and put together an implementation plan.

If you are still carrying out HACCP Studies on other products, then the HACCP Team will need to have sufficient time available for meetings. When all HACCP Plans have been implemented the HACCP Team will still be required to meet in order to discuss maintenance, but this will be on a less frequent basis. In both cases it is important that HACCP Team members do find the time to participate in meetings, and it is therefore best to keep meetings as short as possible. Many companies find that meetings of between a half and one hour's duration work best.

7.2 Monitoring CCPs

Monitoring is one of the most important aspects of any HACCP System. This is how we measure that the CCPs are working. CCP monitors therefore play a key role in the production of safe products.

7.2.1 *Briefing and motivating CCP monitors*

CCP monitors will only perform effectively if they understand not only what they are expected to do and why they are doing it, but also how this fits in with the rest of the HACCP System. An understanding of how essential their role is for the safety of the product is also a key factor in maintaining motivation.

155

Figure 7.7 'Briefing and motivating CCP monitors!'.

It is vital that all your CCP monitors are instructed in basic HACCP philosophy and in particular the importance of accurate monitoring. They must understand what the Critical Limits are for the CCP in question, and how to take corrective action when a deviation occurs. In some cases you will need the CCP monitors to adjust the process in order to maintain control and prevent a deviation from occurring. Here it is important to know that your monitor is capable of the required actions. The detail and accuracy requirements for CCP records must also be agreed. In order to achieve this you will have to ensure that appropriate training is available for all CCP monitors, and this may be carried out by your HACCP Team members. Because of the importance of this role, it is recommended that you not only provide training, but also check understanding and competency in the specific task.

7.2.2 Monitoring sheets

The monitoring sheet should have details of the Critical Limits and corrective action procedures. Target levels within the Critical

Table 7.2 Chocolate chip ice cream – CCP Monitoring sheet

Log Sheet CCP No. 7	Pasteurizer filter inspection	HACCP Plan Ref No. HP001
Monitoring procedure Visually inspect filter to ensure it is intact.	Frequency 2 × daily – at start-up and at shut down	

Corrective action:
Replace filter and contact Operations Manager regarding quarantine of product.

Date and time	Result	Action taken	Signature

Reviewed by:

Title: _____ Signature: _____ Date: _____

Limits can be included if the CCP monitor is to adjust the process in order to maintain control. It is also useful to include details of the monitoring method but this may not be necessary in all cases as long as monitors have been properly trained. There should be sufficient space available to record the necessary data and columns must be included for the monitor to sign off and date each monitoring event. In addition each monitoring sheet must have a cross reference to the HACCP Plan and CCP number.

An example of a CCP monitoring sheet for one of the CCPs for our chocolate chip ice cream product is shown in Table 7.2 although not all CCP monitoring sheets will look like this.

7.2.3 Reporting deviations

A deviation occurs when the Critical Limits are exceeded and the CCP goes out of control. The CCP monitors must understand exactly what constitutes a deviation with reference to the Critical Limits. It is essential that they know when to report a problem and who to report to, so the corrective action reporting structure must be specified. This could be done on the monitoring log sheet or in work instructions.

7.2.4 Feedback on results and corrective action

The monitor needs to see the whole picture and understand what happens to the product, both when it has been produced under control and when a deviation has arisen. This is important from the point of motivation and helps in getting monitors to take responsibility for their part in the proceedings.

Feedback can be given effectively both individually and in groups and it is always important to stress positive aspects, e.g. telling the monitor that his/her fast action saved £s by preventing reject product being produced. This may be done through departmental briefings and performance charts or through written reports being circulated to appropriate personnel. It is also helpful from the motivation point of view if all other staff in the processing area know the importance of the CCP monitor's actions.

7.3 Record keeping

HACCP Principle 6 requires that effective record keeping procedures are established to document the HACCP System. Records need to be kept of all areas which are critical to product safety, as written evidence that the HACCP Plan is in compliance, i.e. verification that the system has been working correctly. This will also support a defence under litigation proceedings. Records will also be useful in providing a basis for analysis of trends (which in turn may contribute towards improvements in the system) as well as for internal investigation of any food safety incident which may occur. The records do not all have to be in typed format and it is likely that you will hold a number of hand-written documents, e.g. Hazard Analysis Charts and CCP monitoring log sheets.

It is extremely useful to allocate a unique reference number to each HACCP Plan. This number may then be used on all pieces of documentation relating to the HACCP Plan and cross-referencing of CCP log sheets, monitor training records, etc. will be made easier.

Specific records which must be kept are the CCP monitoring results including the results relating to any CCP deviations. Here there must also be records of the corrective action procedures which were followed in each case.

The length of time which records must be kept will vary depending on several factors. Firstly there is likely to be a minimum time which records must be kept for legal reasons, and this will partly be determined by the country where your operation is located. The record retention time will also depend on the nature of the product itself, e.g. there is little point in keeping records for production of a sandwich with 2 days' shelf life for as long as the records for production of a canned product which has 4 years' shelf life. In general it is likely that you will need to keep records of CCP monitoring, and in particular records of deviations and corrective actions, for a period of 3 to 6 years.

The types of HACCP records which might be retained are as follows:

1. The HACCP Plan: as the critical document in the HACCP System the current HACCP Plan should be kept together with all data collected during its creation. This will mean the Process Flow Diagram and HACCP Control Chart, plus the Hazard Analysis information (Hazard Analysis Chart if used), details of the HACCP Team who were actually responsible, copies of any Non-Compliance Notes and corrective action details. Details of any monitoring procedures need not be retained with the HACCP Plan providing that they are clearly cross referenced by number or by location. A useful HACCP Documentation program is available for the PC from Campden Food and Drink Research Association. This will save administrative effort, particularly when it comes to updating the HACCP plan.
2. History of amendments to the HACCP Plan: while it is important to hold the current copy of the HACCP Plan, it is

equally useful to have a concise history of any amendments that may have been carried out. Obsolete HACCP Plans will have been destroyed with the exception of the master copy which should be retained by the HACCP Team Leader in a secure location.

3. Critical Control Point (CCP) monitoring records: the amount of paper involved in retaining CCP log sheets may be prohibitive in which case a monthly/three-monthly summary is recommended. This should clearly detail the CCP number, Control Limits, indicate any deviations and corrective actions taken, and persons involved.

4. Hold/Trace/Recall records: in the event of a deviation, at a CCP, it may be necessary to hold the product in quarantine pending a decision as to the means of disposition. If the product has been despatched it will need to be traced and recalled. Records of these activities will need to be retained. It may prove useful in the event of a serious incident if evidence in the form of documented challenge tests on the trace and recall system are available.

5. Training records: evidence that the HACCP Team and other personnel have been trained will almost certainly be needed. A simple record sheet detailing the type of training carried out and signed and dated by both trainer and trainee will suffice. Training records should include HACCP training, auditor training, food hygiene training and so on. It is also important that you keep records which demonstrate that your CCP monitors are fully trained and proficient in carrying out their task(s). It is recommended that the Personnel/Human Resources function is responsible for maintaining training records.

6. Audit records: records of HACCP audit through retention of non-compliance notes and reports. This will be discussed in more detail in Chapter 8.

7. Meeting records: it will be useful to keep concise minutes of HACCP meetings. These should indicate any actions required prior to the next meeting, together with the person responsible for taking the action. The minutes will provide a useful focus for the HACCP Team and help to drive the system forward by ensuring that all Team members have the same understanding of what actions were agreed during the meeting.

8. Calibration records: records relating to any instrumentation associated with CCPs. This includes both processing and monitoring equipment.

9. The HACCP System procedures: you may wish to consider producing a HACCP Procedural Document for your company

Figure 7.8 'Retaining records'.

as a way of drawing together all activities associated with the HACCP programme. It may consist of a HACCP Manual which contains firstly the company's policy on Food Safety Management, signed by its most senior executive. The Manual may then follow on with details of how the company plans to implement HACCP – the Project Plan and contain a master list of site HACCP Plans and their reference numbers. If you only have one HACCP Plan, perhaps you may wish to keep the document itself in the manual. A directory of useful external contacts and training bodies and perhaps the HACCP audit schedule could be considered along with any master copies of data sheets and instructions for filling them out.

Regulatory bodies will be interested in reviewing significant records which relate specifically to establishment of and compliance with critical control points, and less interested in those records which relate to the 'systems' aspect of HACCP.

Those companies who wish to use the HACCP System as a foundation for a quality system however, will need to treat systems related records also as 'significant'. The ISO 9000 record retention period is 3 years.

Records should be stored in an organized manner which enables easy retrieval. Standardized record forms will assist.

161

7.4 Working within your constraints

All production operations are operating under certain constraints and these are most likely to be associated with time and money. When implementing the HACCP Plan it is important to ensure that all the critical issues **can** be addressed while working within your constraints. You have already put a large amount of resource into drawing up the HACCP Plan, through the HACCP Team training requirements and personnel time for the study. Now it is important to ensure that this resource has not been wasted through improper implementation of the HACCP Plan.

If your processing personnel have limited time available it is important to ensure that their time is well spent. Target the resource to managing the critical areas, i.e. the CCPs, and investigate whether time can be saved elsewhere. You should ask whether or not all existing tasks are really necessary for product safety or quality.

There are a number of ways in which a tight budget can be maintained while implementing the HACCP System. It is crucial that you do not try to save money by only implementing selected parts of the HACCP Plan. Instead concentrate on how HACCP can be brought together within your existing operation without additional on-costs. For example, you may not need to create new log sheets for monitoring all the CCPs. It is likely that many of your existing monitoring sheets can either be used directly or amended to take on additional data and/or signature columns (e.g. dating and signing of thermograph charts).

As we have seen, training is essential for the successful implementation of HACCP, but this does not have to be expensive external courses. Some of your HACCP Team members will be able to train other company personnel and conduct briefing sessions. You may also be able to save some time and money by combining training sessions, e.g. food hygiene and HACCP, where the same personnel require different types of training.

If HACCP implementation is carried out to a carefully thought out plan, it does not need to be a drain on your resources, and instead helps to target resources effectively at the areas which really are critical to the safety of your business.

8

HACCP as a way of life – maintaining your HACCP System

Having completed the HACCP Study and ensured that the CCPs are being monitored, many people breath a sigh of relief and congratulate themselves that they are using HACCP to manage food safety. Be careful! The HACCP Study was completed at a point in time and if it is to remain as effective as it was on the day it was written it **MUST BE MAINTAINED**. Like any Quality Management System, the ongoing maintenance of the HACCP System is where the benefit really lies. The initial study will result in a system that will act as a bench mark for the future improvements – driven through identification of weaknesses and by taking corrective action. HACCP should be seen as a way of life throughout the entire company from the moment that the initial studies are completed and the implementation underway. In this chapter we will consider some of the activities that can drive the system forward, making it live instead of being a set of documents on the QA Manager's office shelf, specifically, the HACCP Audit, Analysis of Data, keeping up with new emerging hazards, ongoing training requirements, and how to keep the HACCP Plan up to date.

8.1 Ongoing verification through audit

The HACCP System must include verification procedures (HACCP Principle 7) to provide assurance that the HACCP Plan is being complied with on a day-to-day basis. This can be done most effectively by using an audit method. An **audit** can be regarded as an independent and systematic examination which is carried out in order to determine whether what is actually happening complies with the documented procedures. Also whether the procedures have been implemented such that the stated objectives have been achieved. The benefits of auditing a HACCP System will include:

1. Providing documented evidence of due diligence in managing food safety.
2. Having an independent and objective review of the effectiveness of the HACCP System.
3. Maintaining confidence in the HACCP System through verifying the effectiveness of the controls.
4. Identifying areas for improving and strengthening the system.
5. Continually reinforcing awareness of food safety management.
6. Removing obsolete control mechanisms.

AUDIT:
a systematic and independent examination to determine whether activities and results comply with the documented procedures; also whether these procedures are implemented effectively and are suitable to achieve the objectives.

In HACCP terms, achieving the objectives means managing the manufacture and distribution of safe food products through use of HACCP.

The Audit can be considered as a 'health' check of the HACCP System. It is a means of determining its strengths and weaknesses and, by taking appropriate corrective actions, a route to continuous improvement.

8.1.1 Types of audit used in HACCP

(a) The Systems Audit

If you have chosen to manage HACCP using a quality systems approach, that is, against each of the HACCP Principles, defined procedures are in place which state precisely how HACCP will be implemented and maintained, the systems audit will be used. The purpose of the audit is to find any weakness in the system and to ensure that corrective action is taken. This will entail taking a thorough, systematic and independent review of all or part of the HACCP System. Priorities for corrective actions can be assigned against food safety risk. For example, if you have a clearly defined requirement for a HACCP Team approach, the auditor may want to look at the team structure, team member qualifications and training records, details of who had carried out the HACCP Studies – one team member or with full team input. Both current and historical documentation will be reviewed. This type of audit is most commonly used for ISO 9000 series (Quality Management System) audits.

(b) The Compliance Audit

Again, the audit will be independent, but a more focused, in-depth inspection of the operation against the standards defined in the HACCP Plan. This type of audit will be most commonly used for HACCP, from checking CCP compliance to ensuring that the HACCP Team had originally identified the hazards correctly along with the appropriate controls in the process. In the latter case, the compliance audit will be done either by an internal or external HACCP audit expert.

In summary, the HACCP Compliance Audit could be assessing two areas.

- Compliance with the requirements of the HACCP Principles.
- Compliance with the documented HACCP Plan.

(c) The Investigative Audit

This is an independent investigation into a specific problem area. This type of audit may be used when a CCP regularly goes out of control – investigating the real cause in order to take corrective action, or where a previously unknown problem has arisen.

In implementing and maintaining HACCP, all three types of audit may be used, either on their own, or in combination. Whatever type of audit used, the essential elements will remain the same.

8.1.2 Identification and training of Auditors

HACCP Auditors must be skilled in the techniques of system auditing, knowledgeable in HACCP itself and technically qualified in the area under study. For this reason it is often advisable to use members of the HACCP Team as auditors as many of the required competencies will be the same. However, it can be an advantage to use someone who wasn't on the original HACCP Team and/or a representative from another discipline. They may be more inclined to challenge existing practices and beliefs.

Audit techniques can be taught fairly quickly through attending an ISO 9000 auditor training course and by shadowing experienced auditors. If the auditor is inexperienced in hazard analysis and HACCP techniques then the training period will take considerably longer. Where an audit is to be conducted by more than one person the responsibility for leading the audit should be defined.

For 'in-house' audits, care must be taken to maintain the independence of the auditor; that is, that the auditors do not audit their own departments.

8.1.3 Scheduling of Audits

It is essential that an audit schedule is established. You will want to ensure that the scope of each audit is clearly defined in order that the entire HACCP System is reviewed and no element missed out. It is recommended that a 3-monthly audit of the entire system would be reasonable. It would be possible to perhaps schedule audits of part of the system on a weekly or monthly basis. Auditors can then be assigned to the schedule well in advance.

Let's now consider the steps that will be required in a HACCP Audit (Figure 8.1).

We will now take each of these stages and look in detail at what happens.

A. Audit programme

It is useful to prepare an agenda for the audit programme. This will serve to notify personnel who may be required during the audit, of your intended timetable and for them to ensure that they are available. Include the start and finish times.

You will need also to make sure that you have all documentation required for the pre-audit review. In alerting the auditees to the agenda for the audit, you will be able to request all relevant documentation as indicated.

B. Document review

Before the audit, all documentation relating to the scope of the audit must be reviewed by the auditors. This will be a very important part of the audit as an initial audit checklist can be drawn up during the process. HACCP auditing involves to a large extent an assessment of the people who put the HACCP Plan together, i.e. have they got it right? This begins with the document review.

What documentation should be reviewed? In answering that question, let us consider what would be available. Firstly, the site layout plan, useful to begin to understand the flow of product through the site before the audit. Also, the scale of the operation and other products produced. Secondly, the HACCP Plan. Start

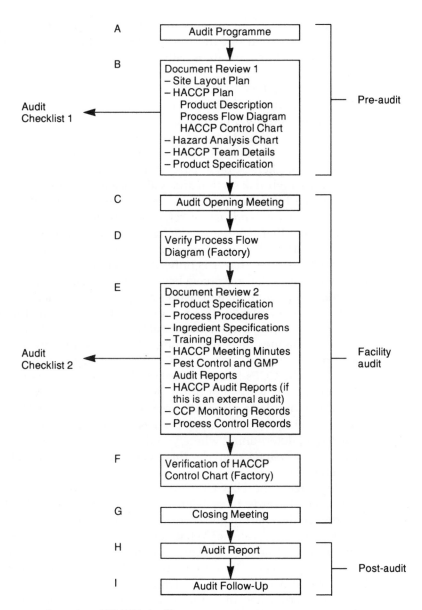

Figure 8.1 Steps in a HACCP Audit.

with the Process Flow Diagram and product specifications relating to it. Compare one against the other, noting whether all elements of the corresponding specifications are included in the Process Flow Diagram and *vice versa*. Consider whether all time/temperature information is adequately covered by the Process Flow Diagram.

167

The initial document review can be done as an initial scan – get a feel for who carried out the HACCP Study, the style, completeness, and also familiarization with the site being audited, and the product and process itself. It will give you an opportunity to carry out some research before the audit.

If you are auditing a HACCP Plan for the first time, an important part of your audit will be to assess the competency of the people responsible for the study. (This is particularly so for external HACCP Audits at other factories within your organization or SQA audits at suppliers.) Take part of the Process Flow Diagram, preferably a high-risk section and without reference to the HACCP Control Chart carry out your own hazard analysis based on your expert knowledge and use of reference material, legislation, etc. Having done that, compare your result with the original Hazard Analysis Chart. At this stage too you will be able to consider whether food safety hazards only have been included or whether quality and legal hazards have been identified. Also, whether the hazards and preventative measures are precisely defined or rather vague and general – is there a preventative measure for each specific hazard? Has the hazard analysis been carried out in an organized manner or is it a jumble of hazards and preventative measures? Following on from this, you will begin to be able to judge how the CCPs have been established. Make a note to check whether records were kept of the decision-making process.

You may decide to assess the competency of the HACCP Team again by taking the CCP Decision Trees and using your own expert knowledge, determining where you think the CCPs are, and why. (Note: As a paper exercise this will only be an indicator of competence.)

In looking at the HACCP Control Chart, make sure that only food safety hazards have been included. Consider each of the columns on the chart, is the corrective action identified going to be effective and is it realistic? What about the people responsible for monitoring and taking corrective action? Make notes of who they are so that you can talk to them during the audit. For example, if the 'Goods-Inwards' clerk is defined as being responsible for checking Certificates of Conformance for certain high-risk raw materials, you will be able to question him or her to assess whether they have been trained, what their terms of reference are, where their CCP log sheets are kept, who reviews them and so on. The same approach can be taken for each CCP. Consider the monitoring procedures and frequency – perhaps a *Salmonella* test is specified and the procedure cross-referenced by a reference number. You will be able during the audit to check in the laboratory that the procedure exists, and/or has been validated.

Check also the frequency of monitoring, training of staff, etc. as previous.

You should by now have a great many questions that you will want to ask during the audit. You may also want to discover what steps were taken to capture any information relating to process control points. This is a useful indicator of the attitude of the HACCP Team – are they really using HACCP to its best effect?

Note: If you feel that the document review has indicated obvious inadequacies, it may be advisable to stop the audit at this point. The deficiencies should be discussed with the HACCP Team, who can then review their HACCP System and implement any further training requirements.

Audit Checklist 1

Many people find that using a checklist is helpful during an audit. One of the most important aspects of an audit is the required organized approach to its execution.

The Process Flow Diagram itself might be useful in drawing up a checklist. One method of drawing up an audit checklist may be as shown in Table 8.1. The 'Considerations' column can be completed

Table 8.1 Example of audit checklist

Process step	Considerations	Auditor's notes
Raw materials (including Goods inwards and storage) List of raw materials here ↓		
Process List of process steps here ↓		
Packaging and despatch List of packaging here ↓		

during the Document Review for each step of the process, the 'Auditors' notes' column, during the audit itself. Audit Checklist 1 is specifically aimed at helping to validate the Process Flow Diagram. Specific considerations may include:

- Raw materials
  - (i) Are they being handled according to specification?
  - (ii) Storage conditions – are they as stated?
  - (iii) Are all raw materials included in the flow diagram?
  - (iv) Are quarantine requirements being adhered to?
  - (v) Should Certificates of Analysis be in place?
- Process
  - (i) Have all activities been included?
  - (ii) Is the Process Flow Diagram correct?
  - (iii) Verify time/temperature controls
  - (iv) Have process capability studies been carried out?
  - (v) Have any changes been made since the Process Flow Diagram was drawn up? If so how were they recorded and approved?
  - (vi) Were any changes discussed with the HACCP Team before implementation?
  - (vii) Are there rework opportunities?
  - (viii)Have they been included?
- Packaging and dispatch
  - (i) Are the packaging materials as specified?
  - (ii) Are storage conditions as stated?
  - (iii) Are distribution procedures in-house or third party?

The above activities can happen in advance of the audit itself. Let's now consider what happens on the day(s).

C. Opening meeting
It is good audit practice to begin with a brief opening meeting. Use it to confirm with the key people being audited (auditees), the audit scope, timetable, and personnel required. Confirm too, the time and location of the closing meeting and who will be needed. Request any additional documentation required for the on site Document Review 2.

D. Validate Process Flow Diagram
It is essential in HACCP to validate the Process Flow Diagram at an early stage, unlike other Quality System audits, where all aspects of the documentation may be considered before going into the factory or process operation. This is simply a matter of walking

through the process from start to finish. However, it may take some time and should not be hurried. Stand and observe what is happening in each area.

The auditor's tools of eyes, ears and mouth are essential to:

- **watch** what is going on;
- **listen** actively to what people are saying;
- **ask** questions, talk to operatives. For example, ask them what they are doing. Do they always do it that way? When might they do it differently?

Check for evidence of any time/temperature stages. Look for opportunities for cross-contamination. What about holding periods? Could there be time enough for toxin formation or spore germination? This may be particularly relevant to high-risk raw materials or part-made product where there is a high degree of handling. Make a note of people with whom you have spoken, check their training records during the second Document Review.

E. Document Review 2

Having established that the Process Flow Diagram is correct, you will be able to carry out a second and more thorough Document Review from a more informed base. This time you should include a full review of operational procedures for CCP monitoring, CCP monitoring records, training records, etc. Check GMP and hygiene maintenance records, pest control and HACCP Team meeting minutes. In the latter case, it may be helpful to get an idea of the decision-making process, who attended the meetings on each occasion and whether difficulties were encountered.

You may want to pick up a few finished products out in the stores during your Process Flow Diagram validation and use their codes to trace records during the second document review and factory audit.

The review will also include previous audit records where non-compliances may have been found. The assurance of the effectiveness of any Corrective Actions taken must be sought. Other quality and safety-related data for review could include a review of customer complaints, customer audit reports, and any minutes of HACCP or Quality Improvement Project meetings relating to the audit.

Audit Checklist 2

Again, it will be useful to take an organized approach to the second stage of the audit and produce a checklist. This may take the form of a matrix against the Process Flow Diagram or perhaps be a list of questions clearly identified in the auditor's notebook.

Some general questions which may be useful to include are:

1. CCPs raw materials
   - Are agreed specifications in place?
   - Supplier Quality Assurance
     (i) have auditors been trained, and how?
     (ii) have all suppliers been audited?
     (iii) have suppliers changed since HACCP Plan development?
     (iv) check visit reports – has all corrective action been followed up as required?
   - Certificates of Conformance
     (i) are these being used?
     (ii) do goods receiving operators know what to do with them?
     (iii) have they been checked as accurate?
2. CCPs Process
   - Are all documents accurate and current?
   - Is monitoring equipment calibrated?
   - Have monitors been trained?
   - Are CCP records being reviewed? By whom?
   - Is the information on the HACCP Control Chart accurate?
   - Are time/temperature parameters being achieved?
   - Are CCP log sheets being filled out correctly?
   - Is frequency of monitoring adequate?
   - Have statistically valid sampling plans been drawn up?
   - What is the general standard of GMP?
   - Is there a hygiene schedule relating to CCPs?
   - Has corrective action been recorded and has the effectiveness been verified?
   - Are the HACCP records clearly identified by unique reference numbers?
   - Are production codes legible on the packaging?
   - Are customer usage instructions clear and accurate?
   - How was shelf life determined?
   - Are the packaging materials as specified?
   - Are good distribution practices being maintained? Check hygiene, handling and temperature if chilled or frozen.
   - Are statistical process control records being used to demonstrate that the process is in control on a day-to-day basis?
   - Do records agree with stated activities?
   - Are there any cross-contamination opportunities?

This list is not exhaustive, but as with hazard analysis, there are many areas to be covered.

F. Validation of HACCP Control Chart
As with the process flow diagram validation – using eyes, ears and mouth to search for evidence of compliance with the HACCP Plan. A few key points to note:

- Investigate any anomalies found during the audit process.
- Note any points of concern that cannot be resolved.
- Ensure that identified deficiencies are clearly understood and supported by evidence (specific examples of correction action not being followed up for example).
- Communicate any deficiencies at the time of discovery and obtain agreement.

G. Closing meeting
This is the first opportunity to present the audit findings and give an overall view of the proceedings. Non-compliances should be discussed together with supporting evidence and a schedule for corrective actions agreed. The recommended corrective actions should be generated by the auditee and agreed by the Departmental Manager and auditor. It is important that recommendations are feasible. An example of a non-compliance note is shown in Table 8.2.

H. Audit reporting
Audit reports should provide evidence of the findings of the audit – primarily what deficiencies have been found in the HACCP System.

While non-compliance notes should be issued ideally on the day of the audit, it may be appropriate for the auditor(s) to issue an audit summary report. This may be useful to company management and also to the HACCP Team and subsequent auditors.

Again a pro forma might be a useful means of summarizing. An example is given in Table 8.3.

The Additional Comments section can be used to note any observations which may not have resulted in a non-compliance note but perhaps where minor corrective actions are needed.

I. Audit follow-up
Outstanding non-compliance notes may be discussed at HACCP Team meetings and if seriously impacting on food safety management, by senior management or board meetings in order to ensure

Table 8.2 Example of non-compliance note

HACCP Audit Non-compliance Note	No:
Location:	Date:
Area under review:	HACCP Plan Ref. No.
Non-compliance:	
Action required by (date):	
Auditors: 1. 2. 3.	
Accepted by Auditee:	
Corrective action:	
Verified (Auditor) Date:	

that timely corrective action is taken. Non-compliance notes should be closed and signed off as soon as the corrective action has been taken. Even so, they will need to be reviewed during any subsequent audit to ensure that the corrective actions taken have been effective on an ongoing basis.

Table 8.3 Example of a HACCP Audit Summary pro forma

HACCP Audit Summary	
Location:	Date of Audit:
Audit Ref. No:	Area under review:
Auditors:	
NCN Ref. No.	Summary of Non-compliances
Additional comments:	
Signed Auditor(s)	Date:
Circulated to:	

8.2 Analysis of data

The HACCP procedures will generate a number of records which should be reviewed on a regular basis. There is nothing worse than seeing records of useful measurements, i.e. data, pile up in the QA

Manager's office, not being used to make process improvements and with no analysis carried out. Some suggested answers to common questions on this data analysis are as follows:

Why analyse data?

- To verify that the HACCP Plan continues to be effective.
- To enable trends to be recognized and corrective action teams to be set up to deal with the cause, e.g. customer complaints and recurring CCP deviations.
- To launch investigatory audits of problem areas.
- To ensure that timely corrective actions are being taken through trace audits of meeting minutes.

What data do you have available?

- CCP log sheets
- Process Control Charts
- Audit Reports – Non-compliance Notes
    (i) Corrective Action reports
- Minutes of food safety-related meetings
    (i) HACCP Teams
    (ii) Hygiene
    (iii) Quality review
- Pest control records
- Customer complaint data

How often should you review data?

- Daily
    (i) CCP log sheets
    (ii) Process Control Charts
- Monthly
    (i) Customer complaints reports
    (ii) Hygiene meetings
- Three-monthly
    (i) CCP deviation summaries
    (ii) Corrective Action reports
    (iii) Audit reports
    (iv) HACCP and quality meetings
    (v) Pest control records
- Annual
    (i) Audit reports
    (ii) Minutes of food safety meetings
    (iii) Customer complaints trend

As appropriate

Who should review it?

- HACCP Team
- Quality Manager
- Operations Manager
- Operations Supervisor
- R & D Personnel
- Sales/Marketing personnel

} As appropriate

8.3 Keeping abreast of emerging hazards

Having established your HACCP System you will need to ensure that you are kept up to date on new emerging hazards which could have an impact on your product. Why will new hazards arise? Let us consider just a few of the possible answers to this question.

1. **New technologies**. This could cover a wide range of activities, but a few recent (within the last 20 years) areas to consider are irradiation, microwaving, sous vide, mycoprotein and advances in aseptic packaging, modified atmosphere packaging (MAP) and extrusion technology. Each bring their own hazards and risks.
2. **New natural foods**. Consider the trend particularly for fewer preservatives and more natural ingredients.
3. **New combinations of foods**. For example, chilled ready-to-eat sandwiches containing unusual combinations of fish, fruit, meat, nuts, eggs, vegetables, mayonnaise and conserves etc. where the interface between foods may present an opportunity for microbiological growth which was not there in the individual components.
4. **Changing legislation**. The banning of additives such as ethylene oxide for the treatment of herbs and spices may have been beneficial from a chemical safety viewpoint but presents difficulties in countries where microbiological decontamination by irradiation is still illegal and no heat processing is available.
5. **New information on existing issues**. Keep updated on information regarding for example, BSE in cattle, causes of microbiological food safety incidents, increased understanding of microorganisms and methods for their detection. Also, the results of any government surveys and research programmes that may be relevant.
6. **New ways of presenting food to the consumer**. Many examples could be considered here, as sales and marketing personnel are always looking for ideas that will increase market share.

Consider the enormous growth of chilled ready meals, new sales outlets such as garage forecourts complete with micro-waves, the restaurant trend for warm meat or fish salads.

A good way to get information on such matters is through Food Research Associations, many of whom regularly circulate abstracts of newly published information. Access to a good reference library may also be helpful. Otherwise use your customers and suppliers as a source of information which is likely to be highly relevant to your products and market. Industry symposia can also be a useful way to meet people with a similar interest. In addition, experienced consultants and government and media published data can be used.

8.4 Updating and amending your HACCP Plan

The HACCP Plan will need to be updated and amended periodic-ally to ensure that it remains current. This is only really common-sense – a HACCP Plan which was drawn up a year ago is unlikely to accurately reflect current activities. In the real world manu-facturing operations change and for various reasons. For example, new raw material types, changes to process controls, CCP deviations, new methods to improve production efficiency, new equipment, factory structural changes, new packaging, extended shelf life and so on. The HACCP Audit may also provide reasons for change but remember that the audit is only a sampling exercise, an indicator of whether the HACCP Plan is being complied with and is correct.

It is recommended that periodic revalidations of the plan are also carried out. Revalidation can be considered as a complete review of the HACCP Plan in order to confirm its accuracy. This is done by the HACCP Team and should be done at least annually. An in-depth inspection is carried out of all HACCP documentation. It may also be a good opportunity for the HACCP Team to consider the effectiveness of the HACCP System, and to determine what new approaches may be needed in the year ahead.

Any changes made to the HACCP Plan will need to be recorded and approved. The revalidation exercise should also be recorded even if no changes to the plan were needed. This may provide useful evidence in the event of a prosecution or customer audit.

A useful method of recording these two activities is to draw up a History of Amendments sheet. This may be the reverse or as a second page to the HACCP Plan approval sheet if this is a separate document. The main elements to include are shown in Table 8.4.

Table 8.4 History of amendments sheet

HACCP Plan Reference: . . . . Page:			
Date:	Amendment	Reason	Approval signature

8.5 Ongoing training requirements

In Chapter 4 we considered initial training needs when embarking on the implementation of HACCP, but what about ongoing training requirements?

8.5.1 Refresher training

It is important that the company updates and refreshes its approach to HACCP on an ongoing basis. A year or two on from implementing HACCP, the company will almost certainly have begun to develop its own interpretation of the HACCP Principles. It will be useful to keep up to date with current international thinking through attendance at industry seminars and literature surveys. This obviously does not need to be done by everyone in the company; most likely it will be a HACCP Team member who on returning should use the new information to brief other company employees.

CCP monitors will also need refresher training in order to maintain their understanding of the HACCP System. This too can be done through internal briefings or by posting information on notice boards.

8.5.2 Training new HACCP Team members and CCP Monitors

This task will get easier as the company becomes more familiar with HACCP. Personnel changes will make it necessary for new people to come into the HACCP Team or new CCP Monitors to be appointed. These new people will not have the advantage of being involved from the beginning so care must be taken to ensure that they have the same level of understanding as their colleagues. HACCP is a team activity and it may be useful when appointing new HACCP Team members to go back through a team-building exercise. This will help to establish the new team relationship – trust and interdependence will not automatically appear with the new member.

8.5.3 Training new staff

In addition to new HACCP Team members and CCP Monitors, the company staff turnover must be considered. At all levels and disciplines of staff, HACCP training will need to be carried out appropriately from spending a whole day briefing a new board director to an hour of awareness training with a cleaner.

8.5.4 New emerging hazards

It is essential that the HACCP Team continually keep abreast of new emerging hazards. This again could be achieved by attending external seminars and reviewing literature. Membership of industry food research associations and professional bodies can be particularly useful.

8.5.5 Ongoing awareness training

In order to keep the HACCP System alive, it will be necessary for the company to promote HACCP on an ongoing basis. This can be done by building HACCP into the annual training programme – linking it with new training initiatives in hygiene or Statistical Process Control for example. Notice boards and suggestion boxes can also be used to good effect.

8.5.6 Design of new training material

Whether you initially did much of the HACCP training 'in-house' or not, you may wish to design internal training materials for future needs. This can be cost effective providing you have people who are suitable to act as trainers for the company. It is a complete waste of time and money to allow ineffective trainers to try to train people. A good investment in using your own training materials will be to train competent trainers. Don't make the mistake of using someone who happens to be available – consider the competencies needed for the role. These include leadership skills, being able to motivate others, communication and interpersonal skills, being able to manage diversity by recognizing and valuing differences in people, and finally having a sound, in-depth knowledge of the subject matter that they are going to train.

External 'Train the Trainer' courses are readily available and last a minimum of 2 days. It will be useful if the designated company trainer(s) have an input into the design of in-house materials. Use of an external consultant may also prove useful if resources are not sufficient within the company. You may alternatively be able to purchase off-the-shelf training packages which you can then adapt. Computer-assisted learning is gaining in popularity and could also be considered.

Ongoing training activities should be seen as a way of continually raising company standards and as a way of ensuring that the HACCP System continues to grow.

8.6 Summary of maintenance requirements

You should now be in a position to pull together a summary of your HACCP Plan maintenance requirements. It may be helpful to keep this list together with the HACCP Plan.

As an example, the HACCP Team at the Iced Delights Ice Cream factory, came up with the following:

Table 8.5 Chocolate chip ice cream – maintenance requirements

Maintenance requirements	*Approved by:* ...*N̶.̶J̶B̶*........ *HACCP Team Leader* *Date:* *14.8.93*
1. Quarterly audit of HACCP Plan *2. Annual plan revalidation* *3. HACCP Plan to be revisited for all process ingredient changes* *4. Quarterly CCP log sheet review for deviation trend analysis* *5. Monthly review of customer complaint data for trends* *6. 6-monthly simulation of trace/recall procedures* *7. Ongoing technical information update through symposia and technical journals* *8. Quarterly analysis of training needs and conduct refresher training of operators as required*	

9

Broader applications of HACCP – using HACCP techniques in other areas

HACCP was originally developed as a technique for the identification and control of food safety hazards and most companies will still want to use it to focus primarily on safety. However, the techniques that you have learned in this book can also be applied to other areas of production, as we will discuss in this chapter. Now that you have learnt the benefits of the HACCP approach, we are sure that you will want to use the principles in areas beyond food safety, but a few words of warning . . .

Safety should always be the primary objective and using HACCP for other issues should not be allowed to complicate matters and cause confusion such that product safety management becomes muddled and ineffective. In order to achieve this it is best to keep the product safety management system completely separate from any other system of control put together using HACCP.

9.1 Using HACCP in targeting resource – a strategy for continuous improvement

If you have read Chapters 1 to 8 before beginning Chapter 9, you will by now have a good understanding of what you need to do to implement and maintain a HACCP System. You may be feeling overwhelmed by what you have to do and be somewhat despondent. Some companies, particularly smaller ones, often think that use of systems such as HACCP is for the large, sophisticated companies with plentiful resources. Other companies, on considering HACCP and being made more aware of hazards and risks, realize that an effective HACCP System relies on firm foundations which they perhaps do not have. The foundations may be considered to be:

1. Working to Good Manufacturing Practice (GMP).
2. Having an established Supplier Quality Assurance System (SQA).
3. Using Statistical Process Control techniques (SPC) to assure process capability and process control.
4. Food safety and quality-related training programmes being built into business strategy – both skills and awareness training.
5. Having a fully developed Product Recall and Incident or Crisis Management Plan in place which is regularly challenged, supported by accurate and complete traceability of raw materials through to distribution to the customer.
6. Regular use of problem solving techniques such as brain-storming, which we have covered previously; also other techniques such as Cause and Effect, Paired Comparison and Pareto, to tackle recurring problems in a way that will ensure that they are permanently resolved, i.e. treating the cause and not the symptoms through daily fire-fighting.
7. Having all quality and safety-related procedures documented.
8. Use of a Quality Management System to pull all of the above activities together.

Perhaps the culture of your company is not quite as it should be – some managers and staff may still be content with the way things have been in the past – and there may be no perception of the need to change to a new way of working.

If you don't have any of the above list of activities in place and want to use HACCP – don't worry, HACCP is the best place to begin. HACCP can be used by everyone and there is no right or wrong time to start using it. The normal use of HACCP is when hygiene is under control and it is fair to say that this view is widely accepted. A common misconception is that if you don't have any written specifications and procedures, and have very poor GMP and hygiene then you are in no position to use HACCP. To the authors, it seems only common sense to say – use HACCP **now** to help you decide where to begin, i.e. in prioritizing against food safety risk and targeting resource.

Hazard analysis of your processing operation will enable you to focus on high priority areas for improvement. To do this you will obviously need to draw an accurate Process Flow Diagram and have calibrated your process equipment. Other than that you need to do very little before starting. Once you have the Process Flow

Table 9.1 Are all the required Preventative Measures in place?

Process step	Hazard	Preventative measure?	Currently in place? Yes/No
Incoming materials Chocolate chips	Salmonella	— Agreed specification	No
		— Certificate of analysis from supplier	Yes
		— SQA visit to supplier	No
Weighing 1 Bagged sugar 2 Chocolate chips	— Ingress of paper from sack into sugar or other foreign bodies	Sieving through 8 mm mesh sieve	Yes
	— Pathogen cross-contamination from operative	Hygiene training	No

Diagram you can carry out a hazard analysis exercise in the normal way. If you have no raw material specifications, use known data from reference books, a hazard database, or bring in a HACCP expert to help you. Once you have identified the hazard (remember to be as specific as possible) you can determine what the preventative measure **should** be. Never put down what your process operation currently uses. Add an additional column then to the Hazard Analysis Chart to indicate whether the preventative measure is currently present (Table 9.1).

The appearance of a 'No' response will indicate that corrective action is needed and that the preventative measure must be put in place. How should you prioritize – after all, there may be a long list of action required? Use the CCP Decision Trees to help you in targeting critical areas requiring control. This may perhaps seem an obvious answer but is particularly helpful where capital expenditure is involved.

The Raw Material CCP Decision Trees will be helpful in providing focus to SQA programmes. This can be taking place at the same time as a production team is drawing up the Process Flow Diagrams and should involve those personnel responsible for purchasing. Many companies purchase hundreds of raw materials (ingredients and packaging). If you have no specifications, a blank pro forma can be sent to all suppliers for completion but using the Raw Material Decision Tree will help you to see where Certificates of Analysis are needed and which suppliers should be audited in order to assess their level of competence. It is important that this activity happens as quickly as possible because you might want to request that your suppliers of high-risk raw materials also use HACCP. They can be working on their HACCP Systems while you are working on yours.

In using hazard analysis and the CCP Decision Trees for both raw materials and process you will also be able to identify training needs. Training can be costly, particularly if done externally and priorities will need to be assessed. You will have identified where basic training in food hygiene is important and, if this involves a large number of people, it may be cost effective for you to conduct this in-house. HACCP, SQA and auditor training may also be needed. By identifying how many suppliers need auditing, you will know what level of resource is needed – whether it can be done by external consultants, or whether several in-house SQA auditors will be needed.

Use of an established technique such as HACCP, early in the development of a company can do a lot in helping to gain commitment for change from all staff. HACCP is common sense – if food safety hazards are identified then they **must** be managed. HACCP can be used to develop a strategy for improvement which is based on a real need to manage food safety.

9.2 Identification of Process Control Points

The hazard analysis approach can highlight 'hazards' at many stages of the process which may not be direct product safety issues. They may still be safety hazards arising at a step which has no CCP following the Decision Tree because of a CCP later in the process, for example *Salmonella* in several different ingredients where there is no cross-contamination risk to the facility and which will be controlled by the product's heat process. However, they may be quality issues (e.g. viscosity, label orientation, etc.), which need to be controlled for a high-quality product. These so-called 'hazards' may either be identified during a safety HACCP, where they would not be directly associated with CCPs, or they could be identified as part of a completely separate exercise focusing on quality.

While these points may be critical to product quality, it is unwise to call them CCPs as this causes direct confusion with the safety management system. Instead, these points are often referred to as 'process' or 'manufacturing' control points and normally have their own system of management.

Using the HACCP techniques independently to capture Process Control Points ensures that they are secured in a systematic manner. As for safety HACCP, the terms of reference for each study need to be clearly defined, and then it is simply a question of following through the hazard analysis and deciding where the elements of control should be situated. In the same way as safety HACCP, the monitoring and control parameters should be established and these could be encompassed in the product specification or in a separate process control system.

If the HACCP Team identifies quality issues during a safety HACCP, it is important to the company's business that these are not lost. In this case the HACCP Team should note them down and pick up on the process control points once the safety management system has been established.

9.3 Prediction of product spoilage

The hazard analysis techniques can also be used to predict product spoilage and set achievable shelf life by establishing appropriate terms of reference.

For microbiological spoilage, in the same way as for safety, you can use hazard analysis to establish which spoilage organisms are likely to be present in the raw materials, and which might survive the process, or which might cross-contaminate from the process environment. You then need to use knowledge of growth rates of these organisms in similar situations (e.g. products with similar intrinsic factors) at the product storage temperature to predict the likely achievable life. This will normally need to be backed up with shelf life experiments, where the product is examined for the microorganisms of concern, or by challenge studies, where organisms are inoculated directly into the product and their growth/survival potential is evaluated.

Using the hazard analysis technique along with knowledge of chemical and physical reactions in food can be used to give predictions of changes, such as in flavour, physical appearance (e.g. colour, texture) and in product taste. The potential for leaching of taints from other product components or from packaging during the shelf life can also be evaluated, but of course if this is a safety issue it should be picked up in the main safety HACCP Study. Again this will normally need to be backed up with shelf life experiments, this time of an organoleptic or analytical nature, but an advantage of using the hazard analysis technique is that confirmatory experiments can be accurately targeted at essential information, thus saving on resources required for a full experimental trial.

9.4 Application to non-foods

As previously stated, HACCP was originally designed for use in food safety and has traditionally been used in that area. However, the techniques are equally applicable to non-food consumer goods, and this is especially true if we remember that HACCP had its route in the engineering system, Failure, Mode and Effect Analysis.

Some of the products in this area are similar to foods in that their safety is directly related to application to and by the consumer, e.g. shampoo or soap which must be safe for direct skin contact, or washing powders which must not leave any residues on fabric which would harm the skin. Other products, such as electrical goods, have a much longer usage life and it is important to ensure that they are not only safe for use initially, but also that they cannot develop any faults which will make them potentially unsafe later in the product life.

Other products may have a potential effect on food, e.g. cling-film, foils, cooking utensils or food storage containers. These must not pass any harmful substances into the food products they contact. Many countries have legislation covering specific substances and migration limits, and the hazard analysis techniques can be used to highlight which substances are likely to be present, along with how they are likely to react under the expected use conditions. For example if heat is applied to a plastic microwave cooking utensil, will any substances pass into the food which is being cooked, and if so will this be harmful to the consumer?

Safety in the non-foods area is further complicated by the fact that some products are unsafe by their very nature, e.g. household bleach. In products such as this the emphasis is placed on instructions for safe use and safe packaging which will neither burst allowing product to escape, nor be accessible to children or individuals who may not understand the safety instructions. Products such as aerosols may be explosive or inflammable, in which case safety instructions are again critical.

The HACCP techniques can be applied to these product areas in exactly the same way as to foodstuffs. The members of the HACCP Team will of course be expert in the particular product area under study, and they will need to consider hazards associated directly with the use of the product, along with indirect or delayed safety hazards. When the hazards have been identified and the risks analysed, CCPs can be established as for food products, and these will require specific control criteria and monitoring systems to be implemented. The actual HACCP Plan should be managed in exactly the same way as we have seen, in earlier chapters of this book, for food products.

It is also possible to use HACCP techniques to identify process control issues for non-food products in the same way as we saw in section 9.2 for foods. Here again it is important not to confuse safety with process control and the systems should ideally be kept separate.

9.5 Other applications

9.5.1 Prediction of malicious tampering opportunities

Use the Process Flow diagram and hazard analysis technique to determine where tampering opportunities exist. Consider the following points:

1. Where might the product be accessed easily?
2. Where in production is it open to the environment?

Figure 9.1 'Prediction of malicious tampering opportunities'.

3. Be aware of situations where operators may feel begrudged.
4. Is the packaging resistant to access and will it indicate if tampering has occurred?

9.5.2 Finding legal control points

Here you can use identical procedures to those which we have described for safety HACCP but will need to redefine 'hazard' as a non-compliance with legal requirements.

9.5.3 Application to plant design

Hazard analysis techniques can be used at the concept stage of equipment and factory design to ensure that plant, equipment and factory do not cause food safety hazards.

9.5.4 Designing preventative maintenance schedules

In the HACCP Study we determined where the equipment and environment were critical to product safety. Carrying out an additional hazard analysis on the equipment operation itself may highlight where it is likely to fail. These two activities will help to establish an effective preventative maintenance programme.

9.5.5 Assessments for health and safety

Again, the 'hazard' is redefined, this time as a health and safety issue. Both the process itself and the control of substances harmful to health will need to be considered in order to assure operator safety and well being.

9.5.6 Evaluation of cleaning procedures

Cleaning procedures may normally be considered as part of the main HACCP Study where they will often be essential in preventing serious microbiological contamination. Cleaning itself may cause a chemical or physical hazard if not properly controlled.

It is important to identify where cross-contamination of any type through poor cleaning can occur. Because of this, it is often helpful to conduct a separate HACCP Study of the cleaning procedures which may result in CCPs being established and added to the HACCP Plan.

10

HACCP and Quality Management Systems – their combined strength

It is often thought that there is little in common between HACCP and other types of Quality Management System (QMS). This chapter will take quite a different view, going so far as to suggest that without the support of systems such as ISO 9000 and laboratory accreditation, the HACCP System will not be as effective as it should be.

10.1 Commonality of approach

What do we mean first of all by a Quality Management System? Simply all of the activities which go on in the company to ensure that it meets its quality objectives. In this respect HACCP can be considered as a Quality Management System in that it is an activity which helps to ensure that the objective of manufacturing safe food is achieved.

Many companies base their QMS on the international standard series of ISO 9000 which is equivalent to EN 29000 and BS 5750 (ISO, 1987). The system can be formally accredited or the requirements used as a framework for an in-company system. The ISO 9000 standard can be and is used across broad spectrums of activity in many organizations. Already, your company may be operating within ISO 9000 or you may alternatively view it as a goal to be reached within the next 1, 2 or even 5 years. Whatever the situation you may have many questions regarding the relationship between HACCP and ISO 9000.

ISO 9000 is a Quality Management System aimed primarily at

preventing and detecting any non-conforming product during production and distribution to the customer, and by taking corrective action to ensure that the non-conformance does not occur again. ISO 9000 means that the product meets its specification 100% of the time. There is obviously the danger here in that if an unsafe product is specified, the Quality System will ensure that you make an unsafe product every time.

How then can you ensure both that you specify a safe product and that you make it every time? **By using HACCP and by managing your HACCP System using ISO 9000.**

ISO 9000 and HACCP, concerned with Quality and Food Safety Management respectively, have much in common. Both systems require the involvement of all company employees, the approach taken is very structured and in both cases involves the determination and precise specification of key issues. Both systems are Quality Assurance Systems, designed to give maximum confidence that a specified acceptable level of quality/safety is being achieved at an economic cost. Quality Control techniques, i.e. statistically valid inspection and testing are used as a vital part of the Quality Assurance System, to monitor that the control points – quality and safety – are being adhered to.

10.2 Using a Quality Management System to manage HACCP

In managing food safety the highest degree of confidence is achieved by:

1. Using a HACCP System which has been established by experts.
2. Ensuring that the HACCP System is maintained 100% of the time by using the ISO 9000 approach to meeting the specification (in HACCP terms, the critical control points).

ISO 9000 is a series of standards. They include the requirements for 20 clauses to be implemented. ISO 9001 contains all 20, whilst ISO 9002 has 18 of the 20 and ISO 9003 only 16. Let's consider how each clause of the ISO 9001 standard can be applied to HACCP (Table 10.1).

Every one of the 20 clauses of ISO 9001 has relevance to HACCP and in many instances it is vital that HACCP is supported by such procedures. For example, HACCP can be very effective but only if:

- calibrated equipment is used;
- people are properly trained;
- documentation is controlled;
- the system is verified through audit and so on.

Table 10.1 ISO 9001 – its application to HACCP

ISO 9001 clause	HACCP application
4.1 Management responsibility	• There should be a quality policy which may include specific references to use of HACCP in managing food safety. The policy will demonstrate management commitment to company employees. • Responsibility and authority within the HACCP System must be defined. • A review of the effectiveness of the System must be periodically carried out by management. This should be done at least annually and results of audits, customer complaints, status of training, status of the HACCP System, can all be discussed.
4.2 Quality System	• HACCP itself is a Quality System but this clause specifically considers all activities which could impact on the 'Quality' (safety) of the product and ensures that they are consistently documented, a quality product is also a safe product.
4.3 Contact review	• Particularly relevant to Supplier Quality Assurance as it considers the relationship between the purchaser and supplier. Are requirements clearly specified and can the supplier meet the requirements? Some raw materials may be Critical Control Points and it will be essential to have tight control over their supply.
4.4 Design control	• The design control clause is not included in ISO 9002 – usually the one that food companies go for. This is a pity because the HACCP process starts at the product concept stage, i.e. the design, and control through a Quality Management System would be a real benefit. Design control must include a hazard analysis risk assessment at the concept stage – has it been designed safely?
4.5 Document control	• All HACCP documents need to be controlled by being reviewed, signed and dated by authorized personnel. This will prevent the use of out of date documents. • Each HACCP document should bear a unique reference number for cross-referencing with CCP log sheets for example.

193

Table 10.1 *continued*

ISO 9001 clause	HACCP application
	• When changes to the HACCP Plans are made new issues must go to listed copy-holders and obsolete documents destroyed.
	• Ad hoc photocopying of 'uncontrolled' copies must be avoided and where necessary these copies should be clearly marked 'Uncontrolled'.
	• Control of artwork for packaging should be reviewed and signed off.
4.6 Purchasing	• Purchasing covers everything from raw materials to subcontractors. Everything purchased should be clearly specified through written specifications.
	• Control of subcontractors should be through assessment and records kept. This will include calibration, process equipment servicing, hygiene and pest control.
4.7 Purchaser-supplied products	• As this will apply to ingredients and packaging materials which are supplied by the purchaser for processing into his products, it is essential to ensure that these items are included in the HACCP assessment and that as much information as is needed is available.
4.8 Product identification and traceability	• Essential within the HACCP System to be able to trace batches of raw materials or products in the event of a failure at a CCP.
	• A written recall plan should be maintained in order to minimize the effect of any failure by being able to trace and withdraw any defective product.
4.9 Process control	• Obviously highly relevant to HACCP and essential to include the following key areas at all stages in the process: (i) Buildings – all facilities from raw material storage areas, through process and despatch. Including employee amenities. (ii) Plant and equipment – process capability, preventative maintenance, hygienic design and cleaning.

ISO 9001 clause	HACCP application
	(iii) Personnel – training, health screening, meeting legislation.
	(iv) Cross-contamination – at all stages where this could be a risk.
	(v) Waste materials – clearly identified and segregated.
	(vi) Computer failure – contingency plans should be in place.
	(vii) Environmental control – atmosphere, ground water.
4.10 Inspection and testing	• Where raw materials are CCPs, these should not be used until confirmation of conformance has been received.
	• Materials used before being certified as meeting specifications should be traceable in order to allow a recall at a later stage if necessary.
	• Finished products should be held until confirmation of all CCPs having been met in full has been received.
	• Records of all inspection and test results should be maintained.
	• Personnel carrying out testing should be trained and qualified appropriately. They should also be assessed as being capable for the job.
4.11 Inspection measuring test equipment	• Effective control of CCPs relies on accurate measuring methods or equipment. All equipment needed to monitor a CCP should be of known accuracy and precision and calibrated on a regular basis.
	• All measuring equipment should be status marked so as to make it clear to all personnel what is calibrated and what is to be used for general guidance only.
	• Equipment must be maintained and stored correctly in-between calibration in order to avoid damage.
	• Records of calibrations should be kept.
4.12 Inspection and test status	• There should be a clearly defined method for identification of the inspection and test status of any raw material, product, or equipment to prevent its being used inadvertently.

Table 10.1 *continued*

ISO 9001 clause	HACCP application
4.13 Control of non-conforming product	• The HACCP Control Chart will define who is responsible for taking corrective action in the event of a deviation. This must include what to do with product made while the system was out of control, i.e. to rework, recycle to reject. • Procedures must be developed to ensure that all non-conformities at a CCP are recorded. This will enable trends to be analysed. • Once any non-conforming product has been brought back into specification it must be tested again to confirm conformance.
4.14 Corrective action	• If a CCP is out of control the underlying cause must be identified in order for the problem to be permanently resolved and not repeated. • Corrective actions also include pest control audits and hygiene audits. • The corrective action taken in the event of any problem arising must be the right corrective action – new hazards could arise if the wrong corrective action is taken. An example of this is to shroud a piece of equipment in polythene because the roof above is leaking. • The effectiveness of any corrective action must be verified for confirmation. • All corrective actions must be recorded.

4.15 Handling, storage, packaging and delivery	• Hazards may arise from improper handling and storage of a product or raw material. Also if the packaging is unsuitable – unable to withstand distribution. Areas for consideration include:
	  – food contact packaging
	  – control of artwork (usage instructions, ingredients and nutritional data)
	  – storage and distribution temperatures
	  – stock rotation
	  – shelf-life
	  – contamination risks
	  – environment and building fabric
	  – hygiene and pest control

ISO 9001 clause	HACCP application
4.16 Quality records	• HACCP records will need to be retained in a controlled manner. They may form part of a due diligence defence or be needed during a regulatory inspection as demonstration of the effective management of food safety. • Quality-related records include product and raw material specifications, the HACCP Plans, Process Control records including CCP log sheets, calibration records, minutes of HACCP/food safety meetings, audits. • Retention time must reflect both statutory regulations and product shelf-life. Three years as a minimum for those records that demonstrate system management.
4.17 Internal Quality Audits	• Process Flow Diagrams must be audited as part of the verification. • The HACCP System itself should be regularly audited by members of the HACCP Team in order to assess whether it is working, correct, and applicable. Internal audits can act as a health check. Documented non-compliances raised must be corrected, allowing continued improvement of the HACCP System. The audit will be what makes the HACCP System live within the company and not remain as documentation on the shelf. • Auditors must be trained and independent of the department being audited and records of audits must be kept.
4.18 Training	• Effective HACCP relies on the participation of knowledgeable and trained people across a wide range of disciplines. • HACCP and Food Safety Management will continue to develop. It is important therefore that future training needs are considered on an ongoing basis. Areas for inclusion may reflect system changes, emerging food safety issues, new processes and corrective action skills. • Training records should be available for all members of staff and include all types of training – in-house, external, skills or awareness activities.

197

Table 10.1 *continued*

ISO 9001 clause	HACCP application
4.19 Servicing	• Often not considered relevant in manufacturing, but as an example, suppliers of vending equipment will be particularly aware of this clause as it requires the servicing of such equipment to be documented and controlled. Such equipment can be a source of hazards if not cleaned and maintained correctly. This needs to be considered in line with the servicing frequency.
4.20 Statistical techniques	• The construction of the HACCP Control Chart requires sampling regimes at each CCP to be documented. • If decisions of conformance are being based upon results of sampling and testing then it must be ensured that schemes are mathematically based i.e. the use of statistical sampling plans. • Other relevant statistical techniques include process capability assessment and statistical process control during CCP monitoring.

In many cases, HACCP is not backed up by such disciplines and in these instances the company concerned may feel complacent in having a HACCP Plan, completely unaware that it cannot be effectively working.

You certainly don't have to have a complete company quality system, certified to ISO 9001 before you start HACCP, but you should be aware of the relationship between the two and how you can use the framework of ISO 9000 as a guideline for installing the procedures which will make your HACCP System secure. An additional bonus in taking this approach is that you will be well down the road towards ISO 9001 accreditation at a later date.

10.3 Laboratory accreditation – should you do it?

10.3.1 What is laboratory accreditation?

Laboratory accreditation is the systematic assessment and validation of a laboratory operation against a specific laboratory quality standard. It is normally carried out by an independent accreditation body and assesses the laboratory operation against a number of key elements, as defined in the laboratory quality standard. The quality standard should itself be based on the international standard 'General Requirements for the Technical Competence of Testing Laboratories' (ISO Guide 25) or the European standard 'General Criteria for the Operation of Testing Laboratories' (EN45001) (EURACHEM/WELAC, 1993). The exact wording of laboratory quality standards will differ but the key elements normally cover the following areas:

- Organization and Management
- Quality Systems
- Audit and review
- Laboratory design and hygiene
- Sample handling
- Equipment
- Calibration
- Methods of analysis
- Quality control
- Records and reports

10.3.2 Why is laboratory accreditation important to HACCP?

The laboratory operation is a critical part of any quality system supplying information to verify that products are within specification. The results of laboratory analysis are particularly important when they are being used to monitor or verify the operation of CCPs, and thus product safety. Here, it is on the basis of results that decisions are made and action is taken so it is vital that they cannot be disputed.

In the case of CCP management it is essential that not only are the laboratory-based tests accredited but also any analytical testing which is carried out on the production line or in the production areas. These must be included in the scope of the accreditation.

Laboratory accreditation is also important where the company plans to use its HACCP System as part of a defence in any litigation case. In this case, the company would need to provide evidence that its HACCP System was operating under control, and that monitoring and verification was being carried out using accredited and assured methods. Independent laboratory accreditation gives confidence in the laboratory operation and helps to support the HACCP System and the litigation defence.

Figure 10.1 'Laboratory accreditation – should you do it?'.

There are many general benefits of laboratory accreditation. Specific benefits to HACCP and product safety are as follows:

- That decisions and action are based on valid results.
- There is confidence that product safety specifications are being met.
- There is assurance that results are accurate and reliable.
- Accreditation will support a defence under litigation procedures.

10.3.3 *Laboratory accreditation – the options*

There are several options available to companies wishing to pursue laboratory accreditation:

Option 1. Independent third party accreditation schemes.
There are a number of laboratory accreditation schemes available based on EN45001 and ISO Guide 25. These are normally operated by coordinating assessment bodies who provide the independent accreditation of a company's laboratory. There is normally an initial fee covering information and administration along with the cost of the accreditation assessment. When a laboratory is granted accreditation there will be ongoing surveillance assessments (normally annual) for which there is also a fee. The independence of this option is one of its key benefits.

Option 2. Writing your own laboratory standard based on ISO Guide 25 or EN45001 and developing a system of assessment against it.
This option loses the independence of third party schemes but can be just as effective provided that all the required elements are fully covered. There are costs associated with the work time necessary to write an effective laboratory standard, along with ensuring the laboratory operation meets the standard, establishing an assessment system, training of auditors and carrying out the assessments and maintaining the system. When this approach is adopted it may be tempting to make the standard more lenient to fit the existing laboratory operation but this will not be of benefit to the company in the long term.

Option 3. Establishing all the elements of a laboratory standard as part of the scope of a formal Quality Management System such as the ISO 9000 series.
This can be straightforward for companies setting up a formal Quality Management System and can easily be added to the scope of an existing system. As for the previous option, it is important to ensure that all the required elements are covered and that the system is not more lenient than an independent laboratory standard.

Option 4. Obtaining a laboratory standard based on ISO Guide 25 or EN45001 and setting up your own system of assessment against it.
In this final option the independence of third party accreditation is again lost but all the required elements can be covered in a

structured manner. Here, the company must establish a system for assessment and ensure that auditors are trained appropriately as well as bringing the laboratory up to standard.

10.3.4 Steps towards laboratory accreditation

Companies wishing to pursue laboratory accreditation will follow through a number of stages. Where Option 1 is chosen the path to laboratory accreditation is straightforward and involves choosing an accreditation body, obtaining a copy of the standard, appraising the laboratory operations and implementing any required changes. When this has been completed the laboratory applies for a formal assessment which is carried out by trained auditors. There are normally some non-compliances which must be corrected before accreditation status is granted, and this is followed by ongoing surveillance.

In Options 2, 3 and 4 the company is involved in developing standards, systems and auditing procedures. The laboratory must be brought in line with the established standard and staff must be trained in the assessment procedures. Following assessment, the laboratory must again maintain the system through ongoing surveillance.

Where a laboratory does not feel able to complete any of the above options initially there are several steps which can be taken towards laboratory accreditation. It must be emphasized that these are just initial steps or procedures and in no way replace a formal accreditation system. These steps include cross-checking of analyses against an accredited laboratory and joining independent quality control testing schemes.

Cross-checking of analyses against an accredited laboratory can give some confidence in the results obtained, but this is only a spot check for the set of samples examined. It will give no indication of the laboratory's ongoing accuracy through repeatability and reproducibility of the test method and results. Cross-checking does not demonstrate that the method can be carried out effectively on other types of samples and inherent sample variability must be taken into account. This is particularly relevant in microbiological analyses where, for example, *Listeria monocytogenes* might be present in one sub-sample but not in the other.

Independent quality control testing schemes are run by organizations who prepare sets of samples with known levels of microorganisms or analytes. These samples are despatched to participating laboratories on a regular basis for analysis by routine procedures. The results are normally communicated back to the quality control organization which then gives an indication of their acceptability and often a comparison with other laboratories. Again, this type of system does not give assurance on the ongoing operational standards of the laboratory but it does give some confidence in the accuracy of the results generated.

10.3.5 *Should you do it?*

From the above discussions you will have seen the importance of accredited laboratory operations and will understand the need to progress the most appropriate option to your company in support of your HACCP System. You will also understand that there are some interim steps which can be taken giving more confidence in the results generated by your laboratory, but that these steps alone cannot give full assurance of the ongoing situation.

There is a strong case for laboratory accreditation in any organization but particularly in one operating a HACCP System for product safety. It is absolutely crucial that the results of all monitoring procedures at CCPs are irrefutable and can be trusted to demonstrate that the system is under control, or can be used as the basis for corrective action decisions. Laboratory accreditation gives confidence in the accuracy of results and an independent system lends support to any necessary defence under litigation procedures.

10.4 Benefits of the combined system – food safety management for the next generation

The main benefit of using the combined system of HACCP, ISO 9000 and an accredited laboratory is confidence; confidence in ensuring that the CCPs are correctly identified and maintained, that the documentation is controlled and, in using both HACCP and ISO 9000, that 100% of the time, your product is safe. The laboratory accreditation ensures that test results are accurate and can be relied upon. Statistically based sampling schedules must be valid in order to meet the requirements of ISO 9000.

Having external independent assessment of the Quality Management and laboratory systems will ensure even greater confidence. To make the system really secure, an independently certified HACCP System would be the final element. Perhaps one day this will be available. Until then, the inclusion of HACCP in the scope of your ISO 9000 system and ensuring that the people carrying out the HACCP Study (the HACCP Team) are both properly trained and assessed as competent, perhaps by external HACCP experts, will ensure safe product every time.

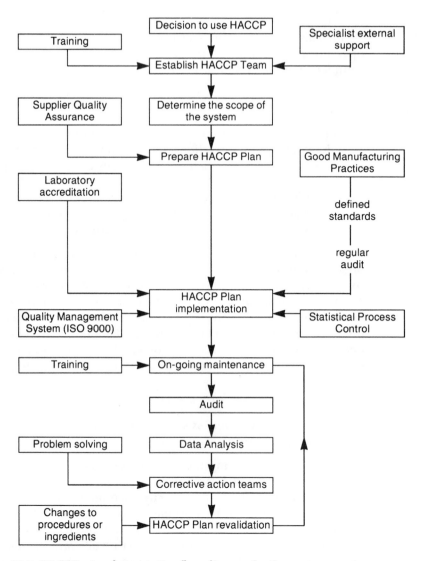

Figure 10.2 HACCP – implementation flow diagram for the next generation.

In working towards food safety management for the future, we believe that there are a number of essential activities which must be in place. This will not only start the process of applying HACCP techniques but will also ensure successful implementation and maintenance. The ideal food safety management system is illustrated in Figure 10.2.

The diagram shows clearly how the various elements work together. At the start of the book, we looked at reasons why you should use HACCP. Having taken the initial decision to do so, it is fundamentally important to spend time on the preparation, through identification and training of the HACCP Team members. Also, through being aware of the limitations of your own resources and finding good external support before you begin.

Supplier Quality Assurance and Good Manufacturing Practice should be reviewed to ensure that procedures are up to required standards as these two disciplines are **essential** support for a HACCP System which is to be effective.

In implementing the HACCP Plan, systems such as Laboratory Accreditation and ISO 9000, and use of Statistical Process Control techniques, will be invaluable in ensuring both the validity and security of the HACCP System. Ongoing maintenance by regular audit, training, use of problem-solving teams to resolve recurring CCP deviations, data analysis and controlled revalidation of the HACCP Plan will make the difference between HACCP being a paper exercise, bringing no real benefits, or instead, becoming part of the culture of your company, providing a foundation for continuous improvement in many areas.

Finally, a few thoughts to bear in mind as you proceed with your HACCP endeavours:

- keep it simple;
- be clear on your objectives;
- choose the right people for the job and train them properly;
- ensure that your HACCP Team know what is expected of them;
- prepare thoroughly – to fail to prepare is to prepare to fail!
- do not make assumptions;
- work in an organized manner;
- make sure that all details are recorded from who was on the HACCP Team to notes on the thought process during hazard analysis;
- challenge existing beliefs – make sure that you have evidence of what is actually happening;
- challenge current practices – are they really acceptable?

We would like to wish you luck in applying HACCP to your operation. We have enjoyed writing this book and hope that you have enjoyed reading it and will go on to use your new found knowledge in HACCP to meet the challenge of product safety.

Appendix A

A.1 Introduction

Five practical case studies have been constructed to illustrate the application of the HACCP Principles to different areas of food and drink production and preparation. The authors of these case study examples are people within the food and drink industry, who have hands-on experience of implementing HACCP. Each example has been carefully chosen so that this appendix represents a wide range of process environments and technologies, and products have been included which are normally considered 'high' or 'low ' risk from the product safety viewpoint.

Case Study 1 Paella – large scale manufacturing, hands on – high risk.
Case Study 2 Hamburger preparation – hands-on in fast-food restaurant – high risk.
Case Study 3 Lime juice cordial – large-scale manufacturing, automated – low risk.
Case Study 4 Potato salad – retail sale, delicatessen and salad bar – low risk.
Case Study 5 Fresh cream gateaux – large-scale manufacturing, hands-on – high risk.

Some points to consider when looking at the case studies are:

- Several different styles are represented. HACCP does not always have to be documented in the same regimented way, but can follow a company style.
- HACCP Teams do not always use the CCP Decision Tree, and may rely on the experience of team members. However, when it is used, the decision tree is a great help in structuring thinking and checking decisions.
- Scope of the HACCP Study must always be clearly defined. All

case studies cover safety hazards, but Case Study 1 only looks at microbiological safety hazards, and Case Study 3 has its scope expanded to cover spoilage in addition to safety. In this example note that only the points critical to safety are called CCPs.

Note: each case study detailed here is theoretical and the findings may not be exhaustive. The contributors are experienced in the products concerned, but the case studies are not necessarily identical to their own company approaches. The examples are not intended as specific recommendations for similar processes/ products, but as a demonstration of the application of the HACCP Principles.

A.2 Case Study 1 – Paella
T. Mayes, Unilever Research Laboratory, Colworth House, England.

A.2.1 Limitations

For reasons of confidentiality some specific aspects of this case study, including the product description, are hypothetical. The overall approach taken is, however, based on a real manufacturing operation.

A.2.2 Case Study

(a) Background

The company concerned (a small specialist manufacturer of chill-stored products) decided to move into the chill, ready-to-eat market and carried out a series of modifications to the factory environment in order to introduce a High Hygiene Area. During product commissioning trials, a HACCP Study was carried out in order to ensure that product safety could be assured. Company management fully supported the HACCP Study.

(b) The HACCP Study Team

The HACCP Study Team consisted of the following:

(i) Company Quality Assurance Manager
(ii) Production Supervisor
(iii) Production Engineer
(iv) Factory Microbiologist
(v) An external Chairman familiar with HACCP
(vi) A Technical Secretary

(c) Terms of Reference

To identify the microbiological hazards and associated Critical Control Points, Critical Limits, Monitoring System and Corrective Actions for ready-to-eat paella.

(d) Product description

Ready-to-eat paella for retail sale. Use by date within 12 days at <7 °C from date of manufacture. Raw materials are listed below:

(i)	Peeled chopped onions	Chill-stored
(ii)	Peeled crushed garlic	Ambient-stored
(iii)	Green and red peppers	Ambient-stored
(iv)	Long-grain rice	Ambient-stored
(v)	Parcooked chicken pieces	Frozen-stored
(vi)	Cooked shelled shrimps	Frozen-stored
(vii)	Cooked mussels	Frozen-stored
(viii)	Frozen peas	Frozen-stored
(ix)	Cooked king prawns	Frozen-stored
(x)	Chicken stock	Ambient-stored
(xi)	Parsley (blanched)	Ambient-stored

(e) Consumer use instructions

Consumer use instructions are: store refrigerated and consume within 3 days of purchase. Microwave on full power (700 W oven) for 3–4 minutes, stirring several times.

(f) Final product microbiological specification

Total Viable Count	$<1 \times 10^3/g$
B. cereus	$< 1 \times 10^2/g$
Salmonella spp.	Absent in 25 g
L. monocytogenes	Absent in 25 g
Coliforms	$<1 \times 10^2/g$
E. coli	$<1/g$

(g) Processing

Refer to the flow diagram in Figure A.1.

All raw materials are sourced from approved suppliers. Equipment is designed to the latest hygiene standards. Process stages 9–16 inclusive are carried out in a High Hygiene Area (HHA), physically segregated from the remaining processing activities. Staff in the HHA work to high standards of hygiene, and

209

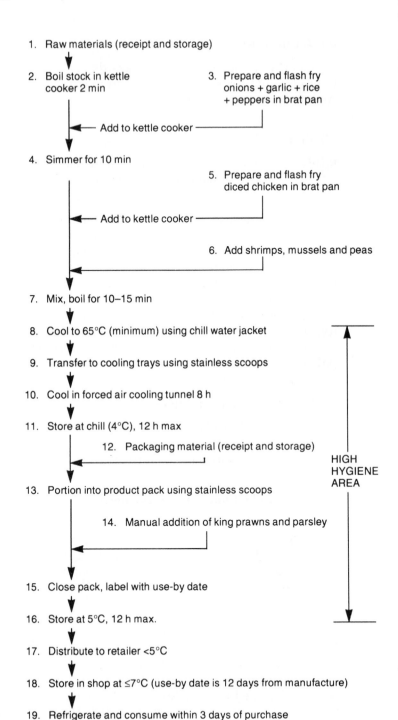

1. Raw materials (receipt and storage)

2. Boil stock in kettle cooker 2 min

3. Prepare and flash fry onions + garlic + rice + peppers in brat pan

← Add to kettle cooker

4. Simmer for 10 min

5. Prepare and flash fry diced chicken in brat pan

← Add to kettle cooker

6. Add shrimps, mussels and peas

7. Mix, boil for 10–15 min

8. Cool to 65°C (minimum) using chill water jacket

9. Transfer to cooling trays using stainless scoops

10. Cool in forced air cooling tunnel 8 h

11. Store at chill (4°C), 12 h max

12. Packaging material (receipt and storage)

13. Portion into product pack using stainless scoops

14. Manual addition of king prawns and parsley

15. Close pack, label with use-by date

16. Store at 5°C, 12 h max.

17. Distribute to retailer <5°C

18. Store in shop at ≤7°C (use-by date is 12 days from manufacture)

19. Refrigerate and consume within 3 days of purchase

HIGH HYGIENE AREA

Figure A.1 Paella – flow diagram.

temperature in the product assembly areas is 10 °C. Product flows logically through the factory.

(h) Hazards of concern

For the purpose of the case study the hazards of concern to the safety of the final product are considered to be:

> *B. cereus*
> *Salmonella* spp.   ⎫ Infectious
> *L. monocytogenes*   ⎬ vegetative
> *E. coli*   ⎭ pathogens (IVP)

A.2.3 Identification of Hazards, Preventative Measures, CCPs, Critical Limits, Monitoring and Corrective Actions

Each process step was discussed by the Study Team and hazards and Preventative Measures identified. The CCP Decision Tree was then used (Table A.1) to identify those process steps that were Critical Control Points – see explanations below. Finally, Critical Limits, Monitoring and Corrective Actions were identified for each CCP. All control data are recorded in Table A.1.2.

Note: in some cases different answers can be obtained from use of the CCP Decision Tree, but this should not affect the identification of CCPs.

Table A.1 Use of CCP Decision Tree

Process Step	Q1	Q2	Q3	Q4	Q5	Comment
1	Yes	Yes	No	Yes	Yes	Therefore not a CCP. (N.B. exceptions to this are king prawns and parsley added at step 14, for these raw materials)
	Yes	Yes	No	Yes	No	Therefore a CCP
2	Yes	Yes	No	Yes	Yes	Therefore not a CCP
3	Yes	Yes	No	Yes	Yes	Therefore not a CCP
4	Yes	Yes	Yes			Therefore a CCP; however hazards controlled by this CCP are also adequately covered subsequently by step 7, so step 4 can, in effect, be removed from the CCP list
5	Yes	Yes	No	Yes	Yes	Therefore not a CCP
6	Yes	Yes	No	Yes	Yes	Therefore not a CCP
7	Yes	Yes	Yes			Therefore a CCP
8	Yes	Yes	Yes			Therefore a CCP
9	Yes	Yes	No	Yes	No	Therefore a CCP
10	Yes	Yes	No	Yes	No	Therefore a CCP
11	Yes	Yes	No	Yes	No	Therefore a CCP
12	Yes	Yes	No	Yes	No	Therefore a CCP
13	Yes	Yes	No	Yes	No	Therefore a CCP
14	Yes	Yes	No	Yes	No	Therefore a CCP
15	Yes	Yes	No	Yes	No	Therefore a CCP
16–18	Yes	Yes	No	Yes	No	Therefore a CCP
19	Yes	Yes	No	Yes	No	Therefore a CCP

Table A.2 HACCP Study table – Paella

	Process step	Hazards	Preventative measures	CCP	Critical limits	Monitoring	Corrective actions
1	Storage of raw materials	Presence of IVP, *B. cereus*	Supplier assurance correct storage conditions	No – but see step 14			
2	Boil stock in kettle	Presence of IVP, *B. cereus*	Boiling of stock	No			
3	Flash fry onions, garlic, rice + peppers	Presence of IVP, *B. cereus*	Raw material supplier assurance	No			
4	Simmer 10 min	Presence of IVP, *B. cereus*	Time/temperature	No			
5	Flash fry chicken	Presence of IVP, *B. cereus*	Raw materials supplier assurance	No			
6	Add shrimps, mussels, peas	Presence of IVP, *B. cereus*	Raw materials supplier assurance	No			
7	Mix, boil 10 min	Presence of IVP, *B. cereus*	Time/temperature	Yes	98°C ± 2°C, 12 min ± 2 min	Chart recorder	Isolate any under-cooked batch. Cook further if still in kettle
			Calibration of temperature probes		Probes to agree with reference	Calibrate 2/year	Recalibrate if required

Table A.2 *continued*

	Process step	Hazards	Preventative measures	CCP	Critical limits	Monitoring	Corrective actions
8	Cool to 65°C min	Recontamination	Temperature	Yes	67°C ± 2°C	Chart recorder Manual check each batch	Re-heat if temperature falls below 65°C
9	Transfer to cooling trays	Recontamination	Hygiene cleaning/ disinfection of trays	Yes	Follow HHA guidelines	Supervision during production Single use of trays between cleaning/ disinfection	Reinforce HHA principles Review c/d procedures
10	Cool in tunnel 8 h	Recontamination and growth	Hygienic design and operation Time/temperature	Yes	Follow HHA guidelines 9 h ± 1 h	Supervision Batch records	Reinforce HHA principles Block product + inform QA
11	Store at chill 4°C/12 h	Recontamination and growth	Hygienic design and operation Time/temperature	Yes	Follow HHA guidelines 4°C ± 1°C, 12 h ± 2 h	Supervision Batch records	Reinforce HHA principles Block product and inform QA

No.	Process step	Hazard	Control measure	Critical	Critical limit/target	Monitoring	Corrective action
12	Packaging materials receipt and storage	Contamination with IVP, B. cereus	Supplier assurance	Yes	Follow HHA guidelines for removal of outer wrapping	Supervision	Reinforce HHA principle
			Supplier certificate – pathogen free		Within microbiological specification	Intake testing according to supplier performance	Do not use material outside specification. Re-audit of supplier to prevent re-occurrence
13	Portion into product pack	Recontamination	Hygienic operation	Yes	Follow HHA guidelines	Supervision	Reinforce HHA principle
			Cleaning/disinfection of dosing equipment		Equipment cleaned/disinfected every 4 h	Supervision Visual check	Reinforce HHA principle
			Time/temperature of product		4°C ± 2°C, 2 h	Batch records	Block product and inform QA
14	Addition of king prawns + parsley	Presence of IVP, B. cereus	Supplier assurance	Yes	Within microbiological specification	Intake testing according to supplier performance	Do not use material outside specification. Re-audit supplier to prevent re-occurrence

Table A.2 *continued*

Process step	Hazards	Preventative measures	CCP	Critical limits	Monitoring	Corrective actions
15 Close pack and label	Recontamination	Hygienic operation		Follow HHA guidelines	Supervision	Reinforce HHA principle
		Hygienic operation	Yes	Follow HHA guidelines	Supervision	Reinforce HHA principles
		Cleaning/ disinfection of equipment		Equipment cleaned/ disinfected every 16 h	Swab tests	Reinforce HHA principles
16– 18 Store at 4°C distribution and retail sale	Growth of contaminants	Time/temperature	Yes	Product temperature 5°C ± 1°C max, 12 days	Date/batch code	Retailer to remove from sale if outside date code
					Temperature recorders	As above
19 Refrigerate and consume within 3 days of purchase	Growth of contaminants	Time/temperature	Yes	6°C ± 1°C, 3 days ± 1 day	Consumer to check refrigeration temperature and storage time	Adjust temperature control on refrigerator Discard product outside date code or stored > 4 days

A.3 Case Study 2 – Hamburger preparation in a fast-food restaurant

D.J. Phillips, Grand Metropolitan Foods Europe, Uxbridge, England.

A.3.1 Introduction

Because the HACCP process is more commonly used for food manufacturing situations where there are usually several discrete processing steps it may appear more difficult to apply to restaurant operations. Generally speaking, there tends to be more product handling in a restaurant operation than in a manufacturing situation and fewer 'process steps' and perhaps a greater opportunity for cross-contamination. It is therefore essential that proper precautions are taken to ensure that food is safe when presented to the consumer. Bryan (1981) quoted a survey carried out in the USA, which identified the 10 most common contributory reasons for food poisoning associated with all types of restaurant operations as being:

- Improper cooling
- Twelve hours or more between preparation and eating
- Infected people handling food
- Inadequate reheating
- Improper hot holding
- Contaminated ingredients
- Food from unsafe sources
- Improper cleaning of equipment
- Raw/cooked cross-contamination
- Inadequate cooking

A HACCP approach aimed at identifying all potential hazards associated with materials, recipes, processes, and product handling, and establishing Critical Control Points to eliminate or reduce the hazards to an acceptable level, is as relevant in restaurant management as it is in food manufacturing.

A.3.2 Hazard analysis of product formulation

A HACCP Study of the recipe should be used to identify:

1. Any potential hazardous ingredients, which would require processing in the restaurant to make them safe.
2. The potential for any of the ingredients to become hazardous during storage in the restaurant or as a result of cross-contamination.

3. All of the time/temperature profiles for both storage, processing and product holding.

The two most important factors affecting product safety of
ingredients before their use in the restaurant are the adequacy of
the Supplier Assurance procedures and the distribution and
storage conditions. Ingredients must only be purchased according
to strict specifications from suppliers that are capable of managing
food safety, and who preferably are applying HACCP to their own
manufacturing processes. Suppliers must be audited regularly to
ensure their compliance with the product specification and their
overall quality system.

   As can be seen from the ingredients table in the example given,
the meat and the bun are the only ingredients that are actually
further processed in the restaurant and therefore the integrity of
the ingredients at delivery plays a major part in ensuring that the
finished product is safe for the consumer. A hazard analysis of the
individual ingredients and the preventative measures required at
the supplier are shown in Table A.3.

A.3.3 *Critical Control Points in product preparation*

An example of the process steps that occur during hamburger
preparation is shown in Table A.4.

   As with any HACCP Process it is very important to validate that
the process sequence is correct and is actually what is happening
in the restaurant, particularly to ensure that no steps have been
omitted. Similarly, it is important to see how product is moved
around the restaurant, how the hygienic practices of the
employees is working, and how equipment is cleaned and stored
before use.

   Each step of the process must then be studied in detail to
identify the presence of hazards or factors that could lead to
hazards occurring, and identify the points at which control can be
applied, together with the Critical Limits, the Monitoring
Procedures and Corrective Actions. A hazard analysis of the
process is shown in Table A.5.

   The hazard analysis confirms that the critical control points fall
into three categories.

1. Prevention of cross-contamination of bacteria or foreign matter
   either by product-to-product or people-to-product routes.
2. Prevention of microbiological growth through abuse of storage
   holding times and temperatures.

Table A.3 Hazard Analysis – hamburger preparation

Ingredients	Hazards	Preventative Measures
Meat patties	Contamination with *Salmonella, E. coli, Staphylococcus aureus*	GMP Product and environmental monitoring Finished product specifications for minimizing pathogen levels
	Bone contamination	Bone elimination devices > 2 mm
Buns	Pathogen contamination	GMP Bake temperature > 85°C
	Foreign matter	GMP Metal detection < 2.5 mm Fe < 3.5 mm non-Fe
Mayonnaise	*Salmonella* from eggs	GMP Positive release or certificates of analysis
	Growth of pathogens	pH < 4.2 Temperature < 4°C Shelf life < 4 months
Lettuce/onion	Pathogens	Chlorination with 100 ppm Chlorine Shelf life < 7 days
	Foreign matter	GMP Metal detection < 2.5 mm Fe < 3.5 mm non-Fe
Tomatoes	Pest infestation/foreign matter	Visual inspection
Ketchup	Toxins in canned tomato paste/foreign matter	Supplier assurance Canning GMPs
Pickles	Foreign matter	GMP

3. Cooking of raw products such as beef to destroy any pathogenic organisms that may be present. In fact, beef is the only product used for hamburgers in the restaurant that is processed to make it safe and this fact reinforces the importance of an effective Supplier Assurance programme for all products to ensure that all potentially hazardous foods and ingredients are properly identified and processed by the supplier to ensure their safety.

Table A.4 Process step table – hamburger preparation

Stage	Mayonnaise	Lettuce	Tomato	Bun	Meat	Pickles	Ketchup	Onion
1 Deliver	1–4°C	1–4°C	Ambient	Ambient	−18°C max	Ambient	Ambient	1–4°C
2 Storage	1–4°C	1–4°C	Ambient	Ambient	−18°C max	Ambient	Ambient	1–4°C
3 Pre-preparation	Transfer to clean, sanitized pans	Transfer to pans	Wash and slice	None	Transfer to freezer cabinet	Transfer to pans	Transfer to dispenser	Transfer to pans
4 Cooking				Toast 66°C	Cook > 68°C			
5 Hold	4 h max at ambient	4 h max at ambient	4 h max at ambient	10 min max hold > 62°	10 min max hold > 62°			4 h max hold
6 Preparation								
7 Assembly/wrap				Hamburger				
8 Hold				> 72°C 10 min max				
9 Service				Customer				

Table A.5 HACCP Control Chart – hamburger preparation

CCP	Process Step	Hazard	Preventative Measure	Critical Limits	Monitoring Procedure	Corrective Action
1	Delivery	Microbiological growth if temperature abused	Temperature control	Meat patties −18°C Lettuce ⎱ 1–4°C Onion Mayonnaise ⎰	Each delivery (Check per Operations Manual procedures)	Reject if outside limit Notify distributor
		Foreign materials	Packaging intact	All packs undamaged and secure	As above	As above
2	Storage	**Cross-contamination** (a) Foreign material	Complete covering of product	No exposed product	Visual	Cover, discard if contamination is evident
		(b) Micro-biological growth if temperature abused	Covering (to prevent contamination)	As above	As above	As above
			Temperature control restricts growth	Meat patties −18°C Lettuce ⎱ 1–4°C Onion Mayonnaise ⎰	Daily temperature checks and record	Alert engineer. Reject if outside limit
			Stock control	Within dates	Use FIFO Daily stock check	Discard products exceeding shelf life

Table A.5 *continued*

CCP	Process Step	Hazard	Preventative Measure	Critical Limits	Monitoring Procedure	Corrective Action
3	Pre-preparation					
	(i) **Mayonnaise**					
	(a) Decant into holding pans	Foreign material	Complete covering of product	No exposed product	Visual	Cover, discard if contamination is evident
		Chemical/micro-biological	Clean and sanitized utensils	Cleaned and sanitized before use	Visual	Do not use. Retraining
		Cross-contamination	Clean, sanitized pans and spatulas	As above	Visual	As above
	(b) Storage (before transfer to preparation table)	Foreign material	Covering of product	No exposed product	Visual	Cover, discard if contamination is evident
		Microbiological growth if contaminated	Temperature control (1–4°C)	4°C max	Visual daily check	Reject if outside limit
	(ii) **Lettuce/ onion/pickles**					
	(a) Fill holding pans	Foreign material	Complete covering of product	No exposed product	Visual	Cover, discard if contamination is evident
			Clean and sanitized utensils	Cleaned and sanitized before use	Visual	Do not use. Retraining

Process step	Hazard	Control measure	Critical limit	Monitoring	Corrective action
(b) Storage	Foreign material	As above	As above	As above	As above
(iii) Tomatoes					
(a) Wash	**Cross-contamination**	Use of dedicated, clean and sanitized sink	Cleaned and sanitized before use	Visual	Do not use. Retraining
(b) Coring/ slicing	**Cross-contamination** Foreign material	Clean, sanitized utensils Equipment clean, sanitized and in good repair	Cleaned and sanitized before use	Visual	Do not use. Retraining
(iv) Bun Storage	Foreign material	Complete covering of product Store 15 cm off floor	No exposed product Food stored off floor	Visual Visual	Cover, discard if contamination is evident Put on trolley. Discard if contamination is evident
(v) Meat patties Storage	Foreign material	Complete covering of product	No exposed product	Visual	Cover, discard if contamination is evident
(vi) Ketchup Decant into bottles	Foreign material Cross-contamination	As above Clean and sanitized utensils Clean and sanitized bottles	As above Cleaned and sanitized before use As above	As above Visual As above	As above Do not use. Retraining As above

Table A.5 *continued*

CCP	Process Step	Hazard	Preventative Measure	Critical Limits	Monitoring Procedure	Corrective Action
4	Meat cooking	Microbiological survival	Correct cooking time/temp	Meat cook-out 68°C MIN	Checks completed minimum 4 × day; record and sign	Refer to equipment Operations Manual
		Cross-contamination	Separate handling of raw and cooked product	Keep raw and cooked meats separate	Visual	Discard if seen. Retraining
				Do not handle raw/cooked meats	As above	As above
				Colour-coded tongs used to handle cooked meat	As above	As above
	Bun toasting	**Cross-contamination**	Correct handling	Staff not handling uncooked food	Visual	Discard if seen. Retraining
5	Holding	Microbiological growth if temperature abused	Temperature	Salad products maximum 4 h at ambient	Use of discard times	Discard product exceeding holding time

No.	Process	Hazard	Control measure	Critical limit	Monitoring	Corrective action
6	Microwaving of bun and meat	Foreign body	Covering of steamer	Buns/meat 68 ± 6°C Holding temperature Covered	Daily temperature checks; record and sign / Visual	Alert engineer. Reject if outside limit / Cover if seen
		Cross-contamination (a) Foreign material	Clean and sanitized equipment	Clean and sanitize before use and ongoing	Visual	Do not use. Retraining
		(b) Micro-biological	Clean and sanitize contact surfaces (hand/work)	Clean and sanitize before use and ongoing (e.g. handle/buttons)	Visual	Do not use. Retraining
7	Preparation	**Cross-contamination** Microbiological/chemical/foreign bodies	(i) Personal hygiene	Clean and sanitized hands	Visual	Do not use. Retraining
			(ii) Clean and sanitized surfaces	Clean and sanitized before use and ongoing regularly	Visual	Do no use. Retraining

Table A.5 *continued*

CCP	Process Step	Hazard	Preventative Measure	Critical Limits	Monitoring Procedure	Corrective Action
8	Assembly/wrap	**Cross-contamination** Foreign material	Wrap intact	Product undamaged and secure	Visual	Discard if contamination is evident. Retraining
9	Holding	Microbiological growth if temperature abused	Temperature/time heat chute 79 ± 6°C	Max holding time 10 min	Daily checks; record and sign	Discard product Troubleshoot procedure. Alert engineer
				Serving temperature 66 ± 17°C	Discard times	
10	Service (if eaten on premises)	**Cross-contamination** (a) Foreign material	General restaurant cleanliness	Restaurant clean and tidy	Visual Signed daily checklist	Rectify/retrain
		(b) Chemical	Care taken with use of chemicals	Use away from customers	Visual	As above

Cross-contamination of products with microorganisms from raw unprocessed food or from staff poses one of the major potential hazards in any restaurant and must be prevented by identifying:

(a) Procedures and practices which may contaminate potentially hazardous foods;
(b) Environmental conditions that may allow the growth and transfer of microorganisms on food contact surfaces.

Typically, such cross-contamination is prevented by:

- use of colour-coded tongs for handling raw and cooked meat, chicken and fish
- three-sink system for washing, rinsing and sanitizing all utensils
- regular use of sanitizers for wiping all product contact surfaces
- stringent application of hand washing and hand sanitizers
- wherever possible, avoiding the introduction of potentially hazardous raw foods such as whole eggs, raw chicken or fish into the restaurant

Control of storage times and temperatures is essential to avoid the uncontrolled multiplication of any bacteria that may be present. This is achieved through:

(a) defining shelf lives and storage conditions of all incoming ingredients, and ensuring that these are adhered to during distribution;
(b) operating to strict 'First in, First out' (FIFO) principles;
(c) defining maximum preparation times and discard times for all products within the restaurant, at all relevant stages of preparation and providing an easy-to-follow system for restaurant staff;
(d) providing hot holding units and steamers capable of maintaining temperatures of $>60\,°C$.

For beef patties, which are produced from 100% beef that has been formed and frozen, cooking in the restaurant is the major control point assuring the absence of pathogens in the finished hamburger. Raw beef may contain *Salmonella* spp., *Staph. aureus*, and *E. coli* 0157, all of which can be effectively destroyed by thorough cooking. However, control still has to commence with the patty manufacturer and with the suppliers of the original beef

227

to minimize the presence of pathogens, and monitoring pro-grammes, specifications and auditing of Good Manufacturing Practices at the manufacturer should all be in place. Cooking temperatures are therefore strictly controlled with all of the meat being cooked to a minimum internal temperature of 68 °C. Broiler speeds are calibrated before start-up and temperatures are regularly checked throughout the day.

A.3.4 Monitoring

Monitoring of all food safety control points can be carried out through the use of check lists which can be used by the restaurant manager. Monitoring of product quality is also carried out throughout the supply and distribution chain to ensure that product specifications, shelf life and temperature criteria are being rigidly complied with. All of the operating procedures are detailed in an Operations Manual which specifies all food safety items, operating procedures and corrective actions.

A.3.5 Record keeping

The monitoring of the CCPs must be properly documented and recorded in a suitable format, validated and signed by the responsible person. Records should be kept for at least 1 year.

A.3.6 Verification

HACCP Systems must be verified to ensure that they are working effectively and should aim to establish that:

(a) appropriate control points have been established to control all known potential hazards;
(b) control measures are working effectively.

Verification is carried out in a number of ways. Firstly, verifica-tion of control points associated with supplier and distribution control is carried out by regular audits of all suppliers and distributor records, quality systems, HACCP Systems, as well as GMP audits. Secondly, at the restaurant level, a team of independ-ent auditors carry out regular audits of every restaurant, checking that every control point is in place and that all Critical Limits are being adhered to. These audits are very detailed and any critical safety factors are highlighted for immediate attention. Thirdly, any customer complaints are systematically analysed to ensure that all hazards have been identified and are being controlled.

Managing food safety effectively is crucial for the success of fast-food businesses; the HACCP Principles of identifying potential hazards and implementing appropriate control measures provide the most efficient means of maintaining such management.

A.4 Case Study 3 – Lime juice cordial
N.S. Hagger, Britvic Soft Drinks Ltd., Chelmsford, England.

A.4.1 Introduction

This case study will provide an insight into the institution of the Hazard Analysis Critical Control Point (HACCP) system, as applied within Britvic Soft Drinks Ltd., through looking at a hypothetical unpasteurized soft drink product – lime juice cordial. Britvic are using HACCP for the control of microbiological, chemical and foreign body hazards, and to prevent product spoilage in addition to food safety. The Britvic HACCP System is illustrated in Figure A.2.

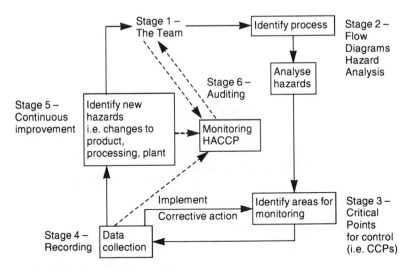

Figure A.2 Britvic HACCP Approach.

A.4.2 Stage 1 – the HACCP Team

The form entitled 'HACCP Team Details' (Figure A.3) is completed. This is to ensure that a record is made of all team members, and the relevant details for that particular HACCP Team are kept together for reference.

229

Location	Britvic Soft Drinks Limited. Factory
Products	Unpasteurized soft drink containing fruit, e.g. lime juice cordial containing 50% juice.
Date	XX/XX/94
Details of Team members	Factory Quality Manager Laboratory Technician (Microbiology) Syrup Room Supervisor Line Engineer Line Supervisor
Details of Team members co-opted	Warehouse checker

Figure A.3 HACCP Team details.

A.4.3 *Stage 2 – Flow Diagrams and Hazard Analysis*

The Hazard Analysis stage consists of identification and description of potential hazards, followed by the assessment of risks associated with the process.

Hazards associated with foods and drinks are normally categorized as microbiological, chemical and foreign body or physical hazards. It is important to note that for this case study, the definition of Hazard is a potential to cause harm in the product in terms of food safety and spoilage.

In order for the HACCP Team to be able to progress towards hazard analysis, first they complete accurate Process Flow Diagrams. The HACCP Team 'walk' the entire process before, during and after completion of the flow diagrams. Flow diagram 1 summarizes processes from raw material receipt to final product delivery for all soft drink products made on this production line. The aim of this Flow Diagram (Figure A.4) is to tune the team into a common understanding of what the production site does and where processes occur on the site.

Copies of relevant engineering diagrams are useful for finer details, which can be transferred in a simplified form to Flow Diagram 1.

Flow Diagram 2 (Figure A.5) details the process of the specific soft drink being considered for this study, i.e. lime juice cordial. The HACCP Team now use their combined knowledge and expertise to describe each activity or operation in its logical sequence in the Flow Diagram, and detail is most important. For the purposes of this case study a basic, non-complicated Flow Diagram has been constructed.

Once both Flow Diagrams are complete, relevant specifications for raw materials, packaging, finished products, storage and delivery are collected together for team use. For this case study, much of the additional information is detailed on the Product Description Sheet (Figure A.6).

Before the hazard analysis stage, the team members familiarize themselves with existing documentation and specifications to understand the process thoroughly and establish what is already in place. The information considered from existing documentation was that:

- the temperature of product throughout manufacturing is ambient;
- the process time is 15 minutes at the batch stirring stage, followed by 1 hour to package the batch;
- there are no 'dead legs' present in the production line;
- there is no rework mechanism;
- the high-care areas include dry pack weighing, batch preparation and product filler to capper;
- the storage of glass bottles is in cardboard boxes in the enclosed warehouse before distribution;
- the cleaning of the process lines is by steam, Cleaning in Place (CIP) and manual breakdown of pipework. The cleaning solution is caustic based.

Starting at the beginning of Flow Diagram 2, each part of the process is taken in order and entered onto the 'part of process' section on the Hazard Analysis Table (Table A.6).

Each potential hazard is then analysed by considering the severity and the likelihood of its occurrence. In other words, each potential hazard is investigated in detail to establish whether or not it is a real hazard.

In Britvic Soft Drinks, the HACCP Team carry out the hazard analysis by assigning specific levels of concern to each potential hazard. These concern levels relate to the Britvic operation and

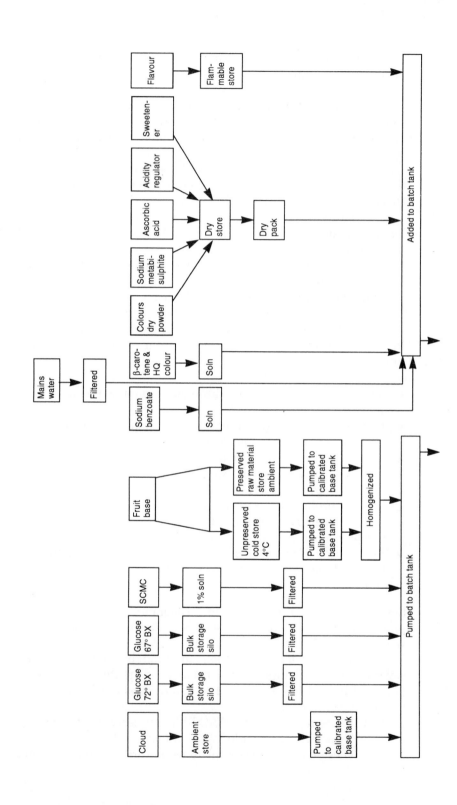

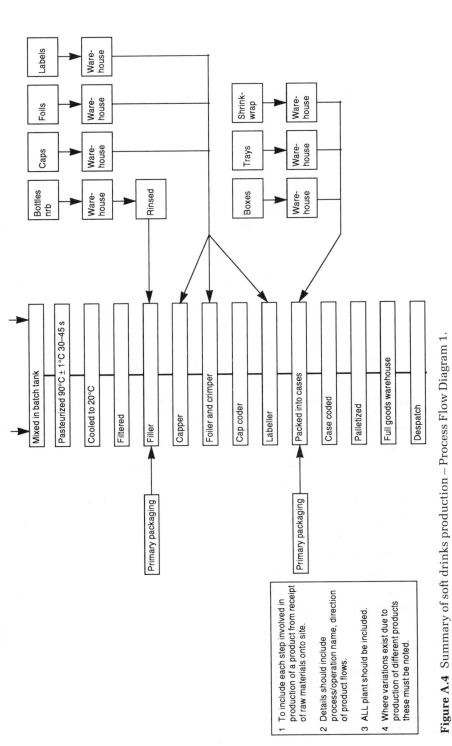

The process flow includes the following steps:

- Mixed in batch tank
- Pasteurized 90°C ± 1°C 30–45 s
- Cooled to 20°C
- Filtered
- Filler
- Capper
- Foiler and crimper
- Cap coder
- Labeller
- Packed into cases
- Case coded
- Palletized
- Full goods warehouse
- Despatch

Raw materials:
- Bottles nrb → Warehouse → Rinsed
- Caps → Warehouse
- Foils → Warehouse
- Labels → Warehouse
- Boxes → Warehouse
- Trays → Warehouse
- Shrink-wrap → Warehouse

Primary packaging (to Filler)
Primary packaging (to Packed into cases)

1 To include each step involved in production of a product from receipt of raw materials onto site.

2 Details should include process/operation name, direction of product flows.

3 ALL plant should be included.

4 Where variations exist due to production of different products these must be noted.

Figure A.4 Summary of soft drinks production – Process Flow Diagram 1.

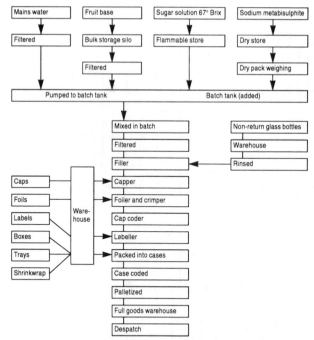

Figure A.5 Lime juice cordial – Process Flow Diagram 2.

---

1. The product is made up of 70° Brix sugar solution, lime juice concentrate, lime flavour, preservative (sodium metabisulphite) and water.

2. Manufactured for the UK.

3. The acid level is of particular importance to product taste.

4. Filtered through a 5-micron filter before filling.

5. Additions are made to the batch tank via a suitably sized sieve.

6. This product is not pasteurized.

7. The product has a 6-month shelf life.

8. The pH is ≃ 2.4.

9. Lime fruit percentage 50%.

10. Sensory flavour when diluted 1 + 4 to conform to accepted standard.

11. Microbiological guidelines:

    Osmotolerant   <1 Yeast   per 100 ml
                     <1 Bacteria   per 100 ml
                     <1 Mould   per 100 ml

12. Pack type and size – glass bottle 1 litre.

13. The product is stored at ambient or chilled once purchased by the consumer.

Figure A.6 Lime juice cordial – product description sheet.

Table A.6 Hazard Analysis – lime juice cordial

Part of process	Hazard	Means of control	Category
1. Raw materials 1.1 Water Mains water incoming	Microbial contamination Chemical contamination Foreign body contamination (insects, debris)	Weekly microbial analysis Daily chemical analysis Filtration	Food safety
Water filters	Microbial growth	Cleaning effect-ively	Quality
Water pump (to batch tank)	Microbial growth Chemical residues	Cleaning effect-ively and speci-fication of food-grade grease	Quality
1.2 Fruit base Incoming ingredients Addition to batch tank	Microbial growth – yeast No hazard identified	Microbial analysis if contamination is suspected	Quality
1.3 Sugar solution Incoming ingredient	Microbial contamination and growth potential – yeast Chemical contamination	Visual inspection and microbial analysis Chemical analysis SQA and agreed specifications	Quality
Bulk storage silo	Increase in microflora Contamination with surface contact chemicals	Microbial analysis Ensure efficiency of CIP chemical drain system Check after each CIP	Quality Food safety
Sugar filter	Microbial growth and therefore cross-contamina-tion	Effective cleaning – checked by microbial swabbing every 2 weeks	Quality
Sugar pumps (to batch tank)	As above	As above plus engineer's visual inspection Microbial swabs every 3 months only	Quality

Table A.6 *continued*

Part of process	Hazard	Means of control	Category
1.4 Lime flavour Incoming ingredient	Chemical contamination (Solvent or non-standard component)	Chemical analysis (HPLC) and SQA (agreed specifications) COSHH compliance (Labelling)	Food safety
Storage (flammable stores)	No food safety or spoilage hazard identified		
Addition to batch tank	Foreign body ingress – human cross-contamination	Correct attire to be worn by all food handlers plus hygiene training	Food safety
1.5 Sodium metabi-sulphite Incoming ingredient	Chemical contamination	Chemical analysis of each incoming batch	Food safety
Addition to batch tank	Foreign bodies from handling – personnel	Correct attire; personnel training and visual inspection of batch	Food safety
1.6 Glass bottles and caps	Foreign body contamination – debris in bottles or 'bird swings'	SQA of glass supplier including audit and agreed specifications. Visual inspection of incoming glass plus bottle rinsing on line	Food safety
2. Batch mixing	No hazard identified		
3. Filter	Foreign body contamination not removed	Ensure integrity of filters through regular engineering inspection	Food safety
4. Filler	Chemical contamination from surface contact	Ensure efficiency of CIP chemical drain system and follow through with a water flush	Food safety

Part of process	Hazard	Means of control	Category
5. Capper	Microbial contamination from dirty caps	Microbial analysis of caps by batch (6 caps < 20 TVC)	Quality
6. Foiler and Crimper	Foreign body – glass	Continuous on-line checks to ensure no signs of neck area chipping	Food safety
7. Packing and Despatch	No hazard identified		

help the HACCP Team to think about what would happen if the potential hazard occurred – would it have a serious outcome or not? The concern level assigned is then used to determine the real hazards, for example, Concern Level 1, the hazard is not realistic – rising to Concern Level 4, there is a real hazard.

Looking more closely at the information on the Hazard Analysis Table (Table A.6), this HACCP Study of lime juice cordial gives some interesting information. Picking out some of the points will show how much useful data has been gathered so far.

1. Mains water contains microbial levels that may affect final product quality.
2. If any of the raw materials used in manufacture of the soft drink are chemically contaminated the highest severity of risk will be realized, i.e. this is a food safety issue.
3. Foreign bodies may enter the process via the raw materials, e.g. debris in water.
4. Microbial growth in sugar needs to be minimized as this type of yeast growth will potentially go on to ferment the final product, leading to product spoilage.
5. The cleaning process needs to be able to remove excess surface contact chemicals in the sugar silos and the filler.
6. The syrup room process of additions to the batch tanks is a critical area – the wrong raw material chemicals must not be used in batch make-up, also the batch is at the stage when the product is most at risk to foreign bodies from human error.
7. The microbial contamination from the capper process could allow all products on line 1 to have mould spores added to each bottle, again causing product spoilage.

8. The crimper, if not carefully maintained, could allow two hazards to be realized: if over-crimping occurs, neck ring glass may be added to bottles, while under-crimping may lead to air ingress into the bottles, potentially causing microbial growth.
9. Foreign-body debris in the non-return bottles needs to be effectively removed or detected.

The Team have been able, through Hazard Analysis, to identify potential hazards by preparing Flow Diagrams and to assess the severity of each hazard by considering the likelihood of that hazard occurring and the risk to the consumer and/or product. The Team then define controls which are relevant and cost effective to control each hazard.

A.4.4 Stage 3 – Control of Critical Points

Following the Hazard Analysis the HACCP Team go on to select those areas as critical for control of food safety, i.e. Critical Control Points (CCPs) – those areas where realistic hazards must be controlled. Control points critical for control of product spoilage are also identified. These are classed as Quality Control Points (QCPs).

The Control Point Information sheet (Tables A.7 and A.8) is completed by selecting from the Hazard Analysis Table (Table A.6) all parts of the process that present a realistic hazard. The remainder of the sheet is then filled in by the Team for each CCP.

The means of control has to be as simple and effective as possible, and once specific parts of the process have been selected either as CCPs or QCPs, the department responsible must be identified. The relevant control systems are then put in place, if not already present.

The key information the HACCP Team have now generated is a clear definition of 'what', 'when', 'where', 'who' and 'how' for each Control Point. These data are then drawn together to document responsibilities and actions in work instructions, such as cleaning schedules, hygiene programmes, and calibration regimes. Documentation is part of the Factory Quality system and is therefore developed in line with the Company's agreed approach to documenting the CP activities to ISO 9000 standard.

The HACCP Team, by using the Control Point Information Sheet (Tables A.7 and A.8) for the production of lime juice cordial, has found 19 Control Points, 10 of which are CCPs associated with chemical contamination or glass faults and debris in the bottles. This is because, with a pH of 2.4, a high sugar content and added preservative the risk of microbiological food

Table A.7 Control Point Information Sheet – Safety

Process step (CCP No.)	Hazard	Means of control	Frequency of control	Specifications for CCP	Department responsible for control	Comments/ action if outside limits
Mains water (1)	Foreign bodies	Water filters	Continuous	Maintenance of water filters daily Filter intact	Engineers	Change filter
	Chemical contamination	Chemical analysis	Minimum daily	EC Regulations	QC Chemical	Liaise with suppliers Agree contract for quality of water
Bulk sugar silo (2)	Chemical contamination from CIP	CIP drain down Water flush	Each clean	No chemical residue detected – visual inspection	Production	Test for detergent residues
Lime flavour (3)	Chemical contamination	Chemical analysis	Every batch of final product	HPLC, standard ingredients detected	QC Chemical	Review supplier contract and specification agreed
Added to batch tank (4)	Foreign bodies – from handling	Correct handling Correct use of protective clothing	Every delivery	Handle to COSHH regulations; Trained operators	Production	Foreign body to be screened from batch
Sodium metabi- sulphite (5)	Chemical contamination	Chemical analysis	Every batch of final product	HPLC, standard ingredients detected	QC Chemical	Review supplier contract

Table A.7 continued

Process step (CCP No.)	Hazard	Means of control	Frequency of control	Specifications for CCP	Department responsible for control	Comments/ action if outside limits
Added to batch tank (6)	Foreign bodies – from handling	Visual inspection of batch and correct attire	Every batch	No foreign bodies from personnel to enter the batch	Production/syrup room	Foreign body to be screened and removed from batch or sourced from final products
Non-return bottles (7)	Foreign bodies – glass	QC checks on line Approved supplier	Continuous	No debris in bottles Annual audit Agreed specification	Production QC	Hold stock – determine level of bottles containing debris Review supplier contract
Filtered (8)	Foreign bodies	Effective filtration	Continuous	Intact filter; maintained daily	Engineers	Change filter
Filler (9)	Chemical contamination from CIP	Chemical drain system CIP to be concluded with a water flush	After each CIP	No chemical residue detected Visual inspection of filler bowl before use	Production and Engineers	Product tested to ensure no foreign chemicals present
Foiler and crimper (10)	Foreign bodies – glass	QC checks on line	Continuous	No chipping of neck area	Production	Hold stock – determine level containing glass/maintain crimper

Table A.8 Control Point Information Sheet – Spoilage

Process step (QCP No.)	Hazard	Means of control	Frequency of control	Specifications for QCP	Department responsible for control	Comments/action if outside limits
Water filters (Q1)	Microbial growth	Cleaning	Daily	No visible debris	Production	Increase cleaning and visible inspection
Water pump (Q2)	Microbial growth	Flush with water	3-monthly	No visible debris	Maintenance	Increase cleaning and visible inspection
Fruit base (Q3)	Microbial growth	Microbial analysis	Only if suspect contamina-tion	< yeast/100 ml	QC Microbiology	Send sample to be confirmed by Central Laboratory
Sugar solution (Q4)	Microbial contamination	Microbial analysis; visual inspection	Every delivery	American Bottlers Standard	QC Microbiology and syrup room	Reject tanker – return to supplier
Bulk storage silo (Q5)	Microbial growth	QC Microbial	Daily	American Bottlers Standard	QC Microbiology	Additional analysis of final product
Sugar filter (Q6)	Microbial growth	Cleaning	2-weekly	Microbial swabbing	QC Microbiology	Increase cleaning frequency
Sugar pumps (Q7)	Microbial growth	Cleaning	3-monthly	Microbial swabbing and Engineer's visual inspection	QC Microbiology and Engineers	Increase cleaning frequency
Capper (Q8)	Microbial contamination	Microbial analysis	Every batch	6 caps analysed < 20 TVC	QC Microbiology	Confirm final product not affected by microbes
Foiler and crimper (Q9)	Microbial growth	QC Microbial analysis	Every batch	No growth	QC Microbiology	detected in caps Increase cleaning and visible inspection

safety issues are small. An additional nine control points were found to be QCPs for the control of spoilage microorganisms (predominantly yeasts).

A.4.5 Stage 4 – Recording

Examples of recording are not included in this case study.

A.4.6 Stage 5 – Continuous improvement

Following implementation of HACCP to Stage 4, recording of information is extremely important to keep the momentum of the System going. In addition, new products, new packages and new processes will inevitably be introduced to a factory and or production line, which will introduce potential new hazards. These new hazards need to be incorporated into the HACCP Study so that new CCPs can be identified and redundant CCPs rejected. This means that a regular review is needed.

The HACCP Team would carry out Stage 2 'The Hazard Analysis' incorporating any potential new hazards, changes to the Flow Diagrams and the Hazard Analysis Table. Depending upon the significance of the hazard, this may be carried out by (i) completely redoing the Hazard Analysis Stage; or (ii) inserting the relevant details onto the existing paperwork. Whichever method is selected, copies of all originals should be maintained for reference. By retaining original copies, historical information is provided for reference in the event of a hazard being realized or if a similar situation arises in the future.

If new CPs are identified, the HACCP Team carry out Stage 3 incorporating the new CPs on the Control Point Information Sheet (Table A.7). Depending on the significance of the hazard, this could mean that the Control Point Information Sheet may need to be (i) completely redone; or (ii) have new/altered CPs inserted. Stage 4 Recording then needs to be updated, and set up for new CCPs as necessary.

Records of HACCP information will eventually build up, and local decisions are made at each factory as to which information is retained.

A.4.7 Stage 6 – Auditing

The auditing of the whole HACCP System ensures that all Critical Control Points are under control and that any corrective action needing to be implemented is carried out. Auditing is therefore part of the continuous improvement plan following the implementation of HACCP. Each department should have a list of CPs relevant to the department's function. The Britvic auditing process is presently carried out by someone external to the site, to ensure the HACCP work is running smoothly and the CPs are being monitored by the relevant departments.

The auditor views and records his or her findings when he or she is satisfied that CPs are being actioned through work instructions, cleaning schedules, hygiene programmes and calibration regimes. The result of the audit is entered onto audit sheets. The Control Point Sheets themselves can be extended and used for this purpose by adding additional columns for audit data and results.

The results of the audit are then discussed with relevant personnel; this may be the whole factory management team or the quality management. An audit performance rating will be given when the auditor has assessed all stages of the HACCP system, i.e. Control of Critical Points, Recording and Continuous Improvement. Copies of audit records are retained by the auditor and factory manager, and a copy is forwarded to the company HACCP Co-ordinator.

In conclusion, the production of soft drinks, with regard to microbial food safety, is considered within the food and drink industry as low risk. However, this case study has briefly shown how manufacture of any product may, through Hazard Analysis of the process and Control Points identification, be used to control not only the risk to food safety, in this case particularly chemical and physical hazards, but also to product spoilage, thus ensuring consumer satisfaction.

A.5 Case Study 4 – Potato salad, retail sale
C.A. Wallace, with assistance from J. Hughes, J. Sainsbury plc, London, England.

A.5.1 Introduction

This case study covers the introduction of a new product to the delicatessen and salad bar counters of a retail supermarket. Hazard analysis had previously been carried out on existing salad products, and the main purpose of this study was to ensure that no new hazards would be introduced which would not be controlled effectively by the existing control mechanisms.

A.5.2 HACCP Team members

The HACCP Team was made up of the following:

- Store Food Safety Officer – Team Leader
- Delicatessen Manager
- Warehouse Manager
- Head Office Technologist

All Team members had a minimum of 3 years' experience in the retailing of fresh food, and had received training in the application of HACCP.

A.5.3 HACCP Study Terms of Reference

The HACCP Study covers food safety hazards from receipt by the store warehouse to consumption by the consumer. The potato salad had already been established as a safe product when supplied, and was covered during manufacture by the supplier's HACCP Plan.

This HACCP Study does not cover spoilage. The HACCP Team proposed to address this separately due to time constraints. As spoilage microorganisms can grow in the product, then storage times and temperatures will become more important, along with the cross-contamination risk, when the spoilage study is carried out.

A.5.4 The Product

The product is a low-pH, chilled potato salad, made up of cooked potato and mayonnaise, and garnished with chives. It is manufactured by an existing approved supplier of prepared salads. The product characteristics are as follows:

(i) pH – 4.0 ± 0.1
(ii) Storage temperature – <5.0 °C
(iii) Pack size – 2 kg
(iv) Pack type – plastic tub with lid
(v) Shelf life – packed product, 15 days at <5.0 °C;
once opened, 4 days at <5.0 °C

The product formulation will not support the growth of pathogens due to its low pH. However, the potential for contamination with pathogens which may survive, and in particular those which have a low infective dose (e.g. *Salmonella* spp.) will need to be considered during the HACCP Study.

A.5.5 The Process

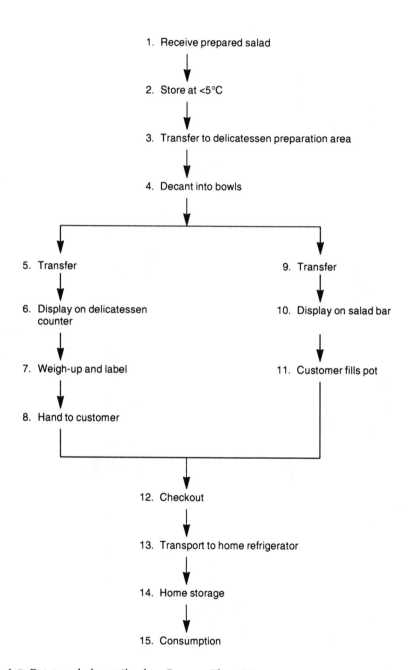

Figure A.7 Potato salad, retail sale – Process Flow Diagram.

A.5.6 Hazard Analysis and CCP Identification

Table A.9 Hazard Analysis and CCP Decision – potato salad retail sale

Process step	Hazard	Preventative Measure	Q1	Q2	Q3	Q4	Q5	CCP?
1. Receive prepared salad	No hazard identified as product on positive release to spec at supplier and manufactured to HACCP System	—						—
2. Store at < 5°C	No hazard identified	—						—
3. Transfer to delicatessen preparation area	No hazard identified	—						—
4. Decant into bowls	– Cross-contamination with pathogens from bowl or utensils	Effective cleaning procedures	Y	Y	N	Y	N	✓
	– Chemical contamination from cleaning residues	Cleaning procedure followed	Y	Y	N	Y	N	✓
	– Cross-contamination with foreign material from environment and operators	Staff personal hygiene procedures and training	Y	Y	N	Y	N	✓
		Good retail practices and environmental management. (Pest control, effective cleaning, preventative maintenance, etc.)						
5. Transfer to delicatessen counter	No hazard identified (preparation area immediately behind counter)	—						—

Process step	Hazard	Control measure					
6. Display on delicatessen counter	– Cross-contamination with pathogens from serving utensils	Effective cleaning procedures	Y	N	Y	N	✓
	– Cross-contamination with pathogens from staff practices	Staff personal hygiene procedures and training	Y	N	Y	N	✓
	– Chemical cross-contamination from cleaning residues	Cleaning procedures followed	Y	N	Y	N	✓
	– Cross-contamination with foreign material from environment and staff	Good retail practices and environment management Staff personal hygiene procedures and training	Y	N	Y	N	✓
7. Weigh-up and label Salad is weighed into pot and lidded. Label placed across lid, sealing edges	– Cross-contamination with pathogens from serving utensils	Effective cleaning procedures	Y	N	Y	N	✓
	– Cross-contamination with pathogens from staff practices	Staff personal hygiene procedures and training	Y	N	Y	N	✓
	– Chemical cross-contamination from cleaning residues	Cleaning procedures followed	Y	N	Y	N	✓
	– Cross-contamination with foreign material from environment and staff	Good retail practices and environment management Staff personal hygiene procedures and training	Y	N	Y	N	✓
8. Hand to customer	No hazard identified	—					—
9. Transfer to salad bar	Cross-contamination with foreign material from environment	Bowls fully covered during transfer	Y	N	Y	N	✓

Table A.9 continued

Process step	Hazard	Preventative Measure	Q1	Q2	Q3	Q4	Q5	CCP?
10. Display on salad bar	– Cross-contamination with pathogens from serving utensils	Effective cleaning procedures	Y	Y	N	Y	N	✓
	– Cross-contamination with pathogens from customers (sneezing, etc.)	Sneeze guards in place Counter height designed to prevent child access	Y	Y	N	Y	N	✓
	– Chemical cross-contamination from cleaning residues	Cleaning procedures followed	Y	Y	N	Y	N	✓
	– Cross-contamination with foreign material from environment and customers	Good retail practices and environment management Effective design of salad bar counter	Y	Y	N	Y	N	✓
11. Customer fills pot	– Cross-contamination with foreign material from environment	Bowls fully covered during transfer	Y	Y	N	Y	N	✓
	– Cross-contamination with pathogens from serving utensils	Effective cleaning procedures	Y	Y	N	Y	N	✓

Process step	Hazard	Control measure			
	– Cross-contamination with pathogens from customers (sneezing, etc.)	Sneeze guards in place; Counter height designed to prevent child access	Y	Y	N ✓
	– Chemical cross-contamination from cleaning residues	Cleaning procedures followed	Y	Y	N ✓
	– Cross-contamination with foreign material from environment and customers	Good retail practices and environment management; Effective design of salad bar counter	Y	Y	N ✓
12. Checkout	No hazard identified	—	—		—
13. Transport to home refrigerator	No hazard identified (spoilage to be considered separately)	—	—		—
14. Home storage	No hazard identified	—	—		—
15. Consumption	No hazard identified	—	—		—

A.5.7 Controlling the CCPs

The HACCP Team found that the CCPs identified were all already in place for other salad products on both the delicatessen and salad bar counters. As no new CCPs were required, it was decided not to construct a HACCP Control Chart specifically for this product, but to add it to the existing documentation. A summary follows for the control of each hazard type requiring a CCP.

(a) Hazard – cross-contamination with pathogens from bowls and utensils
Hazard – chemical contamination from cleaning residues

The Preventative Measures for both of these hazards, which occur at several places in the operation, are similar. Effective cleaning procedures, which are carried out properly by trained staff, are essential to prevent these hazards. The Critical Limits are that each item has been effectively cleaned before each use. This could be monitored on an ongoing basis by the delicatessen staff and intermittently by their supervisor, using visual inspection. Corrective action will include not using any items which have been inadequately cleaned, and retraining staff where appropriate.

(b) Hazard – cross-contamination with pathogens from staff practices
Hazard – cross-contamination with foreign material from staff and environment

The Preventative Measures for these hazards involve hygiene procedures for both staff and environment, also known as Good Manufacturing or Good Retail Practices (IFST, 1991). These procedures will control the availability of items which may enter the product as foreign material, as well as the design of equipment and practices to prevent ingress, eg the covering of bowls during the transfer to the salad bar at process step 9. In addition, the personal hygiene procedures will reduce the potential for cross-contamination from staff.

For effective control of these hazards, the required procedures must be in place and staff must be fully trained. In other words, the Critical Limit is that the procedures are carried out effectively on an ongoing basis. This type of procedure would be monitored on an ongoing basis through visual inspection by the staff themselves and their supervisors, and through intermittent audits by the store Food Safety Officer and Head Office technologists. Corrective action would include immediate correction of any fault and retraining of staff where necessary.

(c) Hazard – cross-contamination with pathogens or foreign material from customers at the salad bar

The Preventative Measures for these hazards relate to the effective design of the salad bar counter, and it is important to get it right before it is brought into use. The main factors are the height of the counter, guards to protect the food and ease of cleaning. Once these have been designed in, the counter requires continuous visual monitoring and action must be taken to correct any fault which is identified.

Note: in every case described above any deviation from the critical limits are recorded in the counter log book, along with the corrective action taken. This is signed off by the member of staff and their supervisor.

A.5.8 Implementation and maintenance

Since the CCPs required are already being implemented for other products on both the delicatessen and salad bar counters, the potato salad product can easily be slotted into the normal management plan.

Maintenance requirements are fulfilled by monthly audits of the systems by the store Food Safety Officer, and by an annual in-depth food safety audit by Head Office technologists. At both of these audits the non-compliances and corrective action log book is reviewed and signed off.

A.6 Case Study 5 – Fresh cream gateaux
S.E. Mortimore, with assistance from the Memory Lane Team, at Cardiff, Wales.

A.6.1 Introduction

This case study covers the large-scale production of a fresh cream and jam gateau.

A.6.2 HACCP Team members

The HACCP Team was organized as follows:

1. Core team
- Factory Production Manager
- HACCP Officer
- Engineering Manager

- SQA Technologist
  2. Co-opted members
  - Cream and Jam Line Supervisor
  - Microbiology Manager

A.6.3 Terms of Reference

The HACCP Study covers food safety hazards of all types – biological, chemical and physical. The HACCP Study did not include any cleaning operations; this was considered in a separate HACCP Plan.

A.6.4 *Product description*

Fresh cream and jam gateau

Facility

The purpose-built factory produces a variety of decorated gateaux for sale to the retail industry. The factory is based on a large new industrial estate and produces both chilled and frozen products.

The product

The product has a fresh cream and jam filling between two sponges. It is a chilled product and must be kept below 5 °C through the distribution chain. The shelf life is 3 days from date of manufacture.

Manufacture

Sponge batters are baked at 150–170 °C through a travelling oven for 18.5 minutes. They are then cooled to ambient, automatically sliced and filled. There is a wide variety of fillings for the sponges. The sponges are flow-wrapped and put into cartons.

Principal hazards and preventative measures

Principal biological hazards are the potential presence of pathogens in various ingredients and cross-contamination during processing. Preventative Measures include approved suppliers and certificates of conformance, sensitive ingredient testing, baking and segregation.

Intended use

The product is targetted at the general public and may therefore be consumed by high-risk individuals. *Salmonella* and *Listeria* control is therefore critical.

HACCP Plan Ref. No. JC 2/1

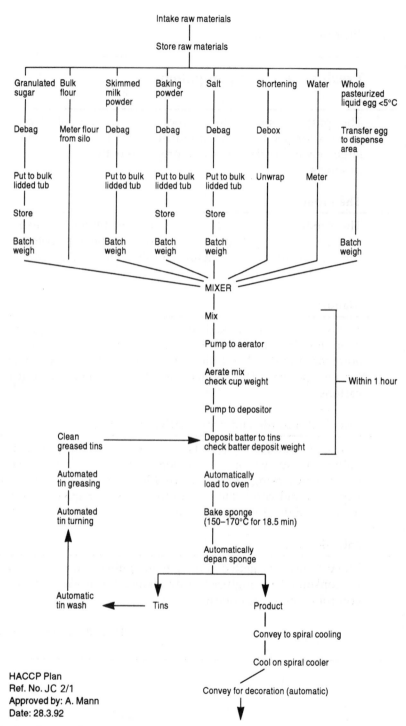

Figure A.8 Sponge base – Process Flow Diagram.

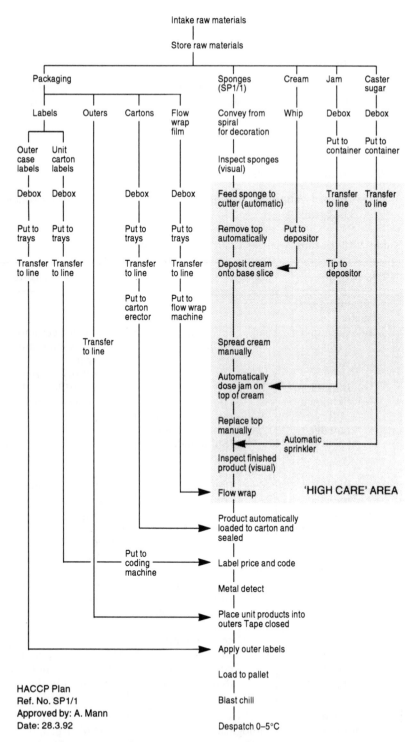

Figure A.9 Fresh cream and jam gateau; assembly and finishing – Process Flow Diagram.

255

A.6.5 The process

As the company produces several varieties of finished product, the sponge bases were considered as a separate Process Flow Diagram, i.e. a modular approach was taken: see Figures A.8 and A.9.

A.6.6 Hazard Analysis

Hazard Analysis was carried out on both of the Process Flow Diagrams.

Table A.10 Hazard Analysis Chart – sponge bases

Process Step	Hazard	Preventative Measure
1. Incoming raw materials		
(a) Granulated sugar	(a) Physical contamination	Visually inspect and check packaging integrity on arrival. Sieve all dry ingredients
(b) Bulk Flour (c) Skimmed milk powder	(b+c) Physical, chemical, microbiological contamination (*Salmonella*)	Obtain certificate of conformance from suppliers. Specify aflatoxin-free grain flour. Carry out SQA audits on all suppliers annually. Baking at Step 12
(d) Baking powder (e) Salt	(d+e) Physical contamination	Visually inspection and check packaging integrity on receipt
(f) Shortening	(f) Chemical (< 5% erucic acid)	Sieve all dry ingredients. Agreed specifications. Certificate of Analysis
(g) Water	(g) Chemical contamination Biological contamination Physical contamination	Certificate of Analysis from Water Authority of an on-site sample
(h) Whole pasteurized liquid egg	(h) Biological contamination (*Salmonella*)	SQA Audit – annually. Certificate of Conformance from supplier. Baking at Step 12
2. Storage of raw materials	Physical, chemical and biological cross-contamination Growth of pathogens	Store as per GMP Manual (a) Whole egg and cream – store at 5°C, covered

Process Step	Hazard	Preventative Measure
3. Debox, debag, decant, etc.	Physical contamination	Hygiene training, sieve dry ingredients
4. Put ingredients into bulk, lidded tubs as appropriate	Physical contamination, microbiological growth	Use only clean, dry containers
5. Store bulk tubs	Physical contamination	Store in clean, covered bins
6. Transfer egg to dispense area	Growth of pathogens	Limit time of storage at ambient
7. Batch weigh/ meter ingredients to mixer	Physical contamination	Hygiene training
8. Mix ingredients	Cross-contamination (unclean mixer) physical, microbial contamination – toxin	Effectively cleaned and well-maintained machinery
9. Aerate mix	No hazard identified	
10. Convey tins to depositor	Physical contamination Chemical contamination	Wash and rinse tins through automated tin wash Grease tins using only food-quality grease
11. Deposit batter to tins	No hazard identified	
12. Bake sponge through oven	Survival of vegetative pathogen spores	Bake sponge at specified time and temperature
13. Depan sponges onto spiral cooler	No hazard identified	
14. Cool sponges on spiral cooler	No hazard identified. However, biological contamination (moulds) would be an issue if spoilage organisms were included in the study	
15. Convey for decoration	Physical cross-contamination	GMP and Environmental Control

Table A.11 Hazard Analysis Chart – cream and jam gateau assembly

Process Step	Hazard	Preventative Measure
1. Intake raw materials (a) Packaging	(a) Chemical, physical, biological contamination	(a) Taint test packaging every delivery and visually inspect. SQA Audit of Food contact packaging suppliers
(b) Sponge bases	(b) No hazard identified	
(c) Pasteurized cream	(c) Biological – vegetative pathogens	SQA visit to Supplier and Certificate of Confirmance by batch
(d) Caster sugar (e) Jam	(d) Physical contamination (e) Physical – insects, large stalks Chemical – pesticide residues	Visually inspect raw material packaging integrity on receipt and examine sample for physical contamination SQA visit to Supplier and Certificate of Conformance by batch
2. Storage of raw materials	Physical, chemical, biological cross-contamination from equipment, environment, people	Dry, ambient warehouse Cream < 5°C
3. Debox, debag	Physical and biological cross-contamination	Hygiene training Regular removal of waste packaging
4. Transfer packaging and ingredients to line	Physical contamination	Keep all containers fully covered
5. Whip and put cream to depositor	Physical and biological cross-contamination	Correct handling procedures Clean hygienic equipment Hygiene training
6. Put caster sugar to sprinkler	No hazard identified	—
7. Put unit carton labels to labelling machine	No hazard identified	—
8. Put packaging to appropriate packing machine	No hazard identified	—

Process Step	Hazard	Preventative Measure
9. Convey sponges for decoration	Physical contamination	Visually inspect sponges – as an indicator
10. Feed sponge to cutter	Physical contamination	Maintain cutter (as GMP)
11. Remove top of sponge	No hazard identified	—
12. Deposit cream onto base slice	No hazard identified	—
13. Spread by hand	Physical and biological cross-contamination	Hygiene training
14. Deposit jam automatically and replace top sponge by hand	As above	As above
15. Sprinkle caster sugar over top	No hazard identified	—
16. Inspect finished product	No hazard identified	—
17. Flow wrap	Incorrect seal leading to biological cross-contamination	Hermetic seal and test
18. Load product to outer carton and seal	Damaged product leading to biological and physical contamination	Sturdy packaging. Travel test before launch
19. Label, price and code	Untraceable product, biological growth (incorrect shelf life code)	Check product label and code
20. Metal detect	Metal contamination not detected	Effective metal detection
21. Place to outers and label	Untraceable product	Check outer code
22. Blast chill (< 5°C)	Microbiological growth	Chill quickly to < 5°C within 2 h max
23. Load to pallet for despatch	Microbiological growth due to incorrect storage and distribution temperature	Maintain temperature < 5°C

A.6.7 *Critical Control Point identification*

The Team used the CCP Decision Tree only to check that their identification of CCPs was correct, the initial identification being carried out using the experience of the Team itself.

Table A.12 HACCP Control Chart – cream and jam gateau

HACCP Plan									
Reference Number JC2/1						Approved by: A. Mann HACCP Team Leader			
						Date: 28/3/92			
Process step	CCP No.	Hazard to be controlled	Preventative measures	Control Critical Limits	Procedures Actions to be taken if deviation occurs	Monitoring Procedure	Frequency	Responsible person(s)	
Incoming raw material Flour	1.1	Aflatoxin	Obtain Certificates of Analysis from suppliers	Aflatoxin: < 10 mg/kg	Reject batch	Inspect Certificate of Analysis	Every batch	Incoming Goods Clerk SQA Manager	
Mains water	1.2	Chemical con-tamination	Carry out on-site micro checks and obtain Certificate of Analysis of local sample-Water Authority	Chemical con-tamination (see spec.) Regulatory Compliance	Contact Water Authority	Testing to include toxic substances Giardia/ Crypto-sporidium. Inspect Certificates of Analysis from Water Authority	Weekly 3-monthly	QA Manager QA Manager	
Jam	1.3	Pesticide residues	Certificates of Analysis from approved supplier	Within legal limits	Contact, Purchasing Manager	Inspect Certificate SQA Audit	Annual Annually	SQA Manager SQA Manager	

Table A.12 continued

HACCP Plan

Reference Number JC2/1

Page 2 of 3

Date: 28/3/92

Approved by: A. Mann

HACCP Team Leader

Process step	CCP No.	Hazard to be controlled	Preventative measures	Control Critical Limits	Procedures Actions to be taken if deviation occurs	Monitoring Procedure	Frequency	Responsible person(s)
Cream	1.4	*Salmonella* and *Listeria*	Supplier Quality Assurance System	Absent/25g Approved supplier	Reject batch Inform purchasing	Laboratory tests *Listeria*, *Salmonella*, Procedure No's xxx SQA audit	Every delivery 6-monthly	QA Manager SQA Manager
Storage of raw materials	2.0	Physical con-tamination, biological growth	Store as specified, i.e. cream < 5°C, egg for specified max time. Keep covered	No physical, chemical con-tamination. Maintain temperature < 5°C	Hold and inform QA Manager	Automatic temperature recorder. Visually inspect label to ensure stock rotation	Daily checks – continue during use. Every batch	Warehouse Manager and Operator
Batch weigh ingredients	3.0	Physical con-tamination	Sieve ingredients	No physical contamina-tion	Reject and check other samples in batch	Check sifter over-size	Half-hourly	Operator
Bake sponge through oven	4.0	Survival of vegetative pathogens	Bake sponge at specified time/temperature	Bake at 70°C for 2 min minimum core temperature	Stop production. Reject faulty product. Adjust oven temperature/time	Automatic chart recorder	Continuous	Operator

HACCP Plan

Reference Number JC2/1

Approved by: A. Mann
HACCP Team Leader

Date: 28/3/92

Process step	CCP No.	Hazard to be controlled	Preventative measures	Control Critical Limits	Procedures Actions to be taken if deviation occurs	Monitoring Procedure	Frequency	Responsible person(s)
Flow wrap	5.0	Biological contamination	Hermetic seal	Intact seal	Stop line, adjust, notify QAM	Visual inspection	Every 15 min	QA Inspector
Label code	6.0	Untraceable product	Product label and code	Correct information, legible label	Stop line, divert product produced. Replace label stock notify QAM	Visual inspection	Every 15 min	QA Inspector
Metal detect	7.0	Metal contamination	Metal detector	Absent – ferrous 2.0 mg Non-ferrous 2.5 mg	Stop line, recalibrate, notify QAM. Hold stock manufactured since previous check	Metal detection check using test pieces. Calibrate metal detector	Every 30 min Daily	QA Inspector Line Engineer
Despatch	8.0	Growth of pathogens	Low temperature during storage and distribution	0–5°C	Hold, inform QAM. Sample and test product	Continuous chart recorder – warehouse and distribution vehicle. Check recorder calibration	Daily review Monthly	Warehouse Manager Transport Manager Warehouse Manager

A.6.8 CCP monitoring

As the HACCP Team expected, the control measures identified during the study were currently in place with the exception of having the Water Authority test a local (factory) sample of water. New log sheets were drawn up for each CCP, each cross-referencing the HACCP Plan number. CCP 'monitors' were given briefings to explain the significance of CCPs on introduction of the new log sheets. They were also retrained in Corrective Action Procedures.

A.6.9 HACCP Plan maintenance

The company HACCP Officer was asked to maintain an audit schedule for the HACCP Plan and each core team member was trained in audit techniques. As the Plan has only nine CCPs, it was decided to carry out a formal audit every month alongside the company formal GMP audit.

The audit includes a review of CCP log sheets, SQA audits, Certificates of Analysis, Corrective Actions taken and the status of any ongoing Improvement Programmes. The results of the audits are discussed at the subsequent board meetings.

Appendix B

Examples of practical hazard control

Hazard	Preventative measures
Hazard category: Biological Heat-stable pre-formed toxins, e.g. *Staphylococcus aureus*, *Bacillus cereus* emetic toxin	Raw materials • Specification for organism and/or toxin • Evidence of control during supplier process • Testing • Certificate of analysis People • Hand wash procedures • Covering cuts/wounds, etc. • Occupational health procedures • Management control of food handlers Build up during process • Control of time that ingredients, intermediate and finished products are held within the organism's growth temperature range • Design of process equipment to minimize dead spaces • 'Clean as you go' procedures
Vegetative pathogens, e.g. *Salmonella* spp., *L. monocytogenes*, *V. parahaemolyticus*, *Y. enterocolytica*, etc.	Raw materials • Lethal heat treatment during process • Specification for organism[a] • Testing[a] • Evidence of control during supplier process[a] • Certificate of analysis[a] • Temperature control to prevent growth to hazardous levels[b] • Intrinsic factors[b] such as pH and acidity; a_w – salt, sugar, drying; organic acids; chemical preservatives • Processes[b] such as irradiation, electrostatic field sterilization, etc.

cont'd

Hazard	Preventative measures

	Cross-contamination at the facility (from the environment and raw materials)
	• Intact packaging
	• Pest control
	• Secure building (roof leaks, ground water, etc.)
	• Logical process flow, including where necessary:
	   (i) segregation of people, clothing, equipment, air, process areas
	  (ii) direction of drains and waste disposal

[a]Critical when your process has no lethal heat treatment
[b]N.B. *Salmonella* spp may cause infection at low numbers in your product. Therefore absolute confidence in your raw materials as supplied is necessary. Remember also that heat-labile toxins will not necessarily be destroyed by other processes/controls such as irradiation or acidity

Hazard	Preventative measures

Spore formers, e.g. *Cl. botulinum*, *Cl. perfringens*, *B. subtilis*, *B. licheniformis*, *B. cereus*	Raw materials
	• Specification
	• Evidence of control during supplier process
	• Testing
	• Certificates of analysis
	• Lethal heat treating during process:
	   (i) $F_0 3$ process required for low acid products for ambient storage
	  (ii) Lethal combination of heat treatment and acidity or sugar level for high acid/sugar products for ambient storage
	 (iii) For products to be stored at chilled conditions ($< 5°C$) a sub-lethal heat treatment may be used but this must be accompanied by intrinsic factors which will prevent the growth of psychrotrophic organisms (e.g. *Cl. botulinum*) during the product shelf life
	 (iv) For all the above processes, pack integrity, cooling water chlorination and cooling container handling are critical
	• Temperature control to prevent growth to hazardous levels
	• Intrinsic factors such as pH and acidity; a_w – salt, sugar, drying; organic acids; chemical preservatives

Hazard	Preventative measures
	• Other processes lethal to the organism of concern, e.g. irradiation, etc.[c]
	Cross-contamination at the facility (from the environment and raw materials)
	• Intact packaging
	• Pest control
	• Secure building (roof leaks, ground water, etc.)
	• Logical process flow, including where necessary:
	(i) segregation of people, clothing, equipment, air, process areas
	(ii) direction of drains and waste disposal
Food-borne viruses, e.g. Hepatitis A, SRSV	• Avoidance of products likely to be grown in sewage-contaminated waters, especially molluscan shellfish
	• Strict SQA control concerning irrigation and wash water of salads and vegetables
	• Consideration given to proven lethal treatments such as irradiation or heat treatment
	• Stringent personal hygiene procedures among food handlers
Parasites	• SQA procedures to include farm animal husbandry and veterinary inspection for control of parasites such as *Toxiplasma gondii*, *Taenia* in beef and pork, and *Trichinella* in pork
	• Freezing ($-18°C$), heating ($> 76°C$), drying and salting
Protozoa, e.g. *Cryptosporidium parvum*, *Giardia intestinalis* (*lamblia*)	• Use of filtered water
	• Pasteurization of raw milk
	• Heat treatment of water used as an ingredient
Mould (mycotoxins), e.g. patulin, aflatoxin, ergot, tricothecenes	• SQA control of harvesting and storage to prevent mould growth and mycotoxin formation in cereals, groundnuts, dried fruit
	• Heat treatment during process to destroy mould and prevent growth in product
	• Controlled dry storage
	• Intrinsic factors to reduce a_w to < 0.7

[c]Remember that heat-labile toxins will not necessarily be destroyed by other processes/controls, such as irradiation or acidity

cont'd

267

Hazard	Preventative measures
Hazard category: physical	
Intrinsic physical contamination of raw materials[d] e.g. Bone – meat/fish Extraneous vegetable matter – fruit stones, stalks, pips, nutshells Glass Wood Metal Plastic Pests	Liquids • Filtering • Magnets • Centrifugal separation Powders • Sifting • Magnets • Metal detection • Air separation Flowing particulates, e.g. nuts, dried fruit, IQF fruit and vegetables • Inspection • Screening • Sifting • Magnets • Metal detection • Washing • Stone and sand traps • Air separation • Flotation • Electronic colour sorting Large solid items, e.g. carcasses, fish, cabbages, cauliflowers, frozen pastry, packaging • X-ray detection • Metal detection • Deboners • Visual inspection • Electronic scanning
Physical cross-contaminants e.g. Glass	• Elimination of all glass except lighting, which must be covered – light breakage procedure • Glass packed products – glass breakage procedures, inversion/washing/blowing of glass packaging before use
Wood	• Exclusion of all wooden materials such as pallets, brushes, pencils, tools from exposed product areas • Segregation of all packaging materials
Metal	• Equipment design – preventative maintenance

[d]N.B. Supplier Quality Assurance procedures should include maximum acceptable levels in specifications. Sampling and visual inspection will supplement above preventative measures

Hazard	Preventative measures
	• Avoidance of all loose metal items – jewellery, drawing pins, nuts and bolts, small tools • Metal detection – sensitivity appropriate for the product, calibrated (3-monthly) and checked (hourly), ferrous, non-ferrous and stainless; fail-safe divert systems; locked reject cages; traceability
Plastic	• Avoidance of all loose plastic items – pen tops, buttons on overalls, jewellery • Breakage procedures in place where hard brittle plastic is used

Pests	• Pest control programme:
	  (i) Prevention – e.g. facility design, avoidance of harbourage areas, waste management, ultrasonic repellants
	  (ii) Screening/proofing – e.g. strip curtains, drain covers, mesh on windows, air curtains, netting
	  (iii) Extermination – e.g. electric fly killers, poisoning, bait boxes, perimeter spraying, fogging

Building fabric	• Design and maintenance
Hazard category: chemical Cleaning chemicals	• Use of non-toxic, food-compatible cleaning compounds • Safe operating practices and written cleaning instructions • Separate storage for cleaning reagents • Covered designated labelled containers for all chemicals
Pesticides, veterinary residues and plasticizers in packaging	• Specification to include suppliers' compliance with maximum legal usage levels • Verification of suppliers' records • Annual surveillance programme of selected raw materials
Toxic metals/PCBs	• Specifications and surveillance where appropriate
Nitrates, nitrites and nitrosamines and other chemical additives	As contaminants: • Specifications and surveillance where appropriate As additives: • Safe operating practices and written additive instructions • Special storage in covered, designated, labelled containers

cont'd

Hazard	Preventative measures

Allergens/food intolerance	• Validation of levels through usage rates, sampling and testing
	• Awareness of the potential allergenic properties of certain ingredients. Special consideration given to adequate labelling, and to the control of the reworking of product in production for the following ingredients
	• Dairy
	    Milk products
	    Cheese products
	    Cream products
	    Whey
	• Nuts and legumes
	    Peanuts/peanut butter, almonds, brazil nuts, cashews, coconuts, hazelnuts, macadamia nuts, pecans, soy/soy flour/soy protein/soybean meal, textured vegetable protein, walnuts
	• Cereal flours
	    Barley, buckwheat, corn, cornstarch, corn meal, corn syrup, oats, rice, rye, wheat
	• Chocolate and cocoa products
	• Eggs
	    Eggs, egg solids, dried eggs
	• Seafood
	    Fish, including shellfish
	• Others
	    Cottonseed, malt, monosodium glutamate, nutmeg, papaya, peaches, potatoes, strawberries, sulphites, tartrazine, tomatoes, wheat germ, yeast

Appendix C

Pathogen profiles

The following profiles of important food poisoning organisms are reproduced by kind permission of Grand Metropolitan Foods Europe. The information contained within the tables is intended as an introduction to the properties of these pathogens and should be used as a general guide only. This information has been drawn from various sources and was up to date when compiled.

Appendix C Pathogen profiles[a]

	Organism			
	Salmonella spp.	*Listeria monocytogenes*	*Yersinia enterocolitica*	*Vibrio parahaemolyticus*
Naturally found	Poultry, domestic and wild animals, man, insects, wild birds	Soil, vegetation, man, sewage, water, animals – ubiquitous	Water, pigs, small rodents, pets	Seafood, coastal marine environments, intestines of marine animals
Associated foods	Raw milk, raw poultry, shell eggs, raw meat	Coleslaw, raw milk, soft cheese, raw meat, ice cream, vegetables	Raw milk, ice cream, vegetables, raw pork	Seafood
Why important	Common food poisoning organism due to poor hygiene or incorrect processing. Severe symptoms. Rarely fatal	Can grow slowly at refrigeration temperatures. Ubiquitous organism. Mortality rate 30% of those infected	Increasing number of reported cases. Gives symptoms similar to appendicitis leading to unnecessary operations	Particularly important in raw seafood. Responsible for 50–70% of enteritis cases in Japan
Infective dose	Low 5–24/ml milk; 4/kg milk powder; 0.4–9.3/ 100 g cheese	Unknown – probably low for immuno-compromized	Unknown – probably high ($> 10^6$)	Not fully established probably high ($> 10^6$) but may be 10^4
Incubation period	12–72 h	8 days–3 months	1–10 days	4–96 h
Symptoms	Nausea, vomiting, abdominal pain, head-ache, chills, diarrhoea, fever. Lasts 2–3 days (or more)	Flu-like illness to meningitis. May cause abortion in pregnant women	Diarrhoea, fever, vomiting, sharp pain in lower right side of abdomen	Acute gastroenteritis: nausea, vomiting, abdominal cramps, fever chills, diarrhoea. Can be fatal

	Gram-negative short rods. Peritrichous flagella 0.5–0.7 × 1.0–3.0 μm	Gram-positive short rods. 0.4–0.5 × 0.5–2.0 μm	Gram-negative short rods. 0.5–1.0 × 1.0–2.0 μm (Pleomorphic forms also appear)	Gram-negative curved or straight rods with flagellum. 0.5–0.8 × 1.4–2.6 μm
Morphology				
Oxygen requirements	Facultative anaerobe	Aerobe or micro-aerophilic	Facultative anaerobe	Facultative anaerobe
Growth temperatures (°C)	Maximum 45–47 Optimum 37 Minimum 5.1	45 25–30 0	44 32–34 0–1	43 37 12.8
pH range	Maximum 9.0 Optimum 6.5–7.5 Minimum 4 (HCl/citric; 4.4 lactic; 5.4 acetic)	9 7–7.5 4.4 at 30°C (pH 5.0 at 4°C)	9 7.0–8.0 4.6 (at 25°C but not at 3°C)	11 7.5–8.5 4.5–5
Minimum a_w for growth	0.95	0.92	0.95	0.94
Maximum salt % allowing growth	8	10	5–8 (7% at 3°C)	8 Halophile (minimum salt 0.5%)

Appendix C continued

	Organism			
	Clostridium botulinum	*Clostridium perfringens*	*Bacillus cereus*	*Staphylococcus aureus*
Naturally found	Soil, fresh water sediments, vegetation, i.e. ubiquitous	Soil, marine sediments, dust, faeces	Soil, vegetation, raw milk	Skin, skin glands and mucous membranes, i.e. nose, throat, cuts, boils, etc.
Associated foods	Improperly processed or contaminated canned foods	Ground beef, chicken, turkey, pork, dairy products	Rice, spices, meat, milk, vegetable products, nuts	Fish, meat, milk, cheese, pasta
Why important	Spores can survive extremes of heat, drying and chemical exposure. Toxin heat-labile but deadly	Common food poisoning organism. Heat-resistant spores. Causes infection by heat-labile toxin formed during sporulation in gut	Heat-resistant spores. Can form toxin in food (emetic or diarrhoeal) or by multiplication in gut (diarrhoeal)	Can easily be passed to food by handling incorrectly. Forms heat-resistant toxin
Infective dose	Very low, 0.2 µg toxin	High: 4×10^9 cells (8–10 mg toxin) medium count in UK implicated food 7×10^5g	1.2×10^3 reported (76% of foods had 10^6/g)	1 mg toxin (1 ng/g food)
Incubation period	< 18–96 h	8–24 h	Diarrhoea toxin 6–15 h emetic toxin 1/2–6 h	2–6 h
Symptoms	Dizziness, blurred vision, inability to swallow → paralysis + death	Diarrhoea, nausea, flatulence	Nausea, vomiting and diarrhoea	Nausea, vomiting and diarrhoea lasting 1–2 days

	Gram-positive spore-forming rods. (Sub-terminal spores) 0.5–2.4 × 1.7–22.0 μm	Gram-positive spore-forming rods. (Sub-terminal spores) 0.9–1.3 × 3.0–9.0 μm	Gram-positive spore-forming rods. 1.0–1.2 × 3.0–7.0 μm	Gram-positive cocci. 0.7–0.9 μm diameter Spherical/ovoid in grape-like clusters
Morphology				
Oxygen requirements	Anaerobic	Anaerobic (may grow in presence of O_2 in log phase)	Facultative anaerobe (i.e. normally aerobic)	Facultative anaerobe
Growth temperatures (°C)	Maximum 48 Optimum 30–37 Minimum 3.3 (non-proteolytic) 10.0 (proteolytic)	50 43–45 12 typical (some 4°C)	49 30 10 typical (some 4°C)	48 37 7–11
pH range	Maximum 9.0 Optimum 6.5–7.0 (proteolytic) 5.0 (non-proteolytic) Minimum 4.6 (proteolytic)	8.3 6–7.5 5.0	9.3 6–7.5 4.35	9.8–10 6.0–7.0 4.0
Minimum a_w for growth	0.94 (proteolytic) 0.97 (non-proteolytic)	0.95	0.912	0.86 (generation time 300 min) (optimum a_w 0.98)
Salt tolerance (%)	10 (proteolytic) 5 (non-proteolytic)	6	10	18.2 (Toxin production 10)

Appendix C *continued*

	Organism			
	Escherichia coli	*Campylobacter jejuni*	Toxigenic moulds	Viruses
Naturally found	Environment – soil, water, faeces/manure. Digestive tract of animals. Raw milk, meat	Soil, water, farm waste. Digestive tract of animals. Raw milk, meat	Soil, dust, manure, animal feeds, stored cereals	Atmosphere, water, on all living organisms
Associated foods	Raw milk, improperly processed or contaminated dairy products, raw meat	Poultry, meats, raw milk	Bread, cheese, jam, etc.	Shellfish, milk, cream, fruit juice, salads, cold meat, ice cubes
Why important	Indicator of poor hygiene or improper processing. Several toxigenic strains producing heat-stable and heat-labile toxins	One of the most important causes of diarrhoea in the world. Do not grow well in foods. Food is vehicle of infection	Grow where many bacteria cannot, i.e. high acid, low a_w foods.	Cause hepatitis A and gastroenteritis. Do not multiply in food – it is just the carrier
Infective dose	High 10^5–10^8/g	Low 5×10^2/g	Varies – low	Varies – low (possibly 100 particles)
Incubation period	8–24 h	48 h–1 week	Varies	Varies

Symptoms	Vomiting, fever, diarrhoea (sometimes bloody), stomach cramps, nausea	Profuse diarrhoea (sometimes bloody), stomach cramps, nausea, dizziness, fever	Production of mycotoxins, e.g. aflatoxin may cause food intoxication. Cancer possible long-term effect	Gastroenteritis, fever, vomiting, diarrhoea
Morphology	Gram-negative short rods. 1.1–1.5 × 2.0–6.0 μm	Gram-negative spirally curved rods. 0.2–0.8 × 0.5–5.0 μm (cocoid/spherical when old)	Many different sizes and shapes may be visible but not always	Many different shapes. 20–80 nm in size.
Oxygen requirements	Facultative anaerobe	Obligate microaerophile Cultured in 6–10% O_2 with 5% CO_2	Aerobic	None. Viruses cannot reproduce themselves but rely on the host
Growth temperatures (°C)	Maximum 45.5 Optimum 30–37 Minimum 2.5	47 42–45 32	Varies	Not applicable – do not grow in food
pH range	Maximum 9.5 Optimum 7 Minimum 4.4	9–9.5 6.5–7.5 4.9–5.3	11.1 Variable 1.6	Survival between pH 3–10
Minimum a_w for growth	0.95	Not known	0.70	No growth in food
Salt tolerance (%)	6–8	2.0	Variable	Variable

Appendix C continued

	Organism			
	Aeromonas hydrophila	*Plesiomonas shigelloides*	*Bacillus subtilis*	*Bacillus licheniformis*
Naturally found	Freshwater, sewage, seawater	Water, aquatic animals, swine, dogs, cats, sheep, monkeys	Soil, vegetation	Soil, vegetation
Associated foods	Seafood, red meat, poultry, raw milk	Oysters and other foods of aquatic origin	Mostly meat, pastry and rice dishes. Custard powder, bread, mayonnaise, pickled onions	Cooked meat, vegetable dishes, boiled sausage, custard pie, bread
Why important	Immunocompromized patients at risk. Capable of growth at refrigeration temperatures. Two toxin types produced	Not very virulent but high incidence in environment. Heat-labile and stable toxins produced	Heat-resistant endospores. Important contaminant in baked products	Heat-resistant endospores. Important contaminant in, e.g. pies, pastries, bread products
Infective dose	Not known	Not known	High 10^5–10^9	Not known. Average no. of cells found in foods causing illness = 10^8/g (high)

Incubation period	Not known	Not known	10 min–14 h (median 2.5 h)	2–14 h (median 8 h)
Symptoms	Diarrhoea, abdominal pain, vomiting, fever. May cause meningitis, septicaemia	Diarrhoea, abdominal pain, vomiting, fever. May cause meningitis, septicaemia	Cramps, vomitting, nausea, occasionally diarrhoea, headache, flushing	Diarrhoea, cramps, vomiting
Morphology	Gram-negative straight rods, rounded end. 0.3–1 × 1.0–4.4 μm	Gram-negative straight rods with rounded ends. 0.8–1.0 × 3 μm	Gram-positive rods spore-forming. 0.7–0.8 × 2–3 μm	Gram-positive spore-forming rods. 0.6–0.8 × 1.5–3 μm
Oxygen requirements	Facultative anaerobe	Facultative anaerobe	Facultative anaerobe	Facultative anaerobe
Growth temperatures (°C)	Maximum 42 Optimum 28 Minimum 1–4	40–44 37–38 8	55 43–46 12	Growth occurs at 30–55 60 maximum
pH range	Minimum 4 Maximum 10	5 7.7	4.6 9.2	Growth occurs between 5.7 and 6.5
Minimum a_w for growth	Not known	Not known	0.901–0.931	Not known; probably 0.95
Salt tolerance (%)	Tolerates 4 No growth at 7.5	Limited growth at 4 but depends on medium	No growth at > 15	7

Appendix C *continued*

	Organism			
	Vibrio vulnificus	*E. coli 0157 H7*	*Cryptospondium parvum*	*Giardia intestinalis (lamblia)*
Naturally found	Saltwater, molluscs, seafood	Dairy cattle, sheep faeces, meat and raw milk	Water, sewage	Water, sewage, small intestine of man, primates, pigs
Associated feeds	Seafood, especially shellfish	Beef and meats, raw milk, hamburgers	Water supplies, raw milk	Water supplies, fruit salad (food handler)
Why important	Invasive and rapidly lethal pathogen. 56% fatal	Enterohaemorrhagic. Severe symptoms, possibly fatal	Oocysts resistant to chemical disinfection. Survive up to 1 year in aqueous solution	Form resistant cysts
Infective dose	Not known	Not known	Low; < 10 oocysts	Low, < 10 cysts
Incubation period	Short, 7 h to several days (median 16–38 h)	3–9 days	2–14 days	1–3 weeks
Symptoms	Fever, chills, hypotension, nausea. Less frequently vomiting, diarrhoea, abdominal pains	Haemorrhagic colitus (HC), haemolytic uremic syndrome (HUS), and thrombotic thrombocytopenic purpura (TPP).	Diarrhoea, abdominal pains, vomiting, may have flu-like symptoms	Chronic diarrhoea

		HC – crampy abdominal pain, watery diarrhoea which becomes very bloody. HUS – bloody diarrhoea, kidney failure, death. TPP – HUS with fever		
Morphology	Gram-negative straight or curved rods. 0.5–0.8 × 1.4–2.6 µm	Gram-negative rod. 1.1–1.5 × 2–6 µm	Oocysts 4–6 µm diameter	10–20 × 5–10 µm Cysts: 12–15 × 8–10 µm
Oxygen requirements	Facultative anaerobe	Facultative anaerobe	Oocysts do not grow in food	Cysts do not grow in food
Growth temperatures (°C)	Minimum 5 Maximum 40 Optimum 37	Minimum 10 Maximum 45 Optimum 37	Oocysts do not grow in food	Cysts do not grow in food
pH range	Not known	Probably 4.4–9.5 (general E. coli)	Oocysts do not grow in food	Cysts do not grow in food
Minimum a_w	Not known	Probably 0.95 (general E. coli)	Oocysts do not grow in food	Cysts do not grow in food
Salt tolerance (%)	Maximum 6 Minimum 0.1 Optimum 1–2	Probably 6–8% (general E. coli)	Oocysts do not grow in food	Cysts do not grow in food
Other control measures			Oocysts resist 60% alcohol. Viability lost by boiling or by drying	

Appendix D

Glossary

Audit A systematic and independent examination to determine whether activities and results comply with the documented procedures; also whether these procedures are implemented effectively and are suitable to achieve the objectives.

Cleaning in Place (CIP) The cleaning of pipework and equipment, while still fully assembled, through the circulation of cleaning chemicals.

Corrective Action Procedures to be followed when a deviation occurs from the critical limits, i.e. the CCP goes out of control.

Critical Control Point (CCP) A point, step or procedure at which control can be applied and a food safety hazard can be prevented, eliminated, or reduced to acceptable levels.

CCP Decision Tree A logical sequence of questions to be asked for each hazard at each process step. The answers to the questions lead the HACCP team to decisions determining which process steps are CCPs.

Critical Limit An absolute tolerance value which must be met for each control measure at a CCP. Values outside the Critical Limits indicate a deviation and potentially unsafe product.

Gantt chart A project implementation timetable. The Gantt chart shows at a glance the timing and dependencies of each project phase.

Hazard A property which may cause the product to be unsafe for consumption.

HACCP Control Chart Matrix or table detailing the control criteria (i.e. critical limits, monitoring procedures and corrective action procedures) for each CCP and preventative measure. Part of the HACCP Plan.

HACCP Plan The document which defines the procedures to be followed to assure the control of product safety for a specific process.

HACCP Study A series of meetings and discussions between HACCP Team members in order to put together a HACCP Plan.

HACCP Team The multidisciplinary group of people who are responsible for developing a HACCP Plan. In a small company each person may cover several disciplines.

Hazard Analysis Chart A working document which can be used by the HACCP team when applying HACCP Principle 1, i.e. listing hazards and describing preventative measures for their control.

Intrinsic factors Basic, integral features of the product, due to its formulation, e.g. pH, a_w.

Monitoring A planned sequence of observations or measurements to assess whether a CCP is under control. Records of monitoring are kept for future use in verification.

PERT chart A diagrammatic representation of the dependency network and critical path to completion of a project plan.

Potable water Wholesome, drinkable water.

Preventative measure A factor which can be used to control an identified hazard. Preventative measures will eliminate or reduce the hazard to an acceptable level.

Process Flow Diagram A detailed stepwise sequence of the operations in the process under study.

Quality Management System A structured system for the management of quality in all aspects of a company's business.

Supplier Quality Assurance (SQA) The programme of actions to ensure the safety and quality of the raw material supply. Includes preparation of and procedures to assess supplier competency, e.g. inspections, questionnaires.

Target level A value within the Critical Limits which can be used to take action and prevent the occurrence of a deviation.

Verification The procedures (other than those used in monitoring) which ensure that the HACCP Study has been carried out correctly and that the HACCP Plan continues to be effective.

Appendix E

Abbreviations and definitions

AEA	Action Error Analysis
ATP	Adenosine tri-phosphate
c	The maximum allowable number of defective sample units (2-class plan) or marginally acceptable units (3-class plan). When more than this number are found in the sample, the lot is rejected
CIP	Cleaning in Place
CCP	Critical Control Point
CFDRA	Campden Food and Drink Research Association
Codex	Codex Alimentarius Commission, an FAO/WHO Organization
EC	European Community
FAO	Food and Agriculture Organization
FDA	The US Food and Drug Administration
FIFO	First in, First out – principles of stock rotation
FMEA	Failure Mode and Effect Analysis
HACCP	Hazard Analysis Critical Control Point
HAZOP	Hazard and Operability Study
HHA	High Hygiene Area
HMSO	Her Majesty's Stationary Office
IAMFES	International Association of Milk, Food and Environmental Sanitarians
ICMSF	International Commission for Microbiological Specifications for Foods
IDF	International Dairy Federation
IFST	Institute of Food Science and Technology, London
ILSI	International Life Sciences Institute
ISO	International Standards Organization
m	A microbiological limit which separates good quality from defective quality (2-class) or from marginally acceptable quality (3-class). Values $\le$ m are acceptable; values $>m$ are either marginally acceptable or unacceptable.

M	A microbiological limit in a 3-class sampling plan which separates marginally acceptable product from defective product. Values $>M$ are unacceptable.
MAP	Modified Atmosphere Packaging
MORT	Management Oversight and Risk Tree
MRL	Maximum Residue Level
PERT	Programme Evaluation and Review Technique
n	The number of sample units examined from a lot to satisfy the requirements of a particular sampling plan.
NACMCF	National Advisory Committee for Microbiological Criteria for Foods (USA)
NASA	National Aeronautics and Space Administration
QMS	Quality Management System
SPC	Statistical Process Control
SQA	Supplier Quality Assurance
SRSV	Small Round Structured Virus
TVC	Total Viable Count
WHO	World Health Organization

References and further reading

References

Beckers, H.J., Daniels-Bosman, M.S.M., Ament, A., *et al* (1985) Two outbreaks of salmonellosis caused by *Salmonella indiana*. A survey of the European summit outbreak and its implications. *International Journal of Food Microbiology*, **2**, 185–95.

Bird, M. (1992) *Effective Leadership*, BBC Business Matters Publications, London.

Brown, M. (1992) *Successful Project Management*, British Institute of Management, Hodder and Stoughton.

Campden Food and Drink Research Association (1992) *HACCP: A Practical Guide*, Technical Manual No. 38.

CDR Weekly, Listeriosis Update, (13) 26 March 1992.

Codex Committee on Food Hygiene (1993) Guidelines for the Application of the Hazard Analysis Critical Control Point (HACCP) System, in *Training Considerations for the Application of the HACCP System to Food Processing and Manufacturing*, World Health Organization, WHO/FNU/FOS/93.3 II.

Council Directive 93/43/EEC (June 14, 1993) on The Hygiene of Foodstuffs, *Official Journal of the European Communities*, July 19, 1993, No. L 175/I.

Council Directive 89/107/EEC (1989) concerning Food Additives Authorised for use in Foodstuffs intended for Human Consumption.

EURACHEM/WELAC (1993) *Accreditation for Chemical Laboratories: Guidance on the Interpretation of the EN 45000 Series of Standards and ISO/IEC*, Guide 25. (Available in the UK from Laboratory of the Government Chemist, Teddington, Middlesex, TW11 0LY.)

ICMSF (1980) *Microbial Ecology of Foods*, Volume 1, *Factors Affecting Life and Death of Micro-organisms*, Volume 2, *Food Commodities*, Academic Press, New York.

ICMSF (1986) *Micro-organisms in Foods 2. Sampling for Microbiological Analysis: Principles and Specific Applications*, 2nd edn, Blackwell Scientific Publications, Oxford.

IFST (1993) *Shelf Life of Foods – Guidelines for its determination and Prediction*, Institute of Food Science and Technology, London.

International Standards Organisation (1987).

(a) ISO 9000 Series, *Quality Management and Quality Assurance Standards: Guidelines for Selection and Use*. (b) ISO 9001, *Quality Systems – Model for Quality Assurance in Design/Development, Production, Installation, and Servicing*.

(c) ISO 9002, *Quality Systems – Model for Quality Assurance in Production and Installation*.

(d) ISO 9003, *Quality Systems – Model for Quality Assurance in Final Inspection and Test*.

IFST (1991) *Food and Drink – Good Manufacturing Practice: A Guide to its Responsible Management*, 3rd edn, Institute of Food Science and Technology, London.

HMSO (1990) Food Safety Act, HMSO, London, UK.

HMSO (1991) Food Safety Act 1990 Code of Practice No. 9: Food Hygiene Inspections, HMSO, London, UK.

Jay, A. (1993) *Effective Presentation*, Pitman Publishing in association with the Institute of Management Foundation, London.

National Advisory Committee on Microbiological Criteria for Foods (1992) Hazard Analysis and Critical Control Point System (adopted March 20, 1992), *International Journal of Food Micro-biology*, **16**, 1–23.

Oates, D. (1993) *Leadership – The Art of Delegation*, The Sunday Times, Century Business.

Pierson, M.D. and Corlett, D.A. (1992) *HACCP Principles and Application*, Van Nostrand Reinhold, New York.

Price, F. (1984) *Right First Time – Using Quality Control for Profit*, Gower, Aldershot.

Rowntree, D. (1981) *Statistics Without Tears*, Penguin.

Shapton, D.A. and Shapton, N. F. (1991) *Principles and Practices for the Safe Processing of Foods*, H.J. Heinz Company, Butterworth-Heinemann, Oxford.

Shapton, N.F. (1989) *Food Safety – A Manufacturer's Perspective*, Hobsons Publishing plc., Cambridge.

Socket, P.N. (1991) A Review: The Economic Implications of Human Salmonella Infection, *Journal of Applied Bacteriology*, **71**, 289–95.

Sprenger, R. (1991) *Hygiene for Management*, 5th edn, Highfield Publications, Rotherham and London.

Suokas, J. and Pyy, P. (1988) Evaluation of the Validity of Four Hazard Identification Methods with Event Descriptions, Research Reports, Technical Research Centre of Finland.

Video

HACCP. Food Quality Management Training Series, Video 3. Available from: Food Quality Management, Lakenmakersstraat 170, B-2800 Mechelen, Belgium. Tel: 32 15 55 72 01. Fax: 32 15 55 79 31.

Further reading

Bryan, F. (1981) Hazard Analysis of Food Service Operations. *Food Technology*, **35**(2), 78–87.

IAMFES (1991) *Procedures to Implement the Hazard Analysis Critical Control Point System*, International Association of Milk, Food and Environmental Sanitarians Inc.. Ames, Iowa, USA.

ICMSF (1988) *Micro-organisms in Foods 4. Application of the Hazard Analysis Critical Control Point (HACCP) System to Ensure Microbiological Safety and Quality*, Blackwell Scientific Publications, Oxford.

Lloyds Register Quality Assurance Ltd. *Quality Systems for the Food and Drink Industries. Guidelines for the Use of BS 5750 Part 2, 1987 in the Manufacture of Food and Drink (ISO 9002: 1987, EN 29002: 1987)*, Issue 2, 1991.

Mayes, T. (1992) Simple User's Guide to Hazard Analysis Critical Control Point Concept for the Control of Microbiological Safety, *Food Control*, 3(1), 14–19.

IFST (1990) Guidelines for the Handling of Chilled Foods, Institute of Food Science and Technology, London.

IFST (1992) Guidelines to Good Catering Practice, Institute of Food Science and Technology, London.

ILSI Europe (1992) A Simple Guide to Understanding and Applying the HACCP Concept, ILSI Europe.

LFRA (in press 1994) Auditing HACCP Systems, Leatherhead Food Research Association, Leatherhead, England.

Index

Supplier Quality Assurance (SQA) 20,
  60–71, 205
  audit 172
  continuous improvement strategy
    185–6
  hazard control 267
  ISO 9001 193
Suppliers
  case studies 218
  pressure for HACCP 15
  prioritization for improvement 17
Surfaces, factory 74
Switzerland 9
Systems audit 164–5

Taenia saginata 41
Tampering opportunities 189–90
Target levels, Critical Limits 120
Tartrazine 47
Team, *see* HACCP Team
Technical expertise 20
Technology 71–3
  developments 177
Terms of reference 80, 81–3, 187
  case studies 209, 244, 252
Testing, *see* Inspection and testing
Thermal processes 71
Third party inspectors, Supplier Quality
    Assurance 70
Third party laboratory accreditation 201
Toxic metals 44–5, 269
  Supplier Quality Assurance 66
Toxicologists 21
Toxoplasma gondii 41
Traceability of products 194, 195
Training
  auditors 165–6
  case studies 244
  CCP monitors 28, 156, 180
  continuous improvement strategy
    186
  costs 162
  in emerging hazards 180–1
  food hygiene 17, 74

  cleaning schedules 75
  HACCP awareness 29, 181
  HACCP Team 24–7, 180
  ISO 9001 197
  new staff 180
  ongoing requirements 179–81
  records 160
  refresher 180
  skills 27, 181
Trichinella spiralis 41
Tricothecenes 42, 267

United Kingdom
  enforcement authorities 15
  food poisoning incidents 9
  Food Safety Act (1990) 13–15
  government 14
United States of America 9, 14
Unsafe products 188
Updates, HACCP Plan 178–9
Upper Action Level 152–3
Upper Warning Level 152–3

Verification
  of HACCP System 6, 145
    case study 228–9
    microbiological factors 114
    ongoing 163–75, 178
  of Process Flow Diagrams 84
Veterinary residues 46, 269
Vibrio
  cholerae 38
  parahaemolyticus 37–8, 265, 272–3
  vulnificus 40, 280–1
Viruses 40–1, 267, 276–7

Warning bands 125
Waste materials 195
Water activity 59
Wood 49–50, 268

X-ray detection 106

Yersinia enterocolitica 39–40, 265, 272–3

Integrated Solid Waste Management: A Lifecycle Inventory

P R White, Environmental Scientist, Procter & Gamble Ltd, UK, M Franke, Environmental Scientist, Procter and Gamble GmbH, Germany and P Hindle, Director of Environmental Quality Europe, Procter and Gamble European Technical Centre, Brussels, Belgium

This book combines the two emerging concepts of Integrated Waste Management (IWM) and Lifecycle Inventory. IWM uses a range of treatment options including recycling, composting, biogasification, incineration and landfilling, to minimise the environmental impacts from solid waste management, at an affordable cost. Lifecycle Analysis is used to predict the overall environmental impacts of waste management systems, in terms of energy consumption, and emissions to air, water and land.
September 1994: 234x156: c.256pp, 30 line illus: Hardback: 0-7514-0046-7: c. £79.00

NEW IN HACCP....

Hazard Analysis Critical Control Point (HACCP) in Meat, Poultry and Seafoods

A M Pearson and T R Dutson, Agricultural Experimental Station, Oregon State University, Oregon, USA

This volume presents the latest information on the HACCP concept and its use in improving the microbiological safety of meat, poultry and seafoods.

Contents: Origin of the HACCP concept. The HACCP concept and how it fits into FSIS programs. Implementation of the HACCP concept on farms and ranches. Implementation of the HACCP program by meat and poultry slaughterers. Implementation of the HACCP program during processing and distribution of meat and poultry products. Implementation of the HACCP program by the fresh and processed seafood industry. Statistical quality control in the HACCP program. Relationship of the HACCP concept to total quality management. The HACCP concept and how it can be used by delicatessens and meat, poultry and fish retailers. The HACCP program and how it can be adapted to restaurants and food service establishments. The HACCP concept and the consumer. Organization and management of the HACCP program by industry. Predictive microbiology and HACCP. National and international cooperation in governmental regulations for meat, poultry and fish inspection.
January 1995: 234x156: c.416pp, 60 line illus,5 halftone illus: Hardback: 0-7514-0229-X: c. £85.00

For further information please contact:

Antonia Sharpe
Chapman & Hall, 2-6 Boundary Row, London SE1 8HN

Tel: 071 865 0066
Fax: 071 522 9623

NEW BOOKS IN FOOD

Related titles from
Chapman & Hall...

Beverages

Technology, chemistry and microbiology
by A Varnam and J Sutherland

Beverages provides thorough and integrated coverage in a user-friendly way, and is the second of an important series dealing with major food product groups. It is an invaluable learning and teaching aid and is also of great use to the food industry and regulatory personnel.
Food Products Series 2: March 1994: 234x156: 480pp, 70 line illus: Paperback: 0-412-45720-2: £24.99

Brewing

M J Lewis and T W Young

This book provides thorough coverage, at an introductory level, of the essentials of brewing science and its relationship with brewing technology. The book will be of interest to students and professionals working in malting, brewing and allied industries, particularly those new to the industry or those training for formal qualifications.
August 1994: 234x156: c.250pp, 100 line illus: Paperback: 0-412-26420-X: c. £19.95

Chemical Engineering for the Food Industry

Edited by P Fryer, D L Pyle, C D Rielly and C A Zaror

This book has arisen from important courses on chemical engineering for the food industry run by the University of Cambridge Programme for Industry. It covers the major principles and applications of process engineering in the food industry and is invaluable for all those embarking on a career in food processing.
November 1994: 234x156: c.340pp, 201 line,6 halftone illus: Hardback: 0-412-49500-7: c. £40.00

Food Industry and the Environment

Practical issues and cost implications
Edited by J M Dalzell

Food manufacturers are now under considerable pressure to ensure that their company's activities are environmentally sensitive, but there is also increased internal pressure to maintain or increase profitability in the face of fierce competition. This book shows how these seemingly conflicting pressures on a business can be reconciled, and describes in a clear and objective way the environmental issues surrounding the food industry.
July 1994: 234x156: c.432pp, 62 line illus,13 halftone illus: Hardback: 0-7514-0031-9: £79.00

Handbook of Organic Food Processing and Production

Edited by S Wright

Significant sales growth of organic products over the last five years has occurred in both the EC and the USA. This factor along with the defining of the word 'organic' by the EC in January 1993 has resulted in the need for this highly practical book which describes authoritatively and comprehensively what is involved in the processing and production of organic food ingredients and products.
Emphasis is placed firmly on technological, economic and regulatory issues with a significant input by both American and EC based authors. Organic food manufacturers, retailers and wholesalers will find the book an important concentrated source of information as will organic farmers and growers and those in academic research institutions.
October 1994: 234x156: c.320pp, 40 line illus,5 halftone illus: Hardback: 0-7514-0045-9: c. £69.00